THE OFFICIAL  GUIDE

GRAND PRIX 2011

This edition published in 2011 by
Carlton Books Limited
20 Mortimer Street
London W1T 3JW

10 9 8 7 6 5 4 3 2 1

itv SPORT

A CIP catalogue record for this book is available from
the British Library.

The publisher has taken reasonable steps to check
the accuracy of the facts contained herein at the
time of going to press, but can take no responsibility
for any errors.

ISBN: 978-1-84732-728-4

Editor: Matthew Lowing
Project Art Editor: Luke Griffin
Designer: Chris Gould
Picture Research: Paul Langan
Production: Kate Pimm
Editorial: Lesley Levene and Chris Parker

Printed in the United Kingdom
by Butler Tanner & Dennis, Frome

With an extra grand prix on the calendar for 2011, the season promises 20 chances
for the drivers to go for glory and for the smaller teams to attempt to close the gap.

THE OFFICIAL itv SPORT GUIDE

GRAND
PRIX 2011

BRUCE JONES

CARLTON
BOOKS

CONTENTS

Lewis Hamilton was in among the thick of the action in 2010 and will be hoping that McLaren will be able to provide him with pace-setting machinery in 2011 so that he can gun for another title.

One of the beauties of the 2010 World Championship was the degree of competition between the top teams. Will it be just as good in 2011?

ANALYSIS OF THE 2011 SEASON

The big question is how can one follow the most scintillating Formula One season ever. The arrival of a new tyre supplier, with Pirelli replacing Bridgestone, ought to spice things up. The return of KERS ought to boost overtaking opportunities too. And unchanged line-ups at the top teams should mean that battle will be rejoined.

The look of dejection on Fernando Alonso's face as he slumped in the paddock after he'd blown his title bid in the Abu Dhabi GP was enough to tell you that the Ferrari driver will be back hunting for glory in 2011, more determined than ever to give it his all in his quest for a third world drivers' title.

Mark Webber, too, is an aggrieved party, as he led the title race for so long yet came up short as his Red Bull Racing team-mate Sebastian Vettel skipped past him and Alonso at that final round to scoop the crown from under their noses. Also, McLaren's Lewis Hamilton and Jenson Button know what it's like to be world champion and, not surprisingly, want to become so again. So the pot is bubbling nicely as six top drivers line up for the three top teams.

There will be challengers from beyond their ranks, and you can be sure that Robert Kubica will be hoping that Renault is able to carry on its progress over the winter and become more competitive in 2011, and thus challenge for wins and not just podium finishes. Then, there is the question of the Mercedes GP challenge. Nico Rosberg is clearly ready to push if the car comes good. His team-mate Michael Schumacher was also showing a useful turn of speed by the end of his comeback campaign, so, if the 2011 Mercedes and its tyres suit him, expect some fireworks from the seven-time World Champion.

Williams, led by Rubens Barrichello (306 grand prix starts and counting), might also gather a healthy collection of points, with Force India's and Sauber's drivers also looking to finish in the top

10 at races to add to their tally. Scuderia Toro Rosso found out last year how hard it is to design and run your own chassis, as they did back when the team was called Minardi, after four years of affiliation with Red Bull Technologies gave them a helping hand.

Then of course there are the three teams that made their World Championship debut last year: Team Lotus, Virgin Racing and HRT. The first two of these showed signs of closing the gap on the midfield teams, but a major financial shortfall looks set to limit HRT's hopes. Talk of their ranks being augmented by a new team centred around 1997 World Champion Jacques Villeneuve came to nothing.

However, the hopes of all teams that didn't find themselves at the front last year will be that the changes to the F1 rulebook might suit them better than their rivals. For 2011, there are a lot of changes, with no double-deck diffusers, no F-ducts plus changed front wing endplates. To maintain standards, there will be a 107% cut-off in first qualifying to exclude cars that are way off the pace.

Two rule changes that are sure to encourage and enable more overtaking are the return of KERS and the introduction of adjustable rear wings. KERS is the energy retrieval system that McLaren used with considerable success when it made its fleeting visit to F1 in 2009. Offering 160bhp more grunt at the press of a button, this power boost has considerable benefits, not only in attack but also in defence. Use of the adjustable rear wing will also be limited, but should offer as much as an extra 9mph down the straights.

Another factor that could change the running order in the season ahead is that there is also a new tyre supplier for 2011, with Pirelli replacing Bridgestone. Anxious not to have the situation in which any team or driver gains an advantage from conducting the initial testing and development work, the teams took steps last season to make sure that all teams receive an equal amount of development data, with a pooling of information after Pedro de la Rosa carried out much of the test mileage. While tyre development will continue through 2011 as Pirelli gains ever more experience, the teams' designers and engineers will have to try and create this year's must-have technical part to find the slightest of advantages needed to mark them out. Last year, it was the F-duct and the blown diffuser. Time will tell what the boffins have in store for 2011.

One of last year's successes was the introduction of ex-F1 drivers to the panel of race stewards, as it brought the experience gleaned from being out there in battle and thus an understanding of why a driver did a certain thing at a certain time. Driving standards will come under extra scrutiny this year, in overtaking, defending position when a driver is being lapped and in the pitlane.

Cost-cutting is always being considered in these beleaguered times, and among the proposals last year were two-day grand prix meetings. The wash-out at the Japanese GP, when qualifying had to be postponed to the Sunday, proved that it can work. The teams, feeling stretched like never before with this year's record calendar of 20 grands prix, are known to be in support of this proposal. With a twinkle in his eye, F1 supremo Bernie Ecclestone suggested last autumn that a short cut, presumably to be used just once each, would liven up the races. Wouldn't that be entertaining...

After a breakthrough season in 2009, Red Bull Racing really came of age last year, but controlling internal strife will be at the top of the job list for 2011 as it looks to match its pace with consistently solid results in order to cement its position and make it two on the trot.

If Sebastian Vettel can achieve the qualifying predominance that he achieved last year, he'll go a long way towards having another title shot.

Here's a team on the crest of a wave. From its transformation from Jaguar Racing to Red Bull Racing in 2005, its drivers had racked up six wins, all in 2009, when it pushed Brawn GP for both the drivers' and constructors' titles. Then came last year, with the Adrian Newey-orchestrated RB6 the class of the field. It achieved nine victories and guided Sebastian Vettel to the drivers' title, with Red Bull Racing's eagerly awaited first constructors' title in the bag with the final round still to run. Actually, such was its dominance, that there could have been more wins, had there not been daft moments such as Vettel having a wheel come loose when leading in Australia and then Vettel and Webber clashing over the lead in Turkey.

So, the big question is whether the same crew can deliver again and also whether it will be the same driver picking up the crown. What lovely questions for team owner Dietrich Mateschitz and team principal Christian Horner to ponder. Don't

they emphasise just how far the team has come from its formative years as Stewart Grand Prix and then Jaguar Racing, when it became increasingly rudderless.

Despite the Overtaking Working Group's efforts, passing in F1 remains something

KEY MOMENTS AND KEY PEOPLE

TEAM HISTORY

Having started life in 1997 as Stewart Grand Prix - set up by three-time World Champion Jackie Stewart and his elder son, Paul - this is a team that won once under that guise, when Johnny Herbert triumphed at the Nurburgring in 1999. However, it changed its identity in 2000 when it became Jaguar Racing, but speed never turned into victory, despite Mark Webber's efforts. Then, in 2005, it changed again, into Red Bull Racing, with that first win in its new guise coming at Shanghai in 2009, courtesy of Sebastian Vettel.

ADRIAN NEWEY

This is a man who has truly earned his place in the pantheon of F1 designers after being responsible for standard-setting cars for Williams, McLaren and now Red Bull Racing. His first job was with Fittipaldi as chief aerodynamicist. That was in 1980 and he then designed sports cars and Indy cars for March, claiming three Indy 500 wins, before returning to F1 and joining Williams in 1990. After five constructors' titles, he joined McLaren and helped them hit the front. In 2006, he moved to Red Bull Racing.

2010 DRIVERS & RESULTS

Driver	Nationality	Races	Wins	Pts	Pos
Sebastian Vettel	German	19	5	256	1st
Mark Webber	Australian	19	4	242	3rd

that is still far less prevalent than desired, so Red Bull Racing's incredible success at claiming pole and/or placing its cars on the front row of the grid is something that it will be seeking to continue. Indeed, a Red Bull RB6 started from pole at 15 of last year's 19 grands prix and teams that had cars that were its equal in race trim were left to rue the disadvantage at which their lowly starting positions put them.

With little changing technically for 2011, save the return of KERS, Newey and the design crew will be able to build on their excellent base of the RB6. Rival teams spent most of last year convinced that there was excessive flexing of its front wing, giving it an aerodynamic advantage, but late-season toughening of the degree of deflection testing did nothing to slow the RB6. So its aerodynamic excellence clearly came not just from wings that bent downwards at speed, much to the chagrin of its rivals.

With Renault engines behind their shoulders, the drivers will probably continue to be a few horsepower down on the drivers with Ferrari and Mercedes V8s, and their straight-line speed might also be limited if their KERS systems aren't as good as their rivals', but expect this year's RB7 to be equally competitive and perhaps even more so. Expect too that their strength will continue to come at circuits with high-speed corners,

such as Sepang, Valencia, Silverstone and Suzuka.

With no change in the team's personnel, there remains one question mark. It's over how its drivers get on and how much they're prepared to cede to each other. Certainly, it was a mess in 2010, when Red Bull's sporting adviser Helmut Marko blamed Webber for the drivers' clash in Istanbul and Horner appeared to side with him, at first. That tension was still being felt by the time of the British GP, when Webber let all and sundry know that his win "wasn't bad for a number two". Perhaps it wasn't the wisest thing, said in the heat of the moment, but Horner will have to make it plain that both are receiving equal equipment and that no decision on tactics seems to favour one driver over another, otherwise Webber, whose contract expires this year, will be angered if Vettel becomes the team's man for the present as well as its man for the future.

FOR THE RECORD

Country of origin:	England
Team base:	Milton Keynes, England
Telephone:	(44) 01908 279700
Website:	www.redbullracing.com
Active in Formula One:	From 1997 (as Stewart until 2000, then Jaguar Racing until 2004)
Grands Prix contested:	242
Wins:	16
Pole positions:	21
Fastest laps:	12

THE TEAM

Chairman:	Dietrich Mateschitz
Team principal:	Christian Horner
Chief technical officer:	Adrian Newey
Head of race engineering:	Ian Morgan
Head of car engineering:	Paul Monaghan
Chief designer:	Rob Marshall
Head of vehicle performance:	Mark Ellis
Head of aerodynamics:	Peter Prodromou
Team manager:	Jonathan Wheatley
Test driver:	tba
Chassis:	Red Bull RB7
Engine:	Renault V8
Tyres:	Pirelli

"We don't underestimate our rivals and, with the performance we have achieved in 2010, they would be foolish to underestimate us."
Christian Horner

Team principal Christian Horner will be hoping to avoid last year's spats between his drivers.

SEBASTIAN VETTEL

He kept it late, but victory at last year's final round made Sebastian the youngest ever Formula One World Champion. This year, he will be out to double up and ensure that he makes fewer of the errors that made last year's passage to the title such a rocky road.

Sebastian all but collapsed after winning last year's final round in Abu Dhabi. Not because he was physically exhausted after racing in the heat as afternoon progressed to nightfall, but because he was emotionally drained. He had held his nerve and earned the sport's biggest prize, but his victory at Yas Marina required more than a peerless drive alone; it required his two arch-rivals, team-mate Mark Webber and Ferari's Fernando Alonso, to mess up, which they did. This was the first time that the 23-year-old had topped the points table.

Obviously, in a formula in which overtaking is rare, any driver who claims pole position 10 times in 19 grands prix ought to end up as the number one. This was even more the case last year than previously as refuelling was banned and so drivers were no longer able to qualify with next to no fuel in their tanks.

Yet, and this is the bit that will make Sebastian squirm, he came close to blowing it, as his first eight pole positions produced just three wins, with the first of his five wins, at Sepang, actually coming from third place on the grid. Many felt that Sebastian had lost his cool under the

Sebastian had much to smile about in 2010, but will he be more serious as champion?

weight of expectation because his car was superior to the rest.

His clash with team-mate Mark Webber in Turkey was the most obvious, but losing control and clattering into Jenson Button at Spa also stands out. Dropping back too far behind the safety car in the Hungarian GP was more a loss of focus.

Sebastian is aware that his career has been financed almost from the outset by Red Bull, and that puts him in a different position to his team-mate, with pressure from within from Red Bull sporting adviser Helmut Marko in particular.

Provided that Adrian Newey delivers another competitive chassis, and provided that no other team finds an advantage, then Sebastian will start 2011 as title favourite.

TRACK NOTES

Nationality:	GERMAN
Born:	3 JULY 1987, HEEPENHEIM, GERMANY
Website:	www.sebastianvettel.de
Teams:	BMW SAUBER 2007, TORO ROSSO 2007-08, RED BULL RACING 2009-11

CAREER RECORD	
First Grand Prix:	2007 UNITED STATES GP
Grand Prix starts:	62
Grand Prix wins:	10
2008 Italian GP, 2009 Chinese GP, British GP, Japanese GP, Abu Dhabi GP, 2010 Malaysian GP, European GP, Japanese GP, Brazilian GP, Abu Dhabi GP	
Poles:	15
Fastest laps:	6
Points:	381
Honours: 2010 FORMULA ONE WORLD CHAMPION, 2006 EUROPEAN FORMULA THREE RUNNER-UP, 2004 GERMAN FORMULA BMW CHAMPION, 2003 GERMAN FORMULA BMW RUNNER-UP, 2001 EUROPEAN & GERMAN JUNIOR KART CHAMPION	

RED BULL GAVE HIM WINGS

Sebastian has been one of the drivers to beat in literally every category in which he has raced, from junior karting right up to F1, and this is why he was signed up by Red Bull after his second season of car racing in the Formula BMW ADAC series in Germany, when he won 18 of the 20 rounds. F3 was next in 2005 and he was placed fifth at his first attempt at the Euro Series, which Lewis Hamilton won. Then Paul di Resta pipped him to the title in 2006. But what helped Sebastian most was becoming test driver for Sauber. He started 2007 in the Renault World Series and was leading this when Robert Kubica injured himself in Canada and Sebastian slotted in to become an F1 driver. It was a one-off, but he replaced Scott Speed at Scuderia Toro Rosso before the year was out and impressed with his speed. Racing full-time with Toro Rosso in 2008, he gave the team its first win, in the rain at Monza, then joined Red Bull Racing for 2009 and added four more.

MARK WEBBER

Mark didn't have it easy on his climb to F1 and needed help from Mercedes to keep his dream going. Fast but unrewarded seemed to be his story, then last year it looked as though it was coming together, only for a late-season dip to cost him dear. This year is his time for revenge.

The received wisdom is that Sebastian Vettel is the faster driver at Red Bull Racing, the driver on whom many of the team were placing their hopes. Then, last year, Mark proved to be the driver who delivered when it mattered. Is he as fast as the German? Perhaps not quite, but we're talking fractions here. Is he a better racer? Perhaps he is, and he certainly made fewer mistakes. Was he looking at his last chance to land the big one? More than likely.

What people forget to take into account when pointing out that Vettel had been the higher ranked of the duo in 2009, finishing second behind Jenson Button with Mark fourth, is that Mark started the year in less than 100% physical condition after his collision with a car when in his bike on an endurance race.

For 2010, there were no such excuses and Mark recovered from a disappointing start to the year to shine as the Red Bull RB6 began to show its supremacy. The thing is in F1, when you have the best car, you have to make the best use of it and Mark did. His determination not to be bettered surfaced in Turkey, when he

Mark had a tempestuous season and is returning determined to finish the job.

refused to let Vettel pass and they clashed. Having been blamed by the team for the collision, paranoia set in as he became convinced that the Austrian powerbase of team owner Dietrich Mateschitz and especially Red Bull motorsport adviser

Helmut Marko favoured Vettel. Typically, his response was clear when he won the British GP. Mark is a tough cookie and his refusal to cede to Lewis Hamilton showed how much the smell of the title had got into his nose.

The big question is whether the team will be fully behind this Aussie battler or allow him to start to feel again that Vettel is the chosen one. Indeed, there was talk last year that Mark might jack it all in and quit the sport if he became champion. But, he didn't, so he's back to try again.

TRACK NOTES

Nationality:	AUSTRALIAN
Born:	27 AUGUST 1976,
	QUEANBEYAN, AUSTRALIA
Website:	www.markwebber.com
Teams:	MINARDI 2002, JAGUAR 2003-04,
	WILLIAMS 2005-06, RED BULL RACING 2007-11

CAREER RECORD

First Grand Prix:	2002 AUSTRALIAN GP
Grand Prix starts:	158
Grand Prix wins:	6
2009 German GP, Brazilian GP, 2010 Spanish GP,	
Monaco GP, British GP, Hungarian GP	
Poles:	61
Fastest laps:	6
Points:	411.5
Honours:	2001 FORMULA 3000 RUNNER-UP,
1998 FIA GT RUNNER-UP, 1996 BRITISH	
FORMULA FORD RUNNER-UP & FORMULA FORD	
FESTIVAL WINNER	

A RACER AND AN ATHLETE

Unlike most of his F1 rivals, Mark didn't spend his childhood racing karts. He did a bit, but Formula Ford was his learning ground and he did well enough to come to race in Britain in a quest to launch his career. Trouble was, his funds started running dry when he was in F3 in 1997 and his career only kept going because Mercedes snapped him up to race sports cars for them. After two years of endurance racing, Mark made it back to single-seaters, becoming a front-runner in F3000. He made it to F1 in 2002 because fellow Aussie Paul Stoddart wanted him for his Minardi team and he did well enough to move on to Jaguar, then Williams. But still those wins didn't come, until the third year of his spell at Red Bull, at the Nurburgring in 2009. Mark is one of those racers who could have made a career in another sport. He became hooked on triathlons, running his own charity event in Tasmania, and one feels that this will be his next challenge when he retires from racing.

McLaren

All the ingredients – two top drivers, one of F1's healthiest budgets and a stable technical line-up – are in place for McLaren to have a great season. Indeed, after a couple of years of being not quite on the pace, it's high time the team started being the class of the field again.

Lewis Hamilton was McLaren's pace-setter in 2010 and will be going all out to give the team more wins and another title in the season ahead.

Observing the pace-setting speed of the Red Bull RB6s last year as they racked up pole position after pole position must have had McLaren, with its sole pole, cursing the day that it let design hero Adrian Newey leave. McLaren did win races, but there were other grands prix when the silver and red cars could scarcely hope even for a healthy helping of championship points.

There's no doubting that McLaren's modus operandi requires that all 550 of its employees will give their all to attempt to overcome any performance shortfalls, as shown by its incredible advances made through the 2009 campaign. However, there are question marks over whether the Neil Oatley-led design team can equal Newey's best offerings.

Certainly, McLaren can be proud that the F-duct system it introduced from the outset of last season was adopted by its rivals through the year, showing that the team still has an innovative approach. However, other teams were innovative too with their blown diffusers. Overall, there is a feeling that McLaren has tended to play it safe over the years rather than take risks in its quest to be fastest. Engineering director Paddy Lowe will have to drive the team hard to change

KEY MOMENTS AND KEY PEOPLE

TEAM HISTORY

Founded by Bruce McLaren in 1966, this is a team that survived his death in a crash when testing at Goodwood in 1970, became regular winners through the 1970s, helping Emerson Fittipaldi and James Hunt become World Champions, then faded. The arrival of Ron Dennis at the helm and John Barnard on the design desk launched a purple patch, with seven drivers' titles being claimed in eight years from 1984. Mika Hakkinen added two more in 1998 and 1999, before McLaren took the battle to Ferrari, Renault and Red Bull Racing through the decade since 2000, overcoming an espionage charge in 2007, then winning the 2008 drivers' title through Lewis Hamilton.

PADDY LOWE

An engineering graduate from Cambridge University, Paddy earned his reputation in the electronics department at Williams. McLaren snapped him up in 1993 and he became head of R&D in the Vehicle Technology division. Promoted in 2001 to be chief engineer in the systems department, Paddy stepped up to be the team's engineering director in 2005, a position he holds to this day.

2010 DRIVERS & RESULTS

Driver	Nationality	Races	Wins	Pts	Pos
Jenson Button	British	19	2	240	4th
Lewis Hamilton	British	19	3	214	5th

FOR THE RECORD

Country of origin:	England
Team base:	Woking, England
Telephone:	(44) 01483 728211
Website:	www.mclaren.com
Active in Formula One:	From 1966
Grands Prix contested:	685
Wins:	169
Pole positions:	146
Fastest laps:	143

THE TEAM

Team principal:	Martin Whitmarsh
Managing director:	Jonathan Neale
Engineering director:	Paddy Lowe
Design & development director:	Neil Oatley
Head of aerodynamics:	John Iley
Head of vehicle design:	Andrew Bailey
Head of race operations:	Simon Roberts
Head of vehicle engineering:	Mark Williams
Team manager:	David Redding
Chief race engineer:	Philip Prew
Test driver:	tba
Chassis:	McLaren MP4-26
Engine:	Mercedes V8
Tyres:	Pirelli

its mindset, but the relative levels of competitiveness among the top teams in 2010 will have proved that this must be done to hit the top again in 2011.

Perhaps McLaren's best hope of rediscovering its cutting-edge form is the reintroduction of KERS, a system that the team used to good effect in 2009. This is very much the sort of technological challenge at which McLaren excels, so its drivers Lewis Hamilton and Jenson Button must be excited that they will find a vital advantage in KERS, at least in the early stages of the campaign.

Then there is the role of teamwork in the decisions made on race strategy by the crew on the pitwall during the race. If conditions were wet or changeable, McLaren proved the most adept last year, showing how Whitmarsh has shaped the team to learn lessons from bygone years, when an inherent caution seemed to hold it back from changing tactics with the ease and confidence of Ross Brawn in his days at Ferrari.

Of course, the team's driving line-up has a huge role to play and it's safe to say that Button and Hamilton showed a healthy level of respect for each other last year in their first championship campaign together. Anyone who saw any of the excellent viral online advertisements that they shot together will have realised that their personal chemistry is natural,

not forced, and this will have benefited Hamilton in particular, especially after he'd started the season without his father as his manager for the first time and could have felt cast adrift.

So, can McLaren produce a champion again? They certainly have drivers good enough to do it but, on the evidence of last year's title bid, it depends whether their management and shrewd race tactics can counteract the best that Newey can produce for Red Bull Racing, whether Hamilton can stay out of the contact zone and whether the team will manage not to repeat mistakes, such as leaving a radiator cover in Button's sidepod, as it did in Monaco, overheating his engine and leading to an early retirement. If Button's experience of a year with the team helps him to be more in tune with the car and thus able to qualify better, it might also depend on how the team manages its drivers should they be equal on points in the title run-in.

"You have to have fundamentally a good car and you have got to have some creative solutions, be they blown diffusers or F-ducts – and hopefully we will have a couple of those and we can be strong."
Martin Whitmarsh

Martin Whitmarsh is anxious to start recording the success that Ron Dennis achieved.

Flashes of blinding speed, plenty of aggression, occasional resignation when the car wasn't competitive and two self-inflicted collisions that left him with damaging non-scores marked Lewis's 2010 campaign. For 2011, if McLaren can deliver, so most certainly will Lewis.

There is undoubtedly a pack of very talented drivers at the top in F1 at present. Lewis is right there with the best of them. Yet, like many a World Champion or star driver in the past, he can only deliver the goods when supplied with the tools with which to do it.

Last year, there were many occasions when, quite simply, McLaren couldn't help him to his dreams. However, like all good World Champions, Lewis delivered when they did, as shown by his wins at Istanbul, Montreal and Spa-Francorchamps. The flip to that was his rash dive up the inside of Felipe Massa into the second chicane on the opening lap of the Italian GP. He crashed out of the following race in Singapore too, but that was more of a racing incident than a rash one as he turned in from the outside line to find that Mark Webber hadn't ceded. On both occasions, though, McLaren team principal Martin Whitmarsh said that he wasn't going to ask Lewis to change his ways, as his desire to attack was what defined him.

Lewis appeared to enjoy not only team-mate Jenson Button's company in their first season together but his technical input too. This will be something on which they can build, with both aware that this is a team that

Lewis will be demanding a car with which he can qualify well and win consistently in 2011.

famously will offer them an equal chance such is its abhorrence of team orders.

To make Lewis's life easier, he will be hoping that McLaren can produce a car that can qualify better than last year's MP4-25, which tended to be relatively better in race trim. Yet, by then, especially on those tracks on which overtaking is limited, the chances of race wins had dwindled.

Being ranked just fourth in last year's championship will only have stoked Lewis's desire to be champion again.

TRACK NOTES

Nationality:	BRITISH
Born:	7 JANUARY 1985, STEVENAGE, ENGLAND
Website:	www.lewishamilton.com
Teams:	McLAREN 2007-11

CAREER RECORD

First Grand Prix:	2007 AUSTRALIAN GP
Grand Prix starts:	71
Wins:	14
	2007 Canadian GP, United States GP, Hungarian GP, Japanese GP, 2008 Australian GP, Monaco GP, British GP, German GP, Chinese GP, 2009 Hungarian GP, Singapore GP, 2010 Turkish GP, Canadian GP, Belgian GP
Pole positions:	18
Fastest laps:	8
Points:	496
Honours:	2008 FORMULA ONE WORLD CHAMPION, 2006 GP2 CHAMPION, 2005 EUROPEAN FORMULA THREE CHAMPION, 2003 BRITISH FORMULA RENAULT CHAMPION, 2000 WORLD KART CUP CHAMPION & EUROPEAN FORMULA A KARTING CHAMPION, 1999 ITALIAN INTERCONTINENTAL A KARTING CHAMPION, 1996 McLAREN MERCEDES CHAMPION OF THE FUTURE, 1995 BRITISH CADET KARTING CHAMPION

HE ASKED AND HE GOT

Not many drivers would, aged just 11, dare to approach an F1 team boss and suggest that he backed them. But Lewis did, to McLaren's Ron Dennis, no less. The rest is history, as Dennis eventually agreed to do so, enabling Lewis not only to continue, but to do so with the best equipment available. World Champion in 2000, he moved on to cars at the end of 2001 and started collecting titles in Formula Renault then F3, often at the second attempt. However, when he reached GP2, F1's feeder formula, he was the dominant character in his rookie season, ending the season as champion. F1 beckoned, with McLaren of course, and history relates that he was soon winning races, and the season ended up being his to lose when he arrived at the final round in Brazil holding the points lead, but Ferrari's Kimi Raikkonen pipped him by a point. There was no mistake in 2008, though, and Lewis continued winning through 2009 once McLaren had made its car competitive.

JENSON BUTTON

The intra-team battle between Jenson and Lewis Hamilton was one of the most eagerly anticipated features of the 2010 season and it highlighted their different talents. In many ways, it boosted Jenson's reputation even more than his 2009 World Championship title.

Prior to Jenson's decision late in 2009 to quit Brawn GP as it became Mercedes Grand Prix and to join McLaren, everyone had their opinion about Jenson and Lewis Hamilton. In truth, most would have put Lewis ahead on points and so the general view was, when Jenson announced that they would be team-mates in 2010, that Lewis would roast him. Jenson is the smooth one, people would say, Lewis the racer.

That opinion is right to an extent, as Lewis remains the more on-the-edge racer, more able to string together a flying lap, but Jenson's more considered driving style showed how it could land results whenever the conditions were wet or wet/dry, as his wins in Melbourne and Shanghai proved.

There were no more wins after that, but Jenson greatly impressed the McLaren team. Added to his on-track ability, Jenson also helped to maintain the non-confrontational atmosphere in the team that had developed after Fernando Alonso's departure. However, unlike Heikki Kovalainen before him, Jenson had to be treated as an equal by Lewis, who, don't forget, didn't win until the seventh round last year, by which time Jenson had already won a couple of grands prix.

Jenson will be looking to improve his form in qualifying in order to boost his challenge.

What was clear is that Jenson and Lewis respected each other and so pooled their knowledge constructively as they fought to rival Red Bull Racing and Ferrari.

Looking ahead to 2011, if they are blessed with pace-setting machinery, Jenson must develop the ability to get heat into his tyres to start matching Lewis in qualifying if he's to come out on top. Perhaps his position will improve as this is his second year with the team. Only time will tell, but Jenson certainly faces 2011 with an enhanced reputation and the extra confidence that this brings. He also brings a smiling face to McLaren, a softer image than Lewis offers, and that's a good thing.

TRACK NOTES

Nationality:	BRITISH
Born:	19 JANUARY 1980, FROME, ENGLAND
Website:	www.jensonbutton.com
Teams:	WILLIAMS 2000, BENETTON/RENAULT 2001-02, BAR/HONDA 2003-08, BRAWN 2009, McLAREN 2010-11

CAREER RECORD

First Grand Prix:	2000 AUSTRALIAN GP
Grand Prix starts:	190
Grand Prix wins:	9
	2006 Hungarian GP, 2009 Australian GP, Malaysian GP, Bahrain GP, Spanish GP, Monaco GP, Turkish GP, 2010 Malaysian GP, Chinese GP
Poles:	7
Fastest laps:	3
Points:	541
Honours:	2009 FORMULA ONE WORLD CHAMPION, 1999 MACAU FORMULA THREE RUNNER-UP, 1998 BRITISH FORMULA FORD CHAMPION & McLAREN AUTOSPORT BRDC YOUNG DRIVER, 1997 EUROPEAN SUPER A KART CHAMPION

FROM CADET KARTS TO THE TITLE

Here was a driver who was clearly a star in a reasonably priced kart. After multiple titles at British and European level, he stepped up to Formula Ford in 1998 when 18, winning the British title and Formula Ford Festival. Jenson then jumped a level to graduate to F3 and was instantly impressive in that. However, after ranking third, it was his test for the Prost F1 team that made people take notice. This led to a trial with Williams and he landed his seat for 2000. He had really impressed by season's end. Then, with Benetton in 2001 and Renault in 2002, Jenson went off the boil. David Richards rated him, though, and signed Jenson for BAR Honda for 2003. After finishing third overall in 2004, the team's form dropped and it took victory in Hungary in 2006 to rebuild his reputation. Then, when all looked bleak, Ross Brawn took over from Honda, the team was renamed Brawn GP and gave him a winning car for 2009. Jenson completed the fairy tale by taking the world title with six wins.

FERRARI

> Ferrari rediscovered its form in 2010 and advanced markedly through the season. Whether this upswing can be turned into regular race-winning form in 2011 remains to be seen, but Fernando Alonso remains extremely hungry so the signs are good for the Tifosi.

With Fernando Alonso at the wheel, the Tifosi can be confident that if the 2011 Ferrari is good enough to win races, then races will be won.

Ferrari doesn't do normal. Its long and illustrious history contains troughs as well as peaks and the undying passion of its supporters, the Tifosi, means that things veer between triumph and disaster, with little settling in between.

So, last year, which was its best since 2008, lurched between euphoria as Fernando Alonso was triumphant on his debut for the team in red, to feeling distraught when watching some dire performances mid-season at Istanbul, Valencia and Silverstone.

Then, of course, came the furore when the team manipulated the German GP at Hockenheim so clumsily in suggesting that Felipe Massa might like to relinquish the lead to team-mate Alonso. So there was a one-two, but it brought upset as well as delight. How typical!

One thing that marks out the management of Stefano Domenicali is that he gets things done without drama or seeking recriminations, as had certain former Ferrari team chiefs, and so the team knuckled down under the technical guidance of Aldo Costa and Alonso got himself back into the title race as the team offered him a car good enough to win at Monza, then Singapore, outstripping McLaren's advances.

KEY MOMENTS AND KEY PEOPLE

TEAM HISTORY
For all of McLaren's success since the late 1960s, Ferrari remains the team with the most of everything, from poles to fastest laps to wins. As it's the only team still going from the first year of the World Championship, this is to be expected. However, its success stems from founder Enzo Ferrari's competitive ambitions. Ferrari began winning in 1951 thanks to Jose Froilan Gonzalez. Then it started producing champions as Alberto Ascari dominated in 1952 and 1953. Juan Manuel Fangio was World Champion in 1956, then Mike Hawthorn (1958), Phil Hill (1961), John Surtees (1964), Niki Lauda (1975 & 1977), Jody Scheckter (1979) and Michael Schumacher (2000–04).

ALDO COSTA
Ferrari's technical director graduated in mechanical engineering and started his career with Abarth in 1987. He reached F1 in 1988, working for Minardi, where he rose from stress engineer to become chief designer. He stayed until 1995, then moved to Ferrari in 1996 to work in its vehicle design office, then the competition arm in 2005, becoming technical director in 2008.

2010 DRIVERS & RESULTS

Driver	Nationality	Races	Wins	Pts	Pos
Fernando Alonso	Spanish	19	5	252	1st
Felipe Massa	Brazilian	19	0	144	6th

After much talk of whether Felipe Massa would be kept on for 2011, even as early as the Malaysian GP in April, as he failed to keep up with Alonso, the Brazilian signed a contract extension to include 2011 in early June. Then, a week later, it was lengthened to include 2012 as well.

However, despite this supposed security of tenure, talk continued for the remainder of the season that he might be replaced. The Ferrari president sent out mixed messages in the closing races, appearing to suggest that he ought to raise his game in one breath, then supporting him in the next. This must have been most unsettling for Massa, but not as much as scoring no wins while Alonso bagged four. Ferrari's fans know just how much pressure the drivers get put under and the overriding desire to be the best again will have them crying out for Alonso to be joined by his good friend and poker partner Robert Kubica for the season after this one. Indeed, that would be the strongest partnership at Ferrari in memory, perhaps even its best ever, so they will just have to wait another year.

One arrival who will certainly play a key role will be Pat Fry, the engineer who was such a long-standing servant at McLaren and is sure to add value to the engineering team and a good helping of the management style that took McLaren back to the top with Lewis Hamilton. Of course, the incoming assistant technical director got to know Alonso in 2007 and so will be able to renew his acquaintance.

One of the keys to success in the year ahead will be how the teams' new cars suit the new Pirelli tyres that will be used in place of Bridgestones. Until racing gets under way, though, nobody will have a clue which team has been most successful in its performance simulations.

There was proof last year that this is a team that is looking to make itself not just fast but consistently fast, so that it doesn't have off days such as the one at the Belgian GP, when its cars were well off the ultimate pace and Massa was able to finish fourth only due to attrition among the front-runners. Whether the Tifosi will accept consistency rather than their diet of highs and lows remains to be seen. They might, after all, be thrown by not being able to play one off against the other.

FOR THE RECORD

Country of origin:	Italy
Team base:	Maranello, Italy
Telephone:	(39) 536 949111
Website:	www.ferrari.com
Active in Formula One:	From 1950
Grands Prix contested:	812
Wins:	215
Pole positions:	205
Fastest laps:	221

THE TEAM

President:	Luca di Montezemolo
Team principal:	Stefano Domenicali
Technical director:	Aldo Costa
Assistant technical director:	Pat Fry
Chief designer:	Nikolas Tombazis
Chief aerodynamicist:	Marco de Luca
Chief engineer:	Mattia Binotto
Head of operations research:	Neil Martin
Sporting director:	Massimo Rivola
Test driver:	Jules Bianchi
Chassis:	Ferrari F11
Engine:	Ferrari V8
Tyres:	Pirelli

"Fernando is an extraordinary driver and an extraordinary person. He demonstrated powers of leadership from both inside and outside the cockpit and we will do all we can to give him and Felipe an even better car in 2011."
Stefano Domenicali

Stefano Domenicali has grown into the role as team principal and the results are flowing.

After two relatively toothless years with Renault, Fernando was back to his snarling, competitive best last year. The former World Champion established himself as the main man at Ferrari in his first season with the Italian team, his title bid only falling at the final hurdle.

Every driver has the vanity to dream of joining Ferrari, winning grands prix and being fêted by a uniquely adoring fanbase. Few achieve even the first of these, but Fernando Alonso had all three sorted by the time he left Bahrain after the opening race of last season.

A comic-book storyline would have Fernando fighting back against the odds to clinch the title at the final grand prix. This didn't quite happen, but the late-season back-to-back wins at Monza and Singapore fanned the flames of hope. Fernando had his swagger back and the tools with which to display his ruthless desire to win.

With Sebastian Vettel, Mark Webber, Lewis Hamilton, Jenson Button and Robert Kubica all at the top of their game, this is a good time for F1 and Fernando is sure to be in there mixing it with them again in 2011.

However, not all was sweetness and light last year, most especially what happened at the German GP, when Ferrari's decision to ask Fernando's team-mate Felipe Massa to cede the lead to him caused upset. Whatever one's view on whether a team should have a right to elect where its drivers finish, what upset many was

Fernando was comfortable at Ferrari from the start and the team reacted to his needs.

Fernando's assumption that it was only natural that his team-mate should move aside "as I was faster". Still, in keeping with the mind games that drivers play, that's what Fernando believed and so the story could be bent to fit it. Self-deceit to bolster

self-confidence is nothing new at the top level of sport, acting or even politics, so it should come as little surprise.

What is clear is that Fernando enjoyed the taste of champagne on the podium again, for the first time since 2008, and is sure to want more in the season ahead.

TRACK NOTES

Nationality:	SPANISH
Born:	29 JULY 1981, OVIEDO, SPAIN
Website:	www.fernandoalonso.com
Teams:	MINARDI 2001, RENAULT 2003–06, McLAREN 2007, RENAULT 2008–09, FERRARI 2010–11

CAREER RECORD

First Grand Prix:	2001 AUSTRALIAN GP
Grand Prix starts:	159
Grand Prix wins:	26

2003 Hungarian GP, 2005 Malaysian GP, Bahrain GP, San Marino GP, European GP, French GP, German GP, Chinese GP, 2006 Bahrain GP, Australian GP, Spanish GP, Monaco GP, British GP, Canadian GP, Japanese GP, 2007 Malaysian GP, Monaco GP, European GP, Italian GP, 2008 Singapore GP, Japanese GP, 2010 Australian GP, German GP, Italian GP, Singapore GP, Korean GP

Poles:	20
Fastest laps:	18
Points:	829

Honours: 2005 & 2006 FORMULA ONE WORLD CHAMPION, 1999 FORMULA NISSAN CHAMPION, 1997 ITALIAN & SPANISH KART CHAMPION, 1996 WORLD & SPANISH KART CHAMPION, 1995 & 1994 SPANISH JUNIOR KART CHAMPION

WORLD CHAMPION IN KARTS AND CARS

Fernando was always a driver in a hurry. Having blazed a trail through the Spanish karting scene, he turned his attention to the World Championship in 1996, when he was turning 15 and won that as well as his third Spanish crown. Clearly, it was time for cars, but he had to wait until he was old enough and duly made his debut in Formula Nissan, bypassing the lower formulae. Champion at his first attempt, in 1999, he graduated to F3000 and impressed with a runaway win at the hardest circuit it visited, Spa-Francorchamps. Flavio Briatore snapped him up and he made it to F1 by the time he was 19, with Minardi. After a year spent as Renault test driver in 2002, he returned with the team in 2003, won world titles in 2005 and 2006, then went to McLaren for more. But although he ranked equal second in the championship, there had been unrest as it wasn't a match made in heaven and it took another spell with Renault in one of the team's less competitive periods before Ferrari signed him for 2010.

FELIPE MASSA

If 2008 had been cruel as he was pipped to the drivers' title by Lewis Hamilton in the dying seconds and 2009 was interrupted by a life-threatening injury, then 2010 was painful in its own way as Felipe had to face up to team orders and the relentless pace of Fernando Alonso.

Life has bestowed fantastic gifts on Felipe, from a happy nature to outstanding skill in a racing car to the breaks that took him to Ferrari. However, now that he is recovered from that Hungarian head injury, his most recent pain stems from an event on the anniversary of that fateful weekend in Hungary. This was last summer's German GP, when he was asked to hand the lead to his team-mate Fernando Alonso, who was vociferous that he was capable of lapping faster than Felipe could at that stage of the race. He yielded to the request and was forced to accept second place. He was disappointed with the team and angry with himself. It became worse when Brazilian fans couldn't forgive him for ceding to the Spaniard and his reputation took a battering.

There had briefly been talk of Robert Kubica taking his place at Ferrari, but Felipe signed a new contract midway through June, lining him up for this year and 2012 as well.

However, that's all behind him now and he ended up having to make up with ranking just 6th overall, some way behind Alonso, McLaren's Lewis Hamilton and

Felipe was made to play number two in 2010 and must fight back to save his reputation.

Jenson Button, Red Bull Racing's Mark Webber and Sebastian Vettel, as well as his own team-mate Alonso.

So, has his confidence been damaged by this episode that edged him out of the title race? Only time will tell.

However, perceptions can be formed and they're then hard to shake off. Yes, there were times when he outpaced Alonso, but one can only feel that Alonso's late-season charge will cement the view that he's the team's rightful lead driver and that Felipe is good only for a supporting role. He won't be the first to have had this inflicted on him, but it's how he responds to the challenge of re-establishing himself that will prove whether Felipe is a driver worthy of becoming champion.

TRACK NOTES

Nationality:	BRAZILIAN
Born:	25 APRIL 1981, SAO PAULO, BRAZIL
Website:	www.felipemassa.com
Teams:	SAUBER 2002 & 2004-05, FERRARI 2006-11

CAREER RECORD	
First Grand Prix:	2002 AUSTRALIAN GP
Grand Prix starts:	134
Grand Prix wins:	11
	2006 Turkish GP, Brazilian GP, 2007 Bahrain GP, Spanish GP, Turkish GP, 2008 Bahrain GP, Turkish GP, French GP, European GP, Belgian GP, Brazilian GP
Poles:	15
Fastest laps:	12
Points:	464
Honours:	2008 FORMULA ONE RUNNER-UP, 2001 EUROPEAN FORMULA 3000 CHAMPION, 2000 EUROPEAN & ITALIAN FORMULA RENAULT CHAMPION, 1999 BRAZILIAN FORMULA CHEVROLET CHAMPION

COMING IN UNDER THE RADAR

Felipe won the Brazilian Formula Chevrolet series in 1999, aged 18. He then headed to Europe in 2000 and won not only the Italian Formula Renault series but the more senior European one too. Felipe then took an unusual route: he raced not in F3 but the F3000 Euro Series, a second-rank series that offered more power but less prestige. Felipe won that and wangled an F1 test ride with Sauber. Kimi Raikkonen had been selected by Sauber as something of an unknown and given an F1 ride for 2001. Felipe followed his lead and was on the grid in 2002, displaying great speed but a wild driving style. Being Ferrari's test driver in 2003 honed his style, before he returned for two years with Sauber. He landed a Ferrari race seat in 2006 and won twice, learning alongside Michael Schumacher. In 2008, Felipe was World Champion for about 10 seconds at the end of the Brazilian GP before Lewis Hamilton passed Timo Glock to outpoint him. Then he suffered his head injury in Hungary in 2009.

Mercedes put its toe in the water last year after taking over the Brawn GP team. Its expectations were probably too high and it was disappointed, but its form started to come good as the season ended, so expect a better showing from its drivers in 2011 with a superior car.

Nico Rosberg was Mercedes GP's pace-setter in 2010, but if the 2011 car suits Michael Schumacher's driving style, then he is sure to challenge.

After Brawn GP's fairy-tale season in 2009 when it was created to save the team that was once Honda Racing from folding and then duly won almost half of the season's races and scooped both the drivers' and constructors' titles, last year was difficult.

One might have thought that the team had to do little more than change the cars' liveries from white, black and acid yellow to Mercedes-Benz's traditional silver and the wins would continue to flow. However, if only Formula One was that simple, as not even one victory came their way. In fact, only three podium finishes did, all third places, even with seven-time World Champion Michael Schumacher at the wheel of one of its cars.

This year, you can be sure, will be different, as many blame last year's drop in form relative to 2009 on the team's technical and design side, which continued to focus on that year's car to ensure that they finished the job and landed that year's titles. Thus the team's 2010 car, the Mercedes W01, suffered.

Whether this is fair comment or not, team principal Ross Brawn, a technically minded man through and through, will have left no stone unturned as he sought to redress that failure and build a superior car for 2011. Certainly he will want to

KEY MOMENTS AND KEY PEOPLE

TEAM HISTORY
Mercedes ran a team in F1 from midway through 1954 to the end of 1955. Then, in reaction to one of its cars crashing into the crowds at Le Mans, it quit. Mercedes would return as an engine supplier from 1994. In the meantime, the BAR team was established in 1999 and this morphed into Honda Racing as the Japanese manufacturer invested more and more. Then, at the end of the 2008 season, it quit. Brawn GP rose from its ashes, won the title with Mercedes engines and then Mercedes bought its way back in and the cars became painted Mercedes' traditional silver for 2010, running as Mercedes GP.

NORBERT HAUG
Norbert started his career as a journalist on the *Sport Auto* and *Auto Motor & Sport* magazines in Germany, then moved to Mercedes-Benz in 1990 to run its motorsport marketing department. However, within three months he was handed the responsibility for all of its motorsport programmes, ranging across F1, Indy cars, sports cars and touring cars, taking over the position when Jochen Neerpasch quit. He has enjoyed considerable success.

2010 DRIVERS & RESULTS

Driver	Nationality	Races	Wins	Pts	Pos
Nico Rosberg	German	19	0	142	7th
Michael Schumacher	German	19	0	72	9th

FOR THE RECORD

Country of origin:	England
Team base:	Brackley, England
Telephone:	(44) 01280 844000
Website:	www.mercedes-gp.com
Active in Formula One:	From 1999
(as BAR until 2005, as Honda Racing until	
2008 and Brawn GP in 2009)	
Grands Prix contested:	207
Wins:	9
Pole positions:	8
Fastest laps:	4

THE TEAM

Team principal:	Ross Brawn
Chief executive officer:	Nick Fry
Vice-president, Mercedes-Benz	
Motorsport:	Norbert Haug
Head of aerodynamics:	Loic Bigois
Head of vehicle engineering:	Craig Wilson
Operations director:	Gary Savage
Sporting director:	Ron Meadows
Chief engineer:	tba
Test driver:	tba
Chassis:	Mercedes W02
Engine:	Mercedes V8
Tyres:	Pirelli

build one that might get the best out of Schumacher, as the German great certainly appeared a shadow of his former self as he failed to match fellow team arrival Nico Rosberg. It's said that Schumacher just couldn't get last year's car's tyres to work, not finding them responsive enough for his liking, and so preventing him from getting the most out of it. This year, perhaps the tyres from new supplier Pirelli will give him more confidence than the Bridgestones did last year, but you can be sure that the 42-year-old will be training flat-out to try and find even the most fractional advantage to help him claw his way back into the mix.

When Schumacher was accused of being past it last summer, Mercedes-Benz motorsport boss Norbert Haug defended him and said that people ought to judge him on the season ahead. Then, if he fails to raise his game, it's highly likely that this will be his last season, and that he will miss the third year of his contract and thus open up a way for the likes of Mercedes protégé Paul di Resta to land a ride for 2012.

Should that happen, rumours will resurface that Schumacher will move into a management role, perhaps eventually replacing Brawn, with whom he worked so closely when they were at Benetton, then Ferrari, combining to produce so many victories through gambling with tactics that were different from their rivals'. Of course, Schumacher learnt about

more than just tactics, and his sheer determination to ensure the maximum input from everyone in the team was another factor that turned Ferrari back into winners.

So, for the second year running there's considerable focus on Schumacher, but it's Rosberg who really deserves more consideration, for if Brawn, Loic Bigois, Craig Wilson and the gang can make the W02 a more competitive package, then perhaps the son of the 1982 World Champion will finally turn his podium visits to ones that take in that long-desired leap up onto the top step as a winner.

This won't be a make-or-break year for Mercedes GP, as the finances are in place to spend what it takes to succeed, but it's an important campaign, as all the characters involved, save Rosberg, are accustomed to winning, and any less surely won't be tolerated for long.

''For 2011, we have been pretty bold on what sort of car we want to create and we've got a good enough engineering structure in place now to support these ideas.''

Ross Brawn

Ross Brawn spent much of 2010 upgrading the team's engineering structure and wants wins.

23

MICHAEL SCHUMACHER

Michael was back in F1, armed with seven world titles and 91 grand prix wins, yet he reached the end of the year without adding any more to his tally. Indeed, if this year's Mercedes doesn't help him rediscover his form, he might be heading back into retirement again.

Any sportsman returning to the sport they left in triumph stands the risk of disappointment. Sure, motor racing ought to be different, as it's not as physically demanding as football or rugby, as technique can make up for some of the gathering years. However, this wasn't any old sportsman, but Michael Schumacher. Poor team-mate (Nico Rosberg), people thought.

Yet, there was no instant domination from Michael. That wasn't a surprise, as the Mercedes W01 wasn't the pick of the crop. That Michael's fans could have lived with. However, he wasn't even the top performer in his own team, with Rosberg outqualifying him 15 times in the 19 rounds and outracing him too.

Michael's defenders said the car hadn't been designed with his driving style in mind. Some said he was tentative as he was still stiff from his tumbles when motorbike racing. Yet he never managed to make up the shortfall.

Worse than that, he produced the dodgiest move of the year when he guided Rubens Barrichello towards the pit wall in Hungary.

As the season approached its close, there was increasing pressure from Mercedes' motorsport boss Norbert Haug for Michael to improve in 2011 or the team might end his three-year contract early. That's to say at the end of this year. Team principal Ross Brawn

Michael still loves F1, but the ex-champion won't rest until he's a winner again.

said: "Michael isn't at his best yet. I'd prefer it if they regularly beat one another. It's not good when one driver is usually behind."

For fans everywhere, let's hope that this racing legend can find his feet again in 2011. And that he doesn't have to resort to the sort of driving he employed against Barrichello.

24

TRACK NOTES

Nationality:	GERMAN
Born:	3 JANUARY 1969, KERPEN, GERMANY
Website:	www.michael-schumacher.de
Teams:	1991 JORDAN, 1991-95 BENETTON, 1996-2006 FERRARI, 2010-11 MERCEDES

CAREER RECORD

First Grand Prix:	1991 BELGIAN GP
Grand Prix starts:	269
Grand Prix wins:	91

1992 Belgian GP, 1993 Portuguese GP, 1994 Brazilian GP, Pacific GP, San Marino GP, Monaco GP, Canadian GP, French GP, Hungarian GP, European GP, 1995 Brazilian GP, Spanish GP, Monaco GP, French GP, German GP, Belgian GP, European GP, Pacific GP, Japanese GP, 1996 Spanish GP, Belgian GP, Italian GP, 1997 Monaco GP, Canadian GP, French GP, Belgian GP, Japanese GP, 1998 Argentinian GP, Canadian GP, French GP, British GP, Hungarian GP, Italian GP, 1999 San Marino GP, Monaco GP, 2000 Australian GP, Brazilian GP, San Marino GP, European GP, Canadian GP, Italian GP, US GP, Japanese GP, Malaysian GP, 2001 Australian GP, Malaysian GP, Spanish GP, Monaco GP, European GP, French GP, Hungarian GP, Belgian GP, Japanese GP, 2002 Australian GP, Brazilian GP, San Marino GP, Spanish GP, Austrian GP, Canadian GP, British GP, French GP, German GP, Belgian GP, Japanese GP, 2003 San Marino GP, Spanish GP, Austrian GP, Canadian GP, Italian GP, US GP, 2004 Australian GP, Malaysian GP, Bahrain GP, San Marino GP, Spanish GP, European GP, Canadian GP, French GP, British GP, German GP, Hungarian GP, Japanese GP, US GP, 2005 US GP, 2006 San Marino GP, European GP, US GP, French GP, German GP, Italian GP, Chinese GP

Poles:	68
Fastest laps:	75
Points:	1441
Honours:	2004, 2003, 2002, 2001, 2000, 1995 & 1994 FORMULA ONE WORLD CHAMPION, 1990 GERMAN FORMULA THREE CHAMPION, 1988 GERMAN FORMULA KONIG CHAMPION

STARTING WITH A DREAM ADVANTAGE

Having millionaires as parents can give a child a huge advantage. Then again, so can having a father who ran a kart circuit, as Michael's did. Bolstered by considerable track time, his natural ability was enough to propel him into car racing, winning the Formula Konig title and shining in Formula Ford in his first season, 1988. That he then came within a few points of winning the German F3 title at his first attempt proved his talent and he'd already been taken on by driver manager Willi Weber. Having won the 1990 German F3 title, Willi guided him into F1 in 1991 when Bertrand Gachot was jailed for assaulting a taxi driver, freeing up a seat at Jordan. He jumped ship to join Benetton for the following race and his four full campaigns with the team yielded two F1 titles before he moved to Ferrari in 1996. Michael made the team win again and then landed five straight titles from 2000 to 2004 before retiring at the end of 2006.

NICO ROSBERG

Imagine the scene: you've built up your reputation with Williams, have signed a deal to transfer to the team that's leading the constructors' championship (Brawn GP, which became Mercedes GP) and then you find out that your new team-mate will be Michael Schumacher...

This was the scenario that presented itself to Nico Rosberg as 2009 approached its close. He had achieved what looked like a dream move from a midfield team - Williams - to a team that was winning grands prix on a regular basis. The team's potential money problems were to be sorted by Mercedes bringing along its manufacturing might. And then came the fly in the ointment, a seven-time World Champion arriving to spoil your fun. Small wonder Nico looked jaded when almost all the media attention at the team launch was focused on his team-mate, not him.

As the form of teams is fickle, it's always said that the best way to judge a driver is against the form of his team-mate. So, it wasn't long before Nico was smiling once the racing season got under way and Schumacher was to be found behind him not only on the grid but also in the races. While race wins weren't coming their way, Nico was on the podium in the third and fourth rounds, and yet, even accounting for taking a few races to shake off the rustiness of being out of racing for three years, Schumacher couldn't match him.

The way Nico met the challenge of his esteemed team-mate last year earned praise.

Although Michael was famous for getting the team to dance to his tune, it wasn't long before the team was looking first to Nico, which was extremely empowering for the younger German.

Furthermore, Nico's calm manner,

analytical brain and guidance from his father, Keke (World Champion in 1982), put him in an increasingly strong position.

It's more than likely that Mercedes GP will have a more competitive car for its second season, so expect Nico to have realistic ambitions to become a race winner at last in 2011. And if Schumacher isn't able to start beating him with a car that is sure to have been designed with Michael's particular driving style in mind, this really will be a feather in Nico's cap.

Nico's highlights in 2010 turned out to be a trio of third-place finishes at Sepang, Shanghai and Silverstone, plus a fighting fourth in Abu Dhabi and, when racing a car not capable of winning, he proved that he's waiting for one that just might be.

WITH GUIDANCE FROM A CHAMPION

Nico's father, 1982 World Champion Keke Rosberg, helped him into kart racing by running a team. This team would include a team-mate: Lewis Hamilton. It's fair to say that Lewis was the faster of the two, but he should have been, as Lewis was five years older. Once he'd turned 17, Nico stepped up to car racing and he was an instant hit, winning the German Formula BMW ADAC Championship. Advancing to F3 in 2003, Nico ranked eighth in the European championship, improving on this in 2004 to come fourth. However, after getting a taste of F1 power with a test for Williams, he moved up to GP2 and had a brilliant 2005 campaign, winning five races and the title ahead of Heikki Kovalainen. Nico was then given his F1 break by his father's most famous old team, Williams, and there he stayed for four years, reaching the podium twice in 2008. Unfortunately, the team was not at its most competitive and all that Nico could do was gather points, which he did with impressive regularity.

TRACK NOTES

Nationality:	GERMAN
Born:	27 JUNE 1985, WIESBADEN, GERMANY
Website:	www.nicorosberg.com
Teams:	WILLIAMS 2006-09,
	MERCEDES 2010-11

CAREER RECORD

First Grand Prix:	2006 BAHRAIN GP
Grand Prix starts:	89
Grand Prix wins:	0
(best result: second, 2008 Singapore GP)	
Poles:	0
Fastest laps:	2
Points:	217.5
Honours:	2005 GP2 CHAMPION,
	2002 FORMULA BMW CHAMPION

LOTUS RENAULT GP

This was a team in turmoil in 2009, laid low by accusations of race-fixing in Singapore in 2008. It took a takeover by Genii Capital to keep the French manufacturer in the sport and the team did well to rediscover the spark that made it great and now has a new name for 2011.

Robert Kubica almost carried Renault's hopes single-handed in 2010 and the team knows that he will reward them if they give him a good car.

When Renault rolled its cars out for the start of last season, it was ironic that they looked more like Renaults than they had for years, as they returned to the yellow, black and white livery in which they raced from their arrival in F1 back in 1977. Of course, it was only ironic, as the team was no longer bankrolled by the French automotive manufacturer but, instead, by a Luxembourg-based venture capital company. Genii Capital had bought 75% of the team in October 2009 and was now charged with saving it. Even more than that, team leader Gerard Lopez was determined not just to keep it going but to achieve good enough results to wipe out the memory of "Crashgate", which haunted the team through 2009. The management team had been accused of suggesting to Nelson Piquet Jr that he should crash at the very point in the Singapore GP that would bring out a safety car and thus propel early-pitting team-mate Fernando Alonso into the lead. To emphasise the

changing of the guard, and thus distance the team further from the scandal that cost former team chief Flavio Briatore and engineering chief Pat Symonds the right to work in F1, he appointed Eric Boullier to be the new man at the helm after a stellar career in team management in F1's feeder formulae. And, you know what, it worked.

KEY MOMENTS AND KEY PEOPLE

TEAM HISTORY

F1 is littered at the moment with teams with confusing identities. Renault introduced turbocharged engines to F1 in 1977. This French team continued until 1985. In the same period, the Toleman team moved from F2 into F1 in 1981. This was sold to Benetton for 1986 and raced on under this name until 2001, helping Michael Schumacher to drivers' titles in 1994 and 1995. Then the Renault name (and finances) were applied to the team in 2002 and this hybrid helped Fernando Alonso to the drivers' title in 2005 and 2006. The French manufacturer pulled the plug at the end of 2009 and it took a takeover by Gerard Lopez to keep it going.

ERIC BOULLIER

Before he was brought in by Genii Capital to run the team for 2010, this hard-working French engineer spent six years running cars for DAMS in a host of international categories, ranging from GP2 to A1GP (helping France to the 2005-06 title) to Formula BMW. He then became the Chief Executive Officer of Gravity Sport Management in 2009, looking after a roster of young drivers.

2010 DRIVERS & RESULTS

Driver	Nationality	Races	Wins	Pts	Pos
Robert Kubica	Polish	19	0	136	8th
Vitaly Petrov	Russian	19	0	27	13th

FOR THE RECORD

Country of origin:	France
Team base:	Enstone, England
Telephone:	(44) 01608 678000
Website:	www.renaultf1.com
Active in Formula One:	From 1977 to 1985, then from 2002
Grands Prix contested:	282*
Wins:	35
Pole positions:	50
Fastest laps:	31

* Note that these figures don't include the 238 races that the team ran as Toleman and Benetton

THE TEAM

Chairman:	Gerard Lopez
Team principal & managing director:	Eric Boullier
Technical director:	James Allison
Deputy technical director:	Naoki Tokunaga
Head of engine operations:	Remi Taffin
Chief designer:	Tim Densham
Head of aerodynamics:	Dirk de Beer
Operations director:	John Mardle
Chief race engineer:	Alan Permane
Sporting director:	Steve Nielsen
Test driver:	tba
Chassis:	Renault R31
Engine:	Renault V8
Tyres:	Pirelli

Money was always an issue for this new-look Renault F1 team and Tarek Obaid, founder of oil and gas exploration company PetroSaudi International, was brought in as a partner mid-season. Indeed, with further cash-flow problems through last year, his appointment could be vital for unlocking Saudi investment.

Yet, with talk of smaller, turbocharged engines being brought back for 2013, there were rumours that Renault the manufacturer might be looking to buy back in. This may yet happen, but the team has a new name – Lotus Renault GP – as Group Lotus has elected not to tie up with Team Lotus but to join the Renault team in its quest to become a winning outfit. Out of deference to the John Player Special Lotus racers of the mid-1980s when Lotus used Renault engines to win races, the cars will race in a black and gold livery.

Last year, without doubt, the team centred around one of its two new drivers: Robert Kubica. He was the ideal driver to help the team through its recovery, offering not just speed but an unfussy nature. Furthermore, the crew knew that if they could make the R30 quick, he'd achieve its maximum. After the fright of his debut, when he finished only 11th in Bahrain, he bounced back to second place in round two in Australia and also made it to the podium twice at Monaco and Spa.

F1 rookie Vitaly Petrov was welcomed for his potential to attract sponsors anxious for exposure in the Russian market. The 2009 GP2 runner-up was something of a disappointment but, just as the team was saying that he'd have to raise his game or lose his ride for 2011, he produced a fifth-place finish at the Hungaroring. Petrov looked to have saved his seat. Talk continued of him being replaced by former Renault racer Heikki Kovalainen, Force India's Adrian Sutil or Nick Heidfeld for 2011. There had even been talk of 2007 World Champion Kimi Raikkonen looking to return to F1 with Renault after a year in the World Rally Championship, but this came to naught. So, with his fighting drive in Abu Dhabi, Vitaly staked his claim.

Surprisingly, just as the team looked to be building on its recovery, managing director Bob Bell, who became principal after Briatore's departure towards the end of 2009, left last October, with the capable Boullier taking on his role as well.

"We look forward to building on what we achieved last year and need to make sure that during the winter we achieve another step that allows us to fight for more podiums and even for wins"
Eric Boullier

Eric Boullier settled in well last year, his first in F1, and is looking to build on it in 2011.

ROBERT KUBICA

Robert is in an exclusive club of drivers who manage to increase their reputation year in, year out. Everyone knew that the Pole didn't have a winning car from Renault last year, but he wrung every last point out of it and Renault did well to keep him, for this season at least.

The winning cars last year came from Ferrari, McLaren and Red Bull Racing, and not from Renault. Yet this talented Polish driver was no stranger to the podium and drove in such a way that it came as no surprise that Ferrari continued to seek his services for this year. He may yet become a Ferrari driver, but for now he's committed to a second season with the Renault outfit.

It must be said that Robert will have been tempted at times to jump ship, as Renault was certainly in flux going into last year after its change of hands, while Ferrari looked rock solid, its level of competitiveness more assured. However, Robert clearly liked what he saw of the team after he joined Renault from BMW Sauber for 2010. He must have liked it even more as the season unfolded and the incoming Eric Boullier guided the team back on to a more even keel. Indeed, by June, he had signed to stay on, and that gave Renault a massive seal of approval.

What Robert will get is the continued position as the number-one driver in a team that has showed the guts to work itself out of its rut. This most unshowy of

Robert remains a driver feared by all of his rivals for being a simple, out-and-out racer.

drivers - he just wants to race and doesn't fuss about the frills and distractions - recognises their spirit and clearly has the ambition to aim higher than the podium finishes achieved last year. If there are points to be scored, he will score them.

Look back at Robert's career record and you will notice another vital factor that augments his undoubted speed: he almost never makes mistakes. Sure, he slid into his pit stop at the Belgian GP, but on a day when some of his leading rivals were slipping up and crashing off the circuit, he still made it to the podium.

So, for a team building itself back up, these are crucial qualities to have. If the car is fast enough to win races, Robert will be first to the finish. If not, he'll still keep the points rolling in. And the team couldn't ask for more than that.

TRACK NOTES

Nationality:	POLISH
Born:	7 DECEMBER 1984, KRAKOW, POLAND
Website:	www.kubica.pl
Teams:	BMW SAUBER 2006-09, RENAULT 2010-11

CAREER RECORD	
First Grand Prix:	2006 HUNGARIAN GP
Grand Prix starts:	76
Grand Prix wins:	1
	2008 Canadian GP
Poles:	1
Fastest laps:	1
Points:	273
Honours:	2005 WORLD SERIES BY RENAULT CHAMPION, 1999 GERMAN & ITALIAN KART CHAMPION & MONACO KART CUP WINNER, 1998 ITALIAN KART CHAMPION & MONACO KART CUP WINNER, 1997 POLISH KART CHAMPION

MOVING ABROAD PAYS OFF

Many drivers gather karting titles on their home patch, then head for the country that will assist their progress the most when they take the step up to car racing. By that stage in his career, Robert had already long been on the road, having left his native Poland behind and based himself in Italy when he was only 13. It paid off, as he landed a top drive in Formula Renault. This certainly wouldn't have happened had he stayed in Poland. Runner-up in Italian Formula Renault in 2002, Robert was signed up by the Renault driver development programme for 2003, only to miss six races after breaking his arm in a road accident. He was back to form in 2005 and won the World Series with Renault, which convinced Sauber to sign him as test driver for 2006. He then got his break mid-season when Jacques Villeneuve was replaced. On the podium in only his third race, his place was consolidated with the team and he stayed for the next three years, winning at Montreal in 2008 to rank fourth.

VITALY PETROV

Vitaly became Russia's first Formula One driver last year with Renault and, with a Russian GP lined up from 2014, he is vital to the team for sponsorship. There were signs too last year that Vitaly is finding his feet, and a two-year deal will give him the chance to progress.

It was an 11th-hour deal that landed Vitaly his Formula One break at the start of last season, but the newly purchased Renault team needed money and he needed a drive, so both parties waited and waited for the deal to be done.

It would be great to say that Vitaly's debut season was a roaring success. However, take away his seventh place in the very wet Chinese GP and bizarrely competitive fifth place at the Hungarian GP and there weren't many championship points. Well, not until it all came right in the final race in Abu Dhabi.

Indeed, Vitaly collected just 27 points to team-mate Robert Kubica's 136. However, Kubica is acknowledged as an exceptional talent and the car was usually only fifth fastest behind the Red Bulls, McLarens, Ferraris and Mercedes, with incursions from Williams and Force India. So, there were scraps to be gathered, not feasts.

The team management spent much of the year saying that it wanted to keep Vitaly "as long as his form improved", which was fair to ask, but only added to the pressure. Perhaps that's why he made his error off the grid at the Japanese GP when he swerved across the nose of Nico Hulkenberg's Williams

The clinching of the deal for a Russian GP has made Vitaly a desirable commodity.

and took them both out of the race. Then, a fortnight later, he pressed too hard in the mixed conditions at the new Yeongam circuit in tricky conditions and slammed his R30 into the wall. Then again, Lewis Hamilton made mistakes in the late-season races with

similar consequences, so perhaps people shouldn't be too hard on Vitaly.

Vitaly earned his place in the final race at Abu Dhabi by holding off title challenger Fernando Alonso for the second half of the race with a flawless drive to sixth place.

F1 is a high-pressure environment and, after signing a deal for 2011 and 2012, Vitaly will return as a far better driver for his second year alongside Kubica. The team will demand more from him, as he needs to be scoring points on a regular basis to bolster their push up the constructors' championship table.

Also, with the deal for the Russian GP at Sochi from 2014 having been signed, he will bring Renault publicity on the fast-growing Russian like never before.

TRACK NOTES

Nationality:	RUSSIAN
Born:	8 SEPTEMBER 1984, VYBORG, RUSSIA
Website:	www.vitalypetrov.ru
Teams:	2010-11 RENAULT

CAREER RECORD

First Grand Prix:	2010 BAHRAIN GP
Grand Prix starts:	19
Grand Prix wins:	0
	(best result: fifth, 2010 Hungarian GP)
Poles:	0
Fastest laps:	1
Points:	27
Honours:	2009 GP2 RUNNER-UP, 2005 RUSSIAN FORMULA 1600 CHAMPION, RUSSIAN LADA REVOLUTION CHAMPION, 2002 RUSSIAN LADA CUP CHAMPION

FROM LADAS TO GP2 GLORY

It has been a long climb from racing in the low-level Russian Lada Cup saloon racing series in 2001 to being on the brink of Formula One. Vitaly tried Formula Renault on his move to single-seaters in 2003, but also went right up the power band and did a Formula 3000 race. He reverted to racing in Russia after two years of racing in European Formula Renault before healthy backing filled his 2006 season with F3000 and later GP2. More GP2 followed in 2007, taking a win for Campos Grand Prix at Valencia, plus a few sports car outings. Vitaly then concentrated on GP2 in 2008 and it paid dividends as he took another win in the GP2 Asia series at Sepang, followed that up with victory in the main series at Valencia and ranked fifth for the Barwa Addax Campos team. Another win at Sepang in the 2008-09 Asian series was followed by two wins in the main 2009 series, at Istanbul and Valencia again, but he couldn't prevent Nico Hulkenberg from lifting the GP2 title.

WILLIAMS

The signs were there last year that Williams was on the verge of returning to the big time. Sadly, the ending of several sponsorship deals has left the team less financially secure and so, perhaps, less likely to continue that advance, with rookie Nico Hulkenberg having to leave.

Rubens Barrichello was credited with much of Williams' improvement last year and his cheery countenance and experience count for a lot.

Had money been no object, the Williams management would have loved to start the 2011 season with the two drivers who served them with such promise last year. Rubens Barrichello brought all the experience of his 18 years in F1, plus his personable nature. Nico Hulkenberg made mistakes but learned from them and showed ever better form as the season advanced, suggesting a top result would be achieved. After all, Williams didn't want to start a season with two drivers new to the team for a second year running, as it had had to do when Barrichello and Hulkenberg filled the seats vacated by its 2009 racers, Nico Rosberg and Kazuki Nakajima.

Yet, with as many as three sponsors – RBS, Philips and Air Asia – leaving Williams at the end of the 2010 season, their original idea of keeping the same driving line-up became untenable. Barrichello would surely be kept on, but young Hulkenberg approached the closing races of his rookie season looking ever more likely for the chop, while newly crowned GP2 champion Pastor Maldonado had the money the team would need to make up some of the shortfall. They would be trading a driver who won the GP2 crown at the first attempt for one who took four goes to achieve the same outcome. But

KEY MOMENTS AND KEY PEOPLE

TEAM HISTORY

Frank Williams ran a team under a series of names, according to the sponsor of the moment, from 1969 to 1976, but he wanted more control after working for Walter Wolf in 1976 and formed Williams Grand Prix Engineering with Patrick Head in 1977. Success soon followed and the first win in 1979 was followed by the first title, thanks to Alan Jones, just a year later. Since then, Williams has been constructors' champion eight times more, with its strongest spells in the mid-1980s and then in the early 1990s.

SIR FRANK WILLIAMS

To start with, Frank competed in saloons and then F3. But he never had the budget to do it properly, so moved into running cars for others and progressed to F2 with Piers Courage in 1968. They moved together to F1 with a Brabham in 1969, but after Courage was killed in 1970 Frank endured some rough years, always short of money. It was only when he teamed up with Patrick Head that things turned around. Frank broke his back in a car crash in 1986, but he has remained at the helm ever since.

2010 DRIVERS & RESULTS

Driver	Nationality	Races	Wins	Pts	Pos
Rubens Barrichello	Brazilian	19	0	47	10th
Nico Hulkenberg	German	19	0	22	14th

money talks in F1 like nowhere else.

There had been discussion about changing engine suppliers for 2011, but the decision was made last autumn to stick with Cosworth and the long-standing engine supplier from Northampton has a clear determination to rebuild its name in F1, and not just as a supplier of engines to tail-end teams. So, clearly, Cosworth has high expectations of its relationship with Williams and both share ambitions to haul in the likes of the Mercedes and Renault teams in 2011.

On the technical side, Sam Michael knows that the team has achieved just one race win since his appointment as technical director in 2004, when Juan Pablo Montoya claimed the last of that year's races at Interlagos. For many seasons, there wasn't much sustenance, and last year it was a case of the Red Bulls, McLarens and Ferraris hogging the headlines, but Williams did, on occasion, get in among those who could claim a good helping of points, with Barrichello breaching the top six three times and Hulkenberg once.

The key will be whether this year's FW33, designed by Ed Wood and Jon Tomlinson under Michael's aegis, will be more competitive than the FW32 and whether they can get it to suit the incoming Pirelli tyres. Certainly, the attention swung towards the FW33 quite early last year when it was clear that the FW32 wasn't going to win races.

Team founders Sir Frank Williams and Patrick Head will never stop striving to move their team back to the front, but the elevation last year of Adam Parr from Chief Executive Officer to Chairman emphasises how he and tech chief Michael are now the duo expected to keep the team striving to get back to the heights it last scaled when Jacques Villeneuve won the team's most recent drivers' and constructors' championship titles in 1997. These were its fifth in a six-year run from 1992 when Nigel Mansell led its dominant attack.

Teams' form ebbs and flows, but almost all of the sport's insiders would love to see Williams do well again as it's a team that goes racing for the right reasons, rather than to help a publicity-seeking billionaire trumpet his name around the world. To Williams, Head et al, it's the winning that counts more than the prize money.

> "We recruited Rubens knowing that he would bring technical expertise, experience and passion. He has delivered everything we could have hoped for and we're delighted that he'll drive for us again."
>
> **Sir Frank Williams**

FOR THE RECORD

Country of origin:	England
Team base:	Grove, England
Telephone:	(44) 01235 777700
Website:	www.attwilliams.com
Active in Formula One:	From 1972
Grands Prix contested:	604
Wins:	113
Pole positions:	125
Fastest laps:	130

THE TEAM

Team principal:	Sir Frank Williams
Director of engineering:	Patrick Head
Chairman:	Adam Parr
Technical director:	Sam Michael
Chief operating officer:	Alex Burns
Chief designer:	Ed Wood
Chief of aerodynamics:	Jon Tomlinson
Senior systems engineer:	John Russell
Team manager:	Dickie Stanford
Test driver:	Valtteri Bottas
Chassis:	Williams FW33
Engine:	Cosworth V8
Tyres:	Pirelli

Team Chairman Adam Parr listens in as Patrick Head imparts his considerable wisdom.

Rubens extended his record as F1's most experienced driver when he topped 300 grand prix starts midway through last season. Now, facing his 19th season of F1, he's as enthusiastic as ever as he eyes his second year with Williams in the expectation of even better results than in 2010.

Two years ago, Rubens wasn't enjoying life as Honda Racing scratched around in search of form. Soon after that, with people suggesting that it was time for Rubens to step aside and let up-and-coming talent have a crack at F1, the decision was taken away from him when Honda Racing quit F1. This was it. He was an F1 driver no more.

Then, of course, Brawn GP rose from the ashes, had a brilliant season and Rubens was a winner again, adding two more wins to end a five-year victory drought. But Rubens was again surplus to requirements, despite showing no lack of speed, as Michael Schumacher and Nico Rosberg arrived at the team and it was rebadged as Mercedes for 2010.

32

When Williams signed him as its lead driver in place of Rosberg, their relationship was one that improved with every race as the FW32 became ever more competitive and he unlocked the form that had been so clear for all to see in the good years with Ferrari. His experience was also invaluable to rookie team-mate Nico Hulkenberg.

That form produced a fourth place at Valencia, followed by a fifth place at

Rubens brings proven speed, experience galore and a strong technical mind.

Silverstone, and that produced a contract extension. His sixth place in Singapore was another top result.

Looking forward, Rubens might have hoped that the team would drop its Cosworth engines for, say, Renault V8s, but

he has that sparkle back in his eyes that suggests he reckons he will be claiming a few scalps in 2011, outracing drivers from the more fancied teams. Then, when the job of helping Williams to be regular podium visitors once more has been done, perhaps he will consider heading back to Brazil to spend more time with his young family.

For now, though, Rubens is simply having too much fun...

TRACK NOTES

Nationality:	BRAZILIAN
Born:	23 MAY 1972, SAO PAULO, BRAZIL
Website:	www.barrichello.com.br
Teams:	JORDAN 1993-96, STEWART 1997-99, FERRARI 2000-05, HONDA RACING 2006-08, BRAWN 2009, WILLIAMS 2010-11

CAREER RECORD	
First Grand Prix:	1993 SOUTH AFRICAN GP
Grand Prix starts:	306
Grand Prix wins:	11
	2000 German GP, 2002 European GP, Hungarian GP, Italian GP, US GP, 2003 British GP, Japanese GP, 2004 Italian GP, Chinese GP, 2009 European GP, Italian GP
Poles:	14
Fastest laps:	17
Points:	654
Honours:	2002 & 2004 FORMULA ONE RUNNER-UP, 1991 BRITISH FORMULA THREE CHAMPION, 1990 EUROPEAN FORMULA OPEL CHAMPION, 1988 BRAZILIAN KART CHAMPION

WINNING OVER THE SPONSORS

Quick drivers often get nowhere if they don't have family money. Rubens might have fallen into this category, but his pace-setting form in karting in Brazil convinced a group of sponsors to try to back him to F1. His part of the bargain was to win races and titles and he duly won the Formula Opel series on his first year in Europe. The following year, he won the British F3 series. Unlike his hero Ayrton Senna, he had to spend a year in the final feeder formula, F3000. Yet, having ranked third in that, he made it to F1 in 1993 before he'd turned 21. Then, just three races into that maiden season with Jordan, he ran second in the European GP at Donington Park before retiring. Over the next six years with Jordan, then Stewart, he proved his speed, but it took a move to Ferrari in 2000 for him to start winning and his best ranking remains runner-up, in both 2002 and 2004 behind Michael Schumacher. It all looked to have come to an end when Honda quit, but in 2009, with Brawn he was back on the winning track.

PASTOR MALDONADO

Pastor was that rare creature hovering around the F1 paddock last year: a driver with money. He is quick, but although his promotion, as GP2 champion, is merited, it's the fact that he has money that has enabled him to join Williams rather than a tail-end team.

Pastor seemed to have become part of the furniture in F1's feeder formulae, racing, crashing and winning in powerful single-seaters in Europe for a number of years. Now, at last, his knocking on the door has been heeded and he's landed an F1 ride.

Four years in GP2 is more than enough for anyone and usually leads to a career in another branch of motorsport, the driver's career report card marked as "Not quite the full ticket. Try sportscars."

Yet, and it is his good fortune that his native Venezuela's industries are backing Pastor to the tune of some $15m, his undoubted speed was finally channelled into a title-winning performance last year. Importantly his wins at Istanbul, Valencia, Silverstone, Hockenheim, Hungaroring and Spa-Francorchamps, all came in the more prestigious feature race on the Saturday rather than the sprint race on the Sunday. It proved he was truly dominant and that this feisty Venezuelan had finally got it all together, and had stopped hurling the car at the barriers.

Because of the sizeable budget that he brings to Williams, it's ironic that Pastor is taking the place of his 2009 team-

Pastor is fast but is going to need to glean as much as possible from his team-mate.

mate Nico Hulkenberg, who outdrove him to become GP2 champion at his first attempt before spending an increasingly promising F1 rookie season with Williams. Alas for the German, he couldn't offer the financial input that Pastor brings.

What Pastor must do in his first year of F1 is to look, listen and learn, not just from team leader Rubens Barrichello but director of engineering Patrick Head as well, because the latter has considerable knowledge to impart. But Pastor will soon learn that Patrick has a towering temper should he resume his crashing ways of old.

Pastor displayed good pace in testing in Abu Dhabi last autumn when he ran both Williams and HRT. What he must do now is glean as much knowledge as he can on how to get the most out of a car that will change through the season as it's developed, which is quite unlike what he'll have experienced in four years in spec-formula GP2.

In addition, Pastor will have to meet the challenge of carrying a nation's hopes on his shoulders.

A DRIVER WHO SHINES AT MONACO

Pastor comes from a family of racers and secured national kart titles before he headed to Italy in 2002 to try junior single-seaters, landing an F1 test with the Minardi F1 team at the end of 2004. As a member of Renault's Driver Development Programme in 2005, he raced in World Series by Renault, but added to this with a Euro F3000 outing at Magione that he won. In 2006, he ranked third in the World Series with a trio of wins. He moved up to GP2 for 2007, won at Monaco, but a broken collarbone ended his season. Back for a full campaign in 2008, Pastor again won at Monaco again and ranked fifth, using Euro F3000 to learn circuits. For 2009, Pastor returned to GP2, but ART Grand Prix team-mate Nico Hulkenberg put him in the shade and he ended up sixth overall, despite winning at Monaco and Silverstone. At the fourth time of asking, he became GP2 champion in 2010, winning at six different circuits as he dominated.

TRACK NOTES

Nationality:	VENEZUELAN
Born:	9 MARCH 1985, MARACAY, VENEZUELA
Website:	www.pastormaldonado.com
Teams:	WILLIAMS 2011

CAREER RECORD

First Grand Prix:	2011 BAHRAIN GP
Grand Prix starts:	0
Grand Prix wins:	0
Poles:	0
Fastest laps:	0
Points:	0
Honours:	2010 GP2 CHAMPION, 2004 ITALIAN FORMULA RENAULT CHAMPION, 2003 ITALIAN FORMULA RENAULT WINTER CHAMPION

FORCE INDIA F1

This is a team that's looking to cement its place in F1's midfield pack after a strong campaign in 2010 helped it to advance from ninth out of 10 teams in 2009 to seventh. However, there has been a wholesale change of its technical side and this might cost it dear.

Adrian Sutil ranked just outside the top 10 last year and displayed the increasing maturity that this ambitious team demands as it aims high.

The Force India cars are easy to identify in their patriotic white, orange and green Indian livery. However, apart from seeing them on TV when either Adrian Sutil or Vitantonio Liuzzi was involved in an accident or was spotted pulling off the track into retirement, they didn't feature on the radar.

The extraordinary thing about this was that they enjoyed more TV exposure in 2009, when they scored far fewer points, even taking the less generous previous scoring system into account, as their points then came from just two late-season races when their form hit a remarkable peak. After all, with no points on the board after 11 rounds, Giancarlo Fisichella suddenly qualified in pole position for the Belgian GP, then led much of the way before being pipped by Kimi Raikkonen's Ferrari.

Last year, Sutil enjoyed a far more consistently competitive season, but he simply wasn't seen on your screens as much, even though he claimed fifth-place finishes at Sepang and Spa-Francorchamps. Meanwhile, Liuzzi raced to seventh in Melbourne, then sixth at Yeongam and the pair produced 11 other top-10 finishes. They had fallen into F1's hinterland, not being close enough to the lead to be considered

KEY MOMENTS AND KEY PEOPLE

TEAM HISTORY
This is a team that has been many things in its 20-year history. Formed from Eddie Jordan's F3000 team, it entered F1 in 1991 as Jordan Grand Prix and was almost straight onto the pace. The following years proved more of a struggle, but the team came good again in 1998 and four grands prix were won before Jordan sold it to Alex Shnaider and it became Midland F1 in 2005. It was soon sold on in 2007 and renamed Spyker in deference to the Dutch sports car company. In 2008, it was taken over by Indian industrialist Vijay Mallya and renamed Force India, with its highlight thus far pole for the 2009 Belgian GP.

MICHIEL MOL
The co-owner of the team made his fortune in the world of e-commerce, with his Lost Boys International company quickly becoming Europe's largest digital agency. Even greater success was then achieved in cross media with Media Republic and by opening a computer games development agency, Guerrilla Games. This gave the ambitious Dutchman the financial clout to buy his way into Formula One when the Force India team was known as Spyker.

2010 DRIVERS & RESULTS

Driver	Nationality	Races	Wins	Pts	Pos
Vitantonio Liuzzi	Italian	19	0	21	15th
Adrian Sutil	German	19	0	47	11th

FOR THE RECORD

Country of origin:	England
Team base:	Silverstone, England
Telephone:	(44) 01327 850800
Website:	www.forceindiaf1.com
Active in Formula One:	From 1991
(as Jordan Grand Prix, Midland F1 in 2005 and then Spyker in 2007)	
Grands Prix contested:	339
Wins:	4
Pole positions:	3
Fastest laps:	3

THE TEAM

Chairman & team principal:	Vijay Mallya
Co-owner:	Michiel Mol
Team director:	Bob Fernley
Chief operating officer:	Simon Roberts
Technical director:	Andrew Green
Team manager:	Andy Stevenson
Chief designer:	tba
Project leader:	Ian Hall
Head of aerodynamics:	Simon Phillips
Chief race engineer:	Dominic Harlow
Test driver:	tba
Chassis:	Force India VJM04
Engine:	Mercedes V8
Tyres:	Pirelli

interesting, not being slow enough to be lapped frequently. You got to see the HRTs, Virgins and Lotuses a fair amount in 2010, not the Force Indias.

What matters to the team, though, and especially to ambitious team owner Vijay Mallya as he heads up the aspirations of a sports-crazy nation, is that progress is made every year. The one thing that might make this trickier in 2011 is that there has been a net outpouring of the technical staff that has yet to be balanced by the arrival of new technical boffins to plug the gap.

Technical director James Key was the first to leave, going to Sauber early last year. Then Mark Smith, who stepped up from being design director to replace him, announced last June that he would be leaving to join Lotus, along with fellow tech team members Lewis Butler and Marianne Hinson. Having joined the team when it was Jordan in 1998, Key's departure removed one of the mainstays of the outfit. Smith went back even further, all the way to Jordan's pre-F1 days in 1990, albeit with seven years away with other teams before rejoining the team in 2008 when it became Force India.

Andrew Green, formerly of Virgin and before that Red Bull Racing, is the main person brought in to replace them, filling the shoes vacated by Smith.

It remains to be seen how much these comings and goings affect this year's VJM04, but one can only surmise that teams with larger budgets than Force India's will continue to poach their technical staff.

One element of Force India that remains a strength is its use of the same drivetrain as McLaren: that's to say Mercedes-Benz horsepower driven through a McLaren transmission. With the return of KERS, which was certainly a McLaren forte in 2009, perhaps Force India's drivers will after all be able to aim at scoring points on a regular basis. However, they will be racing in that roughest arena of all, the midfield, where their drivers are far more likely to get caught up in other drivers' moments of madness or become overambitious at the start and have some of their own.

On this count, Sutil has calmed down from his early F1 days, in 2007, when he was involved in more than a few first-lap clashes, and his more polished performances had him linked with rides at both Renault and Mercedes for 2011.

''When we bought the team, we scored zero points the first year, then 13 in 2009 and five times that last year. We've achieved our racing stripes and I hope that with the Indian GP as a target we can go bigger and better.''
Vijay Mallya

Vijay Mallya's money has stabilised Force India as a midfield runner, but he wants much more.

ADRIAN SUTIL*

German drivers are dominating F1 and Adrian is looking forward to demonstrating again that he can mix it with Michael Schumacher, Sebastian Vettel and Nico Rosberg. After four years in F1, though, he knows he must shine more to land a ride with a top team to rival them.

If Adrian wasn't a German driver plying his craft at a time when Formula One is packed with German drivers, including seven-time World Champion Michael Schumacher and 2010 World Champion Sebastian Vettel, his name would be better known in his own country because Adrian is a very rapid driver.

As he prepares for his fifth year with the team that was Spyker when he joined it in 2007, and became Force India the following year, Adrian is still struggling to put his name up in lights despite some sterling performances. Gone, by and large, are the impetuous collisions and accidents that marked his first few seasons in F1. Instead there are drives such as his run to fifth place in the wet at Sepang, where he displayed controlled speed in changing conditions. There was another masterpiece in mixed conditions to fifth place at Spa-Francorchamps and an excellent run to sixth around the Valencia street circuit.

The trouble is, the car in which he was performing, the Force India VJM03, was no match for the cars from the front-running teams and the best that Adrian could hope for was that some of them would

Adrian was courted by rival F1 teams but is sticking with Force India for one more go.

encounter problems and retire.

Will this year be any different, though? That was the question in Adrian's mind as last season came to a close. He was definitely looking elsewhere, hoping to find more competitive equipment, with

his name linked to rides with Mercedes, if Schumacher elected not to continue after struggling to rediscover his form, and also Renault and Williams.

However, Adrian is staying on with Force India for another crack at the big time and will be hoping that the team's 2011 car proves amazingly suited to the new tyres brought along by Pirelli, allowing him to advance several rungs further up the ladder and achieve his first podium finish.

Adrian knows full well that momentum must be maintained in a driver's career and that the clock is a-ticking.

* Not confirmed at time of going to press.

HITTING ALL THE RIGHT NOTES

With their childhoods spent criss-crossing their own country and later their continent to race karts, it's safe to say that most of today's F1 drivers didn't give all of their school studies their full focus. Adrian is unusual in the ranks for having studied a musical instrument to a high standard. He looked set to follow in his father's footsteps and become a concert musician, but then he had his first experience of karts and decided that was his passion. Having started after his contemporaries, Adrian did well but didn't win titles. However, he was Swiss Formula Ford champion in his first year of car racing, then showed an impressive turn of speed in F3 in 2004 before finishing runner-up in the 2005 European series behind his team-mate, Lewis Hamilton. He tried more power, for Germany in A1GP, then raced in Japan in 2006, winning the F3 title. This gained him a test with the Spyker F1 team and he landed a race seat for 2007, and has stayed with the team ever since as it metamorphosed into Force India.

TRACK NOTES

Nationality:	GERMAN
Born: 11 JANUARY 1983, GRAFELFING, GERMANY	
Website:	www.adriansutil.com
Teams:	SPYKER/FORCE INDIA 2007-11

CAREER RECORD

First Grand Prix:	2007 AUSTRALIAN GP
Grand Prix starts:	71
Grand Prix wins:	0
	(best result: fourth, 2009 Italian GP)
Poles:	0
Fastest laps:	1
Points:	53
Honours:	2006 JAPANESE FORMULA THREE CHAMPION, 2005 EUROPEAN FORMULA THREE RUNNER-UP, 2002 SWISS FORMULA FORD CHAMPION

He's British and he's fast, yet he's reached Formula One with Force India with few F1 fans knowing his name after taking four years away from single-seaters. However, this young Scot outranked Sebastian Vettel last time they raced together in F3 back in 2006.

Motor racing has spent the past decade making itself ever more difficult to understand. Back in the 1980s, the climb to the top would include spells in Formula Three and Formula Two before trying to break into Formula One. Since then, category names have been changed, more and more similar single-seater formulae have been created and there has been the banning of in-season F1 testing, removing the possibility of a quick, rising star spending time cutting his teeth on the extra performance of an F1 car. Without these chances and uniform points of comparison, it's increasingly hard to spot the very best talent on the way up.

Paul is a case in point. Having starred in karts, his form in junior single-seaters was impressive too. But then came that stumbling block that has tripped up many promising careers: the final step before F1. Being unable to move on to GP2 has turned out to be the making of Paul as he was taken under the wing of Mercedes and their belief in him stretched beyond just running him, successfully, in the DTM. Indeed, Mercedes motorsport boss Norbert Haug reckoned Paul's speed would translate well

Paul has great support from Mercedes and will be excited to be back in single-seaters.

to F1 and when Force India signed to run Mercedes engines and transmissions in its cars, this opened a route for Paul to try F1. A three-day test with the team at the end of 2009 led to him becoming test and reserve driver for 2010.

Judging by the speed that Paul showed compared to either Adrian Sutil or Vitantonio Liuzzi in his eight Friday practice runs, expect him to be right in the mix very quickly. That said, he'll have to get his mind around racing a single-seater again after four years of rubbing metal in the DTM.

Making his F1 debut just short of his 25th birthday will mean that Paul brings more experience than some of his contemporaries had when they arrived and his mature approach ought to stand him in good stead.

* Not confirmed at time of going to press.

TRACK NOTES

Nationality:	BRITISH
Born:	16 April 1986, Uphall, Scotland
Website:	www.pauldiresta.com
Teams:	FORCE INDIA 2011

CAREER RECORD	
First Grand Prix:	2011 BAHRAIN GP
Grand Prix starts:	0
Grand Prix wins:	0
Poles:	0
Fastest laps:	0
Points:	0
Honours:	2010 GERMAN TOURING CAR CHAMPION, 2006 EUROPEAN FORMULA THREE CHAMPION & FORMULA THREE MASTERS WINNER, 2001 BRITISH JICA KART CHAMPION, 1998 SCOTTISH OPEN KART CHAMPION, 1997 BRITISH CADET KART CHAMPION, 1995 SCOTTISH CADET KART CHAMPION

IT RUNS IN THE FAMILY

Paul's father Louis raced in Formula Ford, but the family connection runs deeper than that because his cousins are racers Dario and Marino Franchitti. Having spent eight years racing karts, Paul stepped up to Formula Renault when he was 17 and was a winner in his debut season against Lewis Hamilton. More wins followed in 2004 before he graduated to Formula Three in 2005. This was another two-year programme and he lifted the European crown in 2006 ahead of a certain Sebastian Vettel. Then, without the budget to progress to GP2, Paul was signed by Mercedes for its DTM attack, taking to touring cars with aplomb as he ranked fifth in his first season and then was runner-up in 2008 just behind Timo Scheider. The Force India F1 team offered him some test runs in 2009 and expanded his input to Friday runs in 2010 and his speed was impressive enough to land him a race seat for 2011, while he landed the DTM title at his fourth attempt.

SAUBER

Serious investment from Mexican industrialist Carlos Slim has transformed the prospects of this Swiss midfield team and given it hope of a renaissance after its worrying year spent running with almost no visible sponsorship. In Kobayashi and Perez, it has two young chargers.

The only thing that made the notably unsponsored cars stand out last year was Kamui Kobayashi's driving. Expect a new livery for 2011.

Peter Sauber started the 2010 World Championship more than a little worried about financing his team after the end of its BMW-backed days. There would have been some money left over from BMW, but more was needed, especially to fund the development of the 2011 car. Sponsorship logos did appear on the cars, but only in dribs and drabs throughout the season, suggesting that the team's continued existence might be in the balance. Then, late in the season, at the Singapore GP, Sauber seemed unusually relaxed, and the reason for this became apparent when it was revealed that Mexican telecoms giant Telmex would be sponsoring the team in 2011.

More than this, it meant that Carlos Slim – the world's wealthiest man, after overtaking Bill Gates last year – was involved and his ambitions can be matched by the budgets to achieve them. How pleasing that a team that has never really been able to "splash the cash" since its BMW days, will finally be

able to spend as it wishes in its bid to add to the one win it achieved under BMW, at Montreal in 2008. This injection of capital will mean that the days of Sauber having

to hold back on the way it goes about its business and definitely on the way it develops its cars through a season should change for the better.

KEY MOMENTS AND KEY PEOPLE

TEAM HISTORY
Sauber started in sports car racing in the 1970s. A deal to run cars for Mercedes brought it into the spotlight and they won the 1989 Le Mans 24 Hours. There were plans to do F1 together, but this didn't happen and so Sauber made the jump anyhow, for 1993. Quick from the outset, with JJ Lehto and Karl Wendlinger, the team slipped back into the midfield and seldom shone until BMW took it over in 2006. Robert Kubica claimed its lone win in Canada in 2008.

JAMES KEY
Sauber's technical director became involved in racing in 1996, aged 24, with Lotus for its GT racing programme, having been sponsored through university by them. He then broke into F1 in 1998 with Jordan and rose from being data engineer to senior race engineer in 2002. James then moved to the aerodynamics division and was appointed technical director in 2005, staying on through the team's changes to become Spyker and then Force India. He moved to Sauber midway through last season.

2010 DRIVERS & RESULTS

Driver	Nationality	Races	Wins	Pts	Pos
Pedro de la Rosa	Spanish	14	0	6	17th
Nick Heidfeld	German	5	0	6	18th
Kamui Kobayashi	Japanese	19	0	32	12th

Clearly an exceptionally busy individual, with a business empire to run, Slim has appointed Adrian Fernandez as his motorsport representative and the 2000 ChampCar runner-up has based himself in Switzerland to oversee the enterprise. Fernandez will have a close relationship with the team's new signing Sergio Perez, whom he has known since Sergio was a toddler, as Sergio's father worked for him when he was racing in ChampCar.

Fernandez's role may become even more important in 2012, as Peter Sauber stated when BMW bought a stake in the team for 2006 that he wished to reduce his role and, now aged 66, perhaps he'll cede control to the 47-year-old Mexican.

With an eye on the future, there's a second Mexican driver, Esteban Gutierrez, on the team's books as its reserve driver, so one can only feel that the creation of an all-Mexican line-up is but a year away, with 2010 GP3 champion Gutierrez being honed for a race seat in 2012.

The lead driver will be Kamui Kobayashi, who so impressed through the course of last season, leaving Pedro de la Rosa in his shadow and then putting on a masterful performance in the race in front of his home fans in Japan as he battled up the order. There's no doubting his speed, but Kamui will still need to have the rough edges smoothed off his style. His unorthodox style of attack will certainly draw the public's eye to the team's sponsors, as he is already a favourite with TV directors when they know that he is coming up on slower cars.

Technically, the team made good progress through 2010, with the arrival of James Key from Force India as technical director giving them useful impetus, and the pace of their cars in the Japanese GP in particular showing how much progress had been made as they scrapped with Williams and Force India. The return of Nick Heidfeld provided a useful barometer too, to put a value on Kobayashi's speed after de la Rosa was dropped following the Italian GP.

With new funds in place and two young but inexperienced drivers at the wheel, Sauber should be able to cement its place in the midfield and can now afford to work at advancing from there.

"Since James Key has joined us, we have improved significantly on the technical side. Furthermore, Kamui has shown a great development during the season, so I'm very happy that he drives for our team."
Peter Sauber

FOR THE RECORD

Country of origin:	Switzerland
Team base:	Hinwil, Switzerland
Telephone:	(41) 44 937 9000
Website:	www.sauber-motorsport.com
Active in Formula One:	From 1993 (but from 2006 to 2010 as BMW Sauber)
Grands Prix contested:	306
Wins:	1
Pole positions:	1
Fastest laps:	2

THE TEAM

Team principal & owner:	Peter Sauber
Managing director:	Monisha Kaltenborn
Technical director:	James Key
Chief designer:	Christoph Zimmermann
Head of aerodynamics:	Seamus Mullarkey
Head of track engineeringO	Giampaolo Dall'Ara
Team manager:	Beat Zehnder
Test driver:	Esteban Gutierrez
Chassis:	Sauber C30
Engine:	Ferrari V8
Tyres:	Pirelli

Peter Sauber presides over the team he founded, but Telmex money could lead to ceding power.

KAMUI KOBAYASHI

From rank outsider to recognised driver for the future in just one year was quite a transformation for Kamui after his surprise F1 debut in 2009 and it just shows how getting a break on the sport's biggest stage is all it takes for certain drivers to launch their careers.

Going into the 2011 World Championship, nobody bats an eyelid when people talk of Kamui Kobayashi as one of the hot young guns after his solid and occasionally spectacular form in his first full season of F1 with Sauber.

Yet even ardent followers of GP2 were extremely unlikely to have predicted that when he raced in F1's immediate feeder category between 2008 and 2009. He was quick but erratic, and certainly not the first name that they would have picked for hitting the heights in F1. After all, his best GP2 result in his second year was only third place at the Nurburgring, this a step down from the win he achieved at the opening round in 2008 at Barcelona.

What is amazing, considering all that has followed since he was given his F1 break, is that Kamui was on the verge of quitting racing, leaving Europe and heading back to Japan to work in his father's sushi restaurant at the end of 2009. This was when he was thrown an extraordinary lifeline: an F1 ride with Toyota to replace the injured Timo Glock. The way in which he took his chance was remarkable.

Kamui is a driver always worth watching as he races with a never-say-die attitude.

However, when Toyota announced late in the autumn of 2009 that it was pulling out of F1, this left Kamui high and dry. Fortunately, the team helped finance a ride with struggling Sauber, so he wasn't lost to a career in catering.

Sixth place in last year's British GP at Silverstone, up from 12th on the grid, was all the proof that people needed to confirm that this Japanese driver who burst onto the F1 radar so spectacularly for the final two races in 2009 and diced on both occasions with Jenson Button really was no flash in the pan. His fighting drive at Suzuka boosted his reputation further.

Kamui's greatest hope this year as he endeavours to really establish himself in F1 is that Sauber's new financial clout will enable it to keep developing its cars through the year.

TRACK NOTES

Nationality:	JAPANESE
Born:	13 SEPTEMBER 1986, HYOGO, JAPAN
Website:	www.kamui-kobayashi.com
Teams:	TOYOTA 2009, SAUBER 2010-11

CAREER RECORD	
First Grand Prix:	2009 BRAZILIAN GP
Grand Prix starts:	21
Grand Prix wins:	0
	(best result: sixth, 2009 Abu Dhabi GP, 2010 British GP)
Poles:	0
Fastest laps:	0
Points:	35
Honours:	2008 GP2 ASIA CHAMPION, 2005 EUROPEAN & ITALIAN FORMULA RENAULT CHAMPION, 2003 JAPANESE FORMULA TOYOTA RUNNER-UP, 2001 ALL-JAPAN ICA KART CHAMPION, 2000 SUZUKA KART CHAMPION

TAKING A DIFFERENT ROUTE

Kamui stands out from the young Japanese drivers who have come to Europe to contest the junior single-seater series in the hope of making it to F1, simply because he was successful at it. Having shown useful speed in Japan, he based himself in Italy in 2004 at the age of just 17 to race in Formula Renault. The following year was his breakthrough, as Kamui won the Italian and European series. F3 was the obvious next step in 2006 and he spent two years in that, ranking fourth in the 2007 Euro series, before graduating to GP2 for 2008. Although his form was erratic in this, and he did win the second race at Catalunya, his progress was only shown when he won the end-of-season GP2 Asia series. Toyota had already had its eye on him for its F1 team, but his 2009 GP2 form was patchy again and he truly shocked everyone with his two F1 outings at the end of 2009 when he shone in the grands prix in Brazil and Abu Dhabi, battling with Jenson Button in each.

SERGIO PEREZ

The influx of Telmex money to Sauber bought a ride for Sergio. The GP2 graduate has speed aplenty and now must spend his maiden Formula One season gaining as much experience as possible to hone his skills while the team finds its feet again after a year of scant investment.

It has been 19 years since Mexico hosted a grand prix and 30 years since one of its drivers started a round of the World Championship. That was Hector Rebaque, whose final F1 outing was for Brabham at Caesar's Palace in 1981. So, with Mexican billionaire Carlos Slim initiating the country's first push into F1 in decades, it's fitting that there's a Mexican driver as part of this bid.

Sauber has a history of introducing young talent to F1, such as Kimi Raikkonen and Felipe Massa. So it probably took little encouragement from Slim for the team to give Sergio a chance. His pedigree is strong, far stronger than Rebaque's ever was, with considerable experience packed into the career of a driver who has just turned 21.

Looking over his record, there's strong achievement at every level, normally against older rivals. However, it's his form in GP2 that impresses most, as it shows how he has over two years added balance to his speed.

There are two sorts of win in GP2: the ones in the first race and those in the shorter sprint on the Sunday. The latter are less prestigious, as the first

As Mexico's top rookie driver, Sergio must prove that he's worthy of the investment.

eight finishers in the first race line up on the grid in reverse order, thus enabling some drivers who finished only eighth to drive a "wide" car and hold on to take victory on the narrower circuits. Three of Sergio's wins in 2010 were sprints. However, none of these was from pole position and the fact that he achieved them at Silverstone, Hockenheim and Spa-Francorchamps shows that he could perform on the classic circuits where overtaking is still possible. Most notably, his drive from seventh place to first at Hockenheim showed what a fighter he is.

Sergio also won one of the Saturday races, at Monaco, after getting past Dani Clos on the opening lap.

This is a heaven-sent opportunity for Sergio to have a crack at F1 and has gained him a place in Ferrari's Driver Academy. Back in Mexico, they'll be praying that he can develop into their first grand prix winner since Pedro Rodriguez was first to the chequered flag at Spa-Francorchamps for BRM in 1970.

41

NOT AFRAID TO MOVE ABROAD

After karting from the age of seven, Sergio started racing cars from 14. That he did so in the USA, not his native Mexico, is a clear example of his ambition. In 2005, when 15, he raced in the German Formula BMW series. After a further year in the same series, he was given a chance to try more power when he had an outing for Team Mexico in A1GP. Then, he moved to the UK and raced to the National Class British Formula Three title. Aiming for the main crown in 2008, he won four times for T-Sport, but had to settle for fourth overall as Jaime Alguersuari won the title. Sergio then stepped up to GP2 Asia over the winter and won two races. The main GP2 series was his target for 2009 and he showed flashes of speed, but ranked 12th. Then a change of team to Barwa Addax for 2010 helped him as he won four races and ended the year as runner-up to Pastor Maldonado.

TRACK NOTES

Nationality:	MEXICAN
Born:	26 JANUARY 1990, GUADALAJARA, MEXICO
Website:	www.sergioperez.mx
Teams:	2011 SAUBER

CAREER RECORD

First Grand Prix:	2011 BAHRAIN GP
Grand Prix starts:	0
Grand Prix wins:	0
Poles:	0
Fastest laps:	0
Points:	0

Honours: 2010 GP2 RUNNER-UP, 2007 BRITISH FORMULA THREE NATIONAL CLASS CHAMPION

The gap between Scuderia Toro Rosso and its sister team Red Bull Racing opened out to a chasm last year as Italy-based Toro Rosso had to produce its own cars for the first time. This year, we will see whether that gap can be closed or whether it will extend even further.

On a good day last year Toro Rosso's drivers found themselves scrapping with the Force Indias. Time will tell who their rivals will be in 2011.

For a few years, Scuderia Toro Rosso seemed to deny the fact that it was once Minardi. Painted to look like the Red Bull Racing cars and, in fact, being made just like the Red Bulls effected a transformation so complete that any connection was severed in the mind of those watching the grands prix. This was especially so when Sebastian Vettel triumphed at Monza from pole position in the rain for the team in 2008. Last year, a slice of reality returned as the Italian team had to fend rather more for itself, using its own chassis. However, with a larger budget than it ever enjoyed as Minardi, the team has yet to slip down to the tail of the field that was Minardi's traditional position through the years, but last year bore signs that it's gfoing to have to work harder in 2011 last Team Lotus and Marussia Virging Racing make progress..

Just a handful of World Championship points were scored last year, and most of these only because of the new scoring system that awarded points all the way down to 10th, rather than just down to eighth, as before. Sebastien Buemi's eighth place at Montreal was the team's top result, with Jaime Alguersuari finishing ninth in the Malaysian GP and Buemi matching that in the European GP at Valencia. In 2009, Buemi had twice finished in seventh place.

Certainly, with the three new teams

KEY MOMENTS AND KEY PEOPLE

TEAM HISTORY

With the passing of years, people are starting to forget that this is a team that plied its trade for 21 years as Minardi, achieving little but earning respect for its enthusiastic efforts. Since being taken over by Red Bull magnate Dietrich Mateschitz in 2006, it achieved the incredible result of beating its more-fancied sister team, Red Bull Racing, to get to the winner's circle, doing so in 2008 when Sebastian Vettel dominated a very wet Italian GP. Since then, though, with young (cheap) drivers, it has lost ground. Yet for a team that was once Minardi to be stuck in midfield is still a step forward...

GIORGIO ASCANELLI

A design engineer at Ferrari in 1985, Giorgio became head of race operations before joining Benetton in 1989. McLaren snared him in 1991 and he led its active suspension project. Ferrari lured him back in 1995 and he stayed until 2002, when Maserati asked him to lead its sports car programme. After success in the FIA GT series, he came back to F1 with Toro Rosso as technical director in 2007.

2010 DRIVERS & RESULTS

Driver	Nationality	Races	Wins	Pts	Pos
Jaime Alguersuari	Spanish	19	0	5	19th
Sebastien Buemi	Swiss	19	0	8	16th

joining the World Championship last year, Toro Rosso ought to be safe from those bottom spots for now at least, but the big question is whether it can improve its form to get into position to pick up the odd points when the drivers from the top teams stumble and so improve from last year's ranking of ninth place overall.

On the plus side, Scuderia Toro Rosso retains great stability, with Franz Tost remaining as team principal for team owner Dietrich Mateschitz and Giorgio Ascanelli continuing to control the technical side. The drivers are likely to be the same too, with parent company Red Bull stating but not confirming that it is giving its young hotshots Buemi and Alguersuari another chance to develop their craft and perhaps bring one of them up to the standard where they are ready to replace Mark Webber when he comes to retire from Red Bull Racing.

One problem with having two young drivers comes when attempting to evaluate your chassis and its development programme, as neither has sufficient experience to judge it as accurately as a more experienced F1 driver would. Add to this the matter that no one knows quite how good each driver is, as they are only being compared against each other and the outcome can be most confusing.

However, that leaves the question of whether Red Bull considers the team as a team in its own right or only as a finishing school for those reaching the top of its development programme.

Looking ahead to this year, it's hard to know just how good a car Toro Rosso's chief designer Ben Butler will produce to be mated with Ferrari engines and gearboxes, but one can only feel that with Mercedes GP bound to be more consistent, as well as Renault, Williams and Sauber raising their game, life could be increasingly unrewarding for this team, which still operates out of Minardi's modest base at Faenza.

Their speed is unlikely to be anywhere close to the speed of the Red Bull RB7s, but it would be really helpful to all concerned if Toro Rosso's cars were given a livery that was truly different from Red Bull Racing's dark blue with a leaping bull livery, if only so that the cars could be identified easily as the Red Bull boys rejoin the race from mid-race pit stops. Red Bull Light, anyone?

> "My view is that if we're ninth in the World Championship, we've just done our job, not good, not bad. If we're 10th, then we deserve to be shot."
>
> **Giorgio Ascanelli**

FOR THE RECORD

Country of origin:	Italy
Team base:	Faenza, Italy
Telephone:	(39) 546 696111
Website:	www.scuderiatororosso.com
Active in Formula One:	From 1985
	(as Minardi until 2006)
Grands Prix contested:	412
Wins:	1
Pole positions:	1
Fastest laps:	0

THE TEAM

Team owner:	Dietrich Mateschitz
Team principal:	Franz Tost
Technical director:	Giorgio Ascanelli
Team manager:	Gianfranco Fantuzzi
Chief designer:	Ben Butler
Chief aerodynamicist:	tba
Chief engineer:	Laurent Mekies
Technical co-ordinator:	Sandro Parrini
Logistics manager:	Domenico Sangiorgi
Test driver:	Daniel Ricciardo
Chassis:	Toro Rosso STR6
Engine:	Ferrari V8
Tyres:	Pirelli

Franz Tost and team continue to support young drivers, but that means watching their errors.

SEBASTIEN BUEMI*

Reaching Formula One by the age of just 20 is an incredible achievement in anybody's books, but Sebastien now knows that his third year in Red Bull's junior team might be his last hope of impressing sufficiently to earn the right to step up to Red Bull Racing.

Being part of a heavily backed programme for young drivers has its benefits. However, it also has its problems. The main one is that Red Bull uses Toro Rosso as a team with which to "blood" the pick of its young drivers, to give them a taste of Formula One and so see how they can perform on the sport's most high-profile stage. If, like Sebastian Vettel, they turn into diamonds, then they will be promoted to Red Bull Racing. If not, then their careers in F1 might not continue any further, as they may not be so highly rated by other team chiefs or have the backing to find a ride elsewhere.

Certainly, Vettel had a superior car when he raced to victory at the Italian GP at Monza in 2008 before joining Red Bull Racing in 2009. Certainly, too, the subsequent Toro Rosso chassis have not been so competitive since then, most notably in 2010, when they had to be built in-house rather than come via Red Bull Technologies. However, Vettel set a gold standard that neither Sebastien nor his even younger team-mate Jaime Alguersuari look able to equal.

So does Sebastien have a hope of

Sebastien scored Toro Rosso's best result last year but knows he must improve in 2011.

moving on to a team likely to feature closer to the front of the grid in 2012? Time will tell, but what he shows with ever greater authority is that he's a really good racer, a driver in no way overawed

when having to mix it even with Michael Schumacher on occasion in 2010.

With the top five teams – Red Bull Racing, McLaren, Ferrari, Mercedes and Renault – extending their advantage over the midfield teams last year, points were increasingly hard to come by, but Sebastien managed it three times, peaking with eighth place at the Canadian GP, and that's as good a marker as any that he deserves a better car to allow his talents to blossom. First, though, he has to keep his younger team-mate in check in 2011.

* Not confirmed at time of going to press.

TRACK NOTES

Nationality:	SWISS
Born:	31 OCTOBER 1988, AIGLE, SWITZERLAND
Website:	www.buemi.com
Teams:	TORO ROSSO 2009-10

CAREER RECORD	
First Grand Prix:	2009 AUSTRALIAN GP
Grand Prix starts:	36
Grand Prix wins:	0
	(best result: seventh, 2009 Australian & Brazilian GPs)
Poles:	0
Fastest laps:	0
Points:	14
Honours:	2008 GP2 ASIA RUNNER-UP, 2007 EUROPEAN FORMULA THREE RUNNER-UP, 2005 WORLD FINAL & GERMAN FORMULA BMW RUNNER-UP, 2002 EUROPEAN JUNIOR KART CHAMPION, 1999 & 1998 SWISS MINI KART CHAMPION

MAKING A SPLASH IN EVERY FORMULA

Coming from a family steeped in motor racing – his grandfather and great-uncle built an F1 car (the Cegga) in the early 1960s – it wasn't surprising that Sebastien started racing karts as soon as he could. He had talent too and was the European Junior Kart Champion in 2002. Then, as soon as he was old enough to transfer to car racing, he did. That was in 2004 and he immediately finished third overall in the German Formula BMW series, then was runner-up at his second attempt behind Nico Hulkenberg. Next he tried F3 and finished second overall behind Sebastien Grosjean in his second year in the European championship but ahead of Hulkenberg. Having tried more power in A1GP, Sebastien moved up to GP2 and ranked sixth in 2008, winning two of the 20 races. However, since he already had Red Bull backing, he was at the front of the queue when Scuderia Toro Rosso wanted a young hotshot. His form in his debut season, 2009, showed continual improvement as he laid layers of experience on his natural speed.

JAIME ALGUERSUARI*

Flashes of speed in 2010 hint at great things to come from this Spaniard who already has a year and a half of F1 racing experience behind him as he turns 21. He also demonstrated a remarkable ability to finish races and a capacity to be extremely feisty in the heat of battle.

Red Bull has financed Jaime's rise through the ranks, as it has done for so many young drivers over the past decade. However, he is one of few who remain on its books, as he continues to deliver to the standard expected, whereas so many of his Red Bull-backed contemporaries slipped up.

When Jaime was signed midway through 2009 to replace Sebastien Bourdais at Toro Rosso, though, there was much resistance to his graduation to the sport's top stage at the age of just 19. After all, he had conducted only straight-line testing for the team and, hampered by the in-season testing ban, had not been able to have a meaningful outing before relieving the disappointing Frenchman. Yet, even though his debut was to be on the twisty Hungaroring, he didn't get in the way and the critics faded away.

The remaining seven races of the 2009 season were used simply to gain experience to put towards his 2010 campaign and Jaime did well, but did have a big shunt at Suzuka. However, he clearly learnt from it and his form in 2010 has been strong, often matching his more experienced team-mate Sebastien Buemi,

Jaime started to blossom last year when he began to revisit tracks he'd tried in 2009.

and clearly picking up once he reached the circuits on which he raced in 2009 in the second half of the season.

Perhaps the clearest proof that he is one to watch came at the Singapore GP, when he was fifth fastest in practice in the damp, then qualified 11th. Infuriatingly, he had to start the race from the pit lane.

Had the relative competitiveness of the Toro Rosso STR5 not dwindled against its rivals as the season advanced, there would surely have been more points come season's end, when Jaime suffered the pain of being one place out of the points three races in succession, finishing 11th at Suzuka, Yeongam and Interlagos. He then rounded the year out with an excellent ninth place at Yas Marina.

Many feel that it is Jaime rather than Buemi who might stand the better chance of advancing further up F1's ladder and being promoted to Red Bull Racing.

* Not confirmed at time of going to press.

NOT IN HIS FATHER'S TRACKS

With so many drivers following the family tradition, one might have expected Jaime to follow his father, also Jaime, into racing, albeit of the two-wheeled kind. However, after a minimal amount of karting, it was decided that he'd race cars instead, helped by the fact that Jaime Snr was in charge of the World Series by Renault. When he turned 15, Jaime raced in Formula Junior 1.6 in Italy, then tried a race in the European Formula Renault series. For 2006 and 2007, he contested the European and Italian Formula Renault series, gaining valuable track time. Despite scoring three wins in the 2007 Italian series, what followed in 2008 took everyone by surprise. Jaime joined Carlin Motorsport to contest the British F3 series and became champion in his rookie year on tracks he'd never visited, overhauling Oliver Turvey at the final round. Continuing with Carlin in 2009, he raced in the World Series, but was given his F1 break mid-season, snapped up by Toro Rosso to replace Sebastien Bourdais.

TRACK NOTES

Nationality:	SPANISH
Born:	23 MARCH 1990, BARCELONA, SPAIN
Website:	www.jalguersuari.com
Teams:	TORO ROSSO 2009-11

CAREER RECORD

First Grand Prix:	2009 HUNGARIAN GP
Grand Prix starts:	27
Grand Prix wins:	0
Poles:	0
Fastest laps:	0
Points:	3
Honours:	2008 BRITISH FORMULA THREE CHAMPION, 2007 ITALIAN FORMULA RENAULT RUNNER-UP, 2006 ITALIAN FORMULA RENAULT WINTER SERIES CHAMPION

TEAM LOTUS

The team backed off early in its maiden year to focus its design efforts on this year's challenge and so Mike Gascoyne and his drivers will be praying that this, boosted by the deal to run Renault V8s and Red Bull Racing gearboxes, was the right decision to power them forward.

Jarno Trulli and Heikki Kovalainen did all the spadework in 2010 and will be hoping that this is rewarded with a performance breakthrough.

One of the changes for 2011 that owner Tony Fernandes is most pleased about is the team's renaming from Lotus F1 Racing to Team Lotus, which is how it was in its pomp in the 1960s and 1970s. It's not just about strengthening the team's link with its historic and successful past, though, but about having independence in not having to secure a licence deal from road car division Group Lotus.

"I felt that we had come to a point where we were getting very deep in investment and commitment," said Fernandes, "and I didn't feel comfortable having a licence from someone else and we needed to secure our own future."

Proton, owners of Group Lotus, weren't so sure and protested, leading to the possibility of two teams having Lotus in their titles for 2011. Talk of Team Lotus running its cars in black and gold in tribute to Team Lotus's great days in the 1970s were scrapped and it will stick after all to the green and old livery it used in 2010.

Name change or not, the team's intent was made plain when it got Mike Gascoyne to sign a five-year contract extension last September that will keep him with the team until the end of 2015. He is as close to every facet of the team as anyone, so the fact that

KEY MOMENTS AND KEY PEOPLE

TEAM HISTORY
Having entered F1 in 1958, this was *the* team by the early 1960s, as team founder Colin Chapman came up with radical ideas to keep the green cars from Norfolk at the front. Jim Clark helped him gather the drivers' and constructors' titles in 1963 and 1965. Then, regrouping after Clark's death in 1968, Graham Hill helped the team back to the top and Jochen Rindt became champion in 1970, albeit posthumously, then Emerson Fittipaldi and Mario Andretti were crowned in 1972 and 1978, before Ayrton Senna shone in 1985. A lack of funds led to it closing its doors in 1994, but the name was revived for 2010.

TONY FERNANDES
Here is a man who makes things happen. He ignored the nay-sayers when he bought AirAsia a decade ago and turned it into a profit-making enterprise. Having worked for Virgin Atlantic as an auditor, he recognised a prospect when he saw one and leapt in. With money to play with, Fernandes backed the Williams team, then encouraged Malaysian businesses to join him in reviving the Lotus marque in F1.

2010 DRIVERS & RESULTS

Driver	Nationality	Races	Wins	Pts	Pos
Heikki Kovalainen	Finnish	19	0	0	20th
Jarno Trulli	Italian	19	0	0	21st

he is committing his future to Lotus proves that he believes it has a good future.

Perhaps the first step towards the advances required to keep Gascoyne and Fernandes happy was shown when Lotus elected not to continue with Cosworth engines and sought power from Renault instead. Augmenting this, Fernandes' ambitious team harnessed gearboxes and hydraulics from Red Bull Technologies, so expect the drivers to move from the head of the much-lapped tail-end trio of teams that were new to F1 last year towards the midfield. Indeed, many of their problems, lack of in-season testing aside, were caused by hydraulic and gearbox failures, so expect more finishes at the very least in 2011.

Gascoyne reckons this deal with Red Bull Technologies will have other performance benefits, as the designers that he'd have otherwise have had allocated to working on the drive train can be reallocated to working on the aerodynamics. Should the hoped-for gains be realised, then Gascoyne is optimistic that Team Lotus will be able to join the midfield pack and race against the likes of Force India, Sauber, Scuderia Toro Rosso and Williams.

The team has been bolstering the technical side, with Mark Smith moving across from Force India, and others are sure to follow, perhaps eventually young Malaysian mechanics and engineers, as their development is very much part of Fernandes' plan, along with the advance of the team back towards the front of the grid.

By retaining drivers Heikki Kovalainen and Jarno Trulli, both of whom remained buoyant through not only the embarrassment of being so far off the pace but also retirement after retirement during 2010, the team has drivers who will bring their experience to bear. These one-time grand prix winners deserve a good step forward to put a smile back on their faces, and the possibility of going racing with the expectation of scoring championship points would be the target they're looking for.

Points proved beyond the duo last year, but 12th place for Kovalainen in the Japanese GP was celebrated as though it was a win, as it secured the team 10th place, ahead of Virgin Racing and HRT in the constructors' championship and thus a share of travel money. Its ambitions for 2011 will be to move yet further up the table.

Thanks to the entrepreneurial Fernandes' links, the team signed a deal with Creative Artists' Agency, the leading Hollywood sports and entertainment agency, so look for a new and exciting approach to publicising and branding the team in the season ahead.

''We did a good job in 2010 with what we had, but you're only a new team once and you've got to go on and be a proper team.''
Mike Gascoyne

FOR THE RECORD

Country of origin:	England
Team base:	Hingham, England
Telephone:	(44) 01953 851411
Website:	www.lotusf1racing.my
Active in Formula One:	From 2010*
Grands Prix contested:	19
Wins:	0
Pole positions:	0
Fastest laps:	0

* THIS TEAM HAS NOTHING TO DO WITH THE LOTUS TEAM THAT RAN FROM 1958 to 1994

THE TEAM

Team owner & team principal:	Tony Fernandes
Chief executive officer:	Riad Asmat
Chief technical officer:	Mike Gascoyne
Chief operating officer:	Keith Saunt
Technical director:	Mark Smith
Team manager:	Graham Watson
Chief designer:	Lewis Butler
Head of aerodynamics:	Marianne Hinson
Chief engineer:	Jody Egginton
Test driver:	tba
Chassis:	Lotus T128
Engine:	Renault V8
Tyres:	Pirelli

Team owner Tony Fernandes listens as Mike Gascoyne (right) cracks a joke over the intercom.

JARNO TRULLI

Smooth, measured and still capable of outstanding flying laps in qualifying, Jarno is facing his second year at the tail end of the grid with the Lotus team, but he's cheered by the prospect of a far more competitive car and hoping for both a change of luck and some reliability.

They say that you make your own luck in sport. If that's the case, then this likeable Italian hasn't been reading the instructions properly, as his luck was rotten throughout his 2010 campaign.

Sure, driving for rookie Team Lotus, he wasn't expecting top results, not even point-scoring drives, but Jarno did expect at least to finish races. Yet, if things went wrong with one of the two dark green and yellow Lotuses, it was invariably the one with his name on the side. Yes, he led to his own demise in the Monaco GP when he assaulted Karun Chandhok's Hispania in the closing laps, but the rest of his race retirements were out of his control.

What will have concerned Jarno was that although he was usually ahead of his team-mate Heikki Kovalainen in qualifying, the Finnish driver was usually ahead of him in the races.

Both drivers were aware that 2010 was very much a learning year and hopefully the experience that they gained will be put to better effect in 2011 as they head out to battle in a car that will undoubtedly have received more of tech chief Mike

Jarno had to learn to be philosophical in 2010 but won't stand for many more failures.

Gascoyne's magic than last year's T127 did. After all, the mantra through last season was very much "we're simply preparing for next year".

If you're picking drivers for a team new to F1, your best bet is to choose drivers who have plenty of F1 experience - Jarno has now contested 238 grands prix - who are also amenable people. Jarno is very much that sort of driver. Indeed, having faced the possible loss of his place in F1 following Toyota's 11th-hour withdrawal at the end of 2009, when almost all the rides with other teams had been taken, perhaps he appreciates his place at motor racing's top table more than most and will be determined to make one last push for glory before he retires to tend his vineyards.

TRACK NOTES

Nationality:	ITALIAN
Born:	13 JULY 1974, PESCARA, ITALY
Website:	www.jarnotrulli.com
Teams:	MINARDI 1997, PROST 1997-99, JORDAN 2000-01, RENAULT 2002-04, TOYOTA 2005-09, LOTUS 2010-11

CAREER RECORD	
First Grand Prix:	1997 AUSTRALIAN GP
Grand Prix starts:	238
Grand Prix wins:	1
	2004 Monaco GP
Poles:	4
Fastest laps:	1
Points:	246.5
Honours:	1996 GERMAN FORMULA THREE CHAMPION, 1995 ITALIAN KARTING CHAMPION, 1994 EUROPEAN & NORTH AMERICAN KARTING CHAMPION, 1991 WORLD KARTING CHAMPION

GET ME TO FORMULA ONE, FAST

There are many levels of kart racing, but even fervent car racing fans take notice when a kartist becomes World Kart Champion. Jarno was one such, doing so at the age of 17. He didn't have the backing to try car racing until he was 21, moving directly to German F3 midway through 1995, once he was signed up by Flavio Briatore. He was an instant hit, winning races before the year was out ahead of the more experienced Ralf Schumacher. Jarno claimed the German title in 1996 ahead of Nick Heidfeld. Reckoning that this meant he was ready for F1 after just one and a half years of car racing, Jarno joined Minardi for 1997. A chance to swap mid-season to the Prost team after Olivier Panis was injured gave Jarno his break and he immediately led the Austrian GP. Sadly, over the intervening years his ability has seldom been matched with a competitive car and it seems inconceivable that he has won only once - for Renault at Monaco in 2004 - and is better known for qualifying laps. His final year with Toyota brought second place in Japan and two thirds.

HEIKKI KOVALAINEN

Never before had Heikki had to drive so hard for so few results, but the 2010 season with Team Lotus was one that rebuilt his dented reputation after he'd come off very much second best to Lewis Hamilton during his two World Championship campaigns for McLaren.

Such was the rush to start the Team Lotus F1 from scratch that little was expected of it last year, especially with a total lack of in-season testing. Heikki was thus plunged into a situation a world away from his two seasons at McLaren. In whichever way he looked at it, all was very, very different. And yet, with possible victories not even a blip on the radar, Heikki knuckled down and simply got on with the job in hand, usually with a smile on his face.

In many ways, it will have been frustrating, plunged from feast to famine, but in other ways it was liberating, as few had any expectations of the team. The target in races wasn't victory or even a podium finish but simply to be the highest-placed of the drivers from the three new teams. This he managed more than any of his fellow tail-end Charlies, winning the self-appointed class nine times across the 19 grands prix.

For 2011, many of these endeavours will have been rewarded by a car that is markedly better, as chief technical officer Mike Gascoyne decided relatively early last season to focus most of the design team's attention on 2011's car. Then, of

Heikki will be attempting to drag this still-young team towards the midfield this year.

course, all was propelled another stage forward with the signing of a technical agreement with Red Bull Racing. This will lead to a massive step forward and should ensure that Lotus starts to battle its way into the midfield with the likes of

Scuderia Toro Rosso, offering more for Heikki to fight for.

What Heikki showed last year was an enjoyment at not being overpowered by a team-mate, as he was so comprehensively by Lewis Hamilton at McLaren in 2008 and 2009. Instead, he more than matched Jarno Trulli at Lotus. Heikki's confidence was boosted and he drove some excellent races. Frustratingly, he will be remembered best for being used as a launching ramp by Mark Webber in Valencia and for his engine catching fire in Singapore.

TRACK NOTES

Nationality:	FINNISH
Born:	19 OCTOBER 1981, SUOMUSSALMI, FINLAND
Website:	www.heikkikovalainen.net
Teams:	RENAULT 2007, MCLAREN 2008-09, LOTUS 2010-11

CAREER RECORD	
First Grand Prix:	2007 AUSTRALIAN GP
Grand Prix starts:	71
Grand Prix wins:	1
	2008 Hungarian GP
Poles:	1
Fastest laps:	2
Points:	105
Honours:	2005 GP2 RUNNER-UP, 2004 FORMULA NISSAN WORLD SERIES CHAMPION, 2004 CHAMPION OF CHAMPIONS AT RACE OF CHAMPIONS, 2000 NORDIC KARTING CHAMPION

FROM MACAU TO McLAREN

Heikki's friends in rural Finland dreamed of being rally drivers, but he always aimed for F1. He had to travel long distances to race karts, but it paid off as he was Nordic Karting Champion when he was 18. He raced in British Formula Renault in 2001 and displayed increasing speed as he ranked fourth. His team, Fortec, even gave him an end-of-season F3 outing at Macau. Ranking third in British F3 in 2002, he rounded out the year by finishing second in Macau. Two years of World Series by Nissan followed, and he was runner-up and then champion. However, it was his form in the multi-discipline Race of Champions when he beat Michael Schumacher that made his name. He landed a seat with a top GP2 team for 2005 and won five races, but ended as runner-up behind Nico Rosberg. After a year as a Renault test driver, the team gave him his F1 break in 2007 and he joined McLaren in 2008, even taking victory in Hungary. But he was overshadowed by Lewis Hamilton.

It was widely believed that not all of the three teams new to F1 last year would make it to the end of the season, with HRT appearing the weakest of the trio. However, it survived and now faces a huge challenge to find greater speed and definitely some reliability for 2011.

Bruno Senna brought a famous name to HRT, but he and his three fellow drivers could do little but attempt to stay out of trouble and finish.

The much-lauded Team US F1 didn't even make it to the start of the 2010 World Championship, so the Hispania Racing Team at least won one race in its maiden season. Not a grand prix, obviously, but the race to make it to the starting grid. However, the fact that the Spanish team approached last year known as Campos Meta F1 demonstrates just how times were tough from the outset, as it had to change to HRT and so never raced under that name.

The history books will show that former F1 racer Adrian Campos had to hand over the reins to his original partner Jose Ramon Carabante in mid-February as the money simply wasn't in place for him to continue. The team was then renamed Hispania Racing Team after his own company, Grupo Hispania. He immediately signed ex-Force India principal Colin Kolles to oversee it.

Dallara built the chassis, which was a wise move, as it helped the team not only to save the enormous start-up costs of buying all the hardware and facilities to build its own car but to concentrate on setting up the team's operational side, letting the world's leading single-seater manufacturer do the stuff it knows best. All parties were aware that Dallara hadn't built an F1 chassis since 1998, when it built the car for Honda's abortive bid to enter F1 in its own right, but it had the wind tunnel and all other leading manufacturing facilities required.

Geoff Willis, formerly of Williams, BAR and

KEY MOMENTS AND KEY PEOPLE

TEAM HISTORY
In years to come, it will appear that this was a team with no history until it made it to the grid for last year's F1 World Championship. However, it was born out of Campos Racing, a team that had run cars in the junior single-seater formulae since 1998. It helped Marc Gene to the Open Fortuna by Nissan title in 1998, then Fernando Alonso to the same in 1999. After that, it focused on GP2 from its inception in 2005 and won the teams' title in 2008 after running Lucas di Grassi and Vitaly Petrov to four wins. The team was then sold to Alejandro Agag and raced on as Barwa Addax.

COLIN KOLLES
This Romanian dentist started his own team to run in German F3 in 2000 and did well. However, his F1 break came when Alex Shnaider bought Jordan and he ran the team through its metamorphoses into Spyker and Force India. Then, for 2010, he was given the task by Jose Ramon Carabante of making HRT work.

2010 DRIVERS & RESULTS

Driver	Nationality	Races	Wins	Pts	Pos
Karun Chandhok	Indian	10	0	0	22nd
Christian Klien	Austrian	3	0	0	27th
Bruno Senna	Brazilian	18	0	0	23rd
Sakon Yamamoto	Japanese	7	0	0	26th

FOR THE RECORD

Country of origin:	Spain
Team base: Madrid, Spain & Greding, Germany	
Telephone:	(49) 8463 602679
Website:	www.hispaniaf1team.com
Active in Formula One:	From 2010
Grands Prix contested:	19
Wins:	0
Pole positions:	0
Fastest laps:	0

THE TEAM

Team owner & chairman:	Jose Ramon Carabante
Team principal:	Colin Kolles
Technical director:	Geoff Willis
Technical co-ordinator:	Jacky Eeckelaert
Team manager:	Boris Bernes
Chief designer:	tba
Chief aerodynamicist:	tba
Chief engineer:	Antonio Cuquerella
Test driver:	tba
Chassis:	HRT F111
Engine:	Cosworth V8
Tyres:	Pirelli

Red Bull Racing, was brought in after the season got under way as technical director, taking over the reins from Daniele Audetto, who saw the car through its gestation at Dallara. Willis was disappointed with what he saw in the chassis and felt that it had little chance of challenging.

There was talk last year of the possibility of the team buying the stillborn 2010 Toyota chassis, perhaps even to help the Japanese manufacturer to prepare for the new engine regulations for 2013. This came to naught and a deal was struck to continue with Cosworth power but with gearboxes from Williams, which ought to boost both reliability and performance.

There's always a queue of drivers waiting to break into F1 and HRT is a likely way in, but its lack of obvious investment may have deterred some. However, looking to 2011, many felt that the team should take a wise old head to help develop the car and the team's structure and a rookie with money to help pay the bills. This is why Pedro de la Rosa, who lost his ride with Sauber last year, was thought to be a sensible candidate for helping his country's only F1 team advance. That and the fact the development skills he honed over seven years as a test driver for McLaren plus his testing experience for Pirelli last year would undoubtedly help improve this year's HRT if he is signed up.

The team certainly won't want the disruption that it endured last year when it ran four different drivers, with Karun Chandhok being dropped to make way for the money-bearing Sakon Yamamoto who was then stood down with alleged food poisoning at the Singapore GP to enable the more experienced Christian Klien to propel the car more speedily.

With money playing a part in almost every decision that this team makes, Narain Karthikeyan was the only driver that the team had signed as this book closed for press. With just one season of F1 to his name, he's neither a rookie nor vastly experienced, but he does bring plenty of welcome backing, from Tata.

As we closed for press, there was talk that Vitantonio Liuzzi wouldn't be retained by Force India, despite having a contract and would be placed by them with HRT so that he could remain in F1.

''We're not in a hurry to announce our drivers as the deadline is three days before the first race. The 2011 car? We'll have one and are in the process of manufacturing it.''
Colin Kolles

Colin Kolles runs the sporting side of the team, leaving worries about finances to the owners.

NARAIN KARTHIKEYAN

After five years away from Formula One, competing in a wide variety of racing categories across the globe, Narain is back on the Grand Prix scene just in time to compete in his inaugural home grand prix, with the money he brought crucial for the HRT team's survival.

It's safe to say that Narain Karthikeyan's signing for struggling HRT in the first week of January came as a major shock, as his name hadn't even been in the frame as a long list of drivers were discussed who might help this year-old team battle its way into a second season. After all, although Narain had kept his toe in the single-seater pond by racing and winning in the Superleague Formula, his greater success appeared to be happening in NASCAR truck racing in the USA.

Furthermore, as Narain will have just turned 34 when he starts his second season of Formula One, he was no longer seen as an up-and-coming star. However, his long-standing relationship with HRT's team principal Colin Kolles, plus a big push for India to have one of its own racing in its inaugural grand prix, at the end of this October combined to give him his second shot at the big time.

Dubbed 'The World's Fastest Indian', as a twist of the title of a recent film about record-breaking motorcyclist Burt Munro, Narain certainly brings years of experience and, as anyone who has watched him race knows, a truly spectacular driving style.

After five years out of F1, Narain has every reason to smile that he's made it back

He also returns as a point-scorer, having raced to fourth place in the 2005 US GP. Delighted as Narain would have been with the points – this was the race which was the race which was boycotted by all but six cars.

Narain's target must be to get up to speed and then help the team advance to the level that it can do well in the one race that really counts for he and his sponsor Tata, the Indian GP in October.

Narain will simply be pleased that he has fulfilled his promise to return to F1, while his wit will be welcomed in the paddock.

Narain has stated that he simply wants to get out there and be sure that he's still around at the end of each grand prix. Having been accused of being less than fit enough to race at his best for a grand prix distance in 2005, you can be sure that Narain will have been in the gym and will be looking to silence those accusing him of being just a pay driver.

A LONG TIME COMING

If all had gone to plan, Narain would have reached F1 far earlier than 2005. He headed to Britain to race in junior single-seaters in 1993 and his plan wouldn't have included a wait of more than a decade to graduate to F1. His journey took him back to Asia before trying British F3 against Jenson Button and others. From there, Narain advanced in 2001 to race Formula Nippon in Japan before settling on the Europe-based World Series by Nissan as his route to F1 and he ranked fourth in 2003. Having fallen two positions in 2004, he might have been facing a fourth year in this feeder formula, but Alex Shnaider had just taken over Jordan and he jumped at the opening. Unfortunately, it lasted only a year before he became Williams test driver and shone in A1GP, winning twice for India. After being reunited with Kolles for the 2009 Le Mans 24 Hours, Narain looked to the NASCAR series in 2010 and made quite an impression.

TRACK NOTES

Nationality:	INDIAN
Born:	14 JANUARY 1977, CHENNAI, INDIA
Website:	www.narainracing.com
Teams:	JORDAN 2005, HRT 2011

CAREER RECORD

First Grand Prix:	2005 AUSTRALIAN GP
Grand Prix starts:	19
Grand Prix wins:	0
	best result: fourth, 2005 United States GP
Poles:	0
Fastest laps:	0
Points:	5
Honours:	1996 FORMULA ASIA CHAMPION, 1994 BRITISH FORMULA FORD WINTER SERIES CHAMPION

VITANTONIO LIUZZI*

If there was bad luck to be had or a collision to be caught up in last year, it seemed that Vitantonio would be there. Fortunately, so was the speed, with flashes shown here or there. But then it looked as though he would be edged out of the team and placed with HRT instead.

When Vitantonio slammed his Force India into the barriers at last year's Brazilian GP, after a trackrod failed, it summed up his season. The speed was there from the Italian driver, but it was team-mate Adrian Sutil who kept recording the points-scoring drives.

A driver's career will always be on a knife edge, as speed alone is not enough and there's usually another driver waiting in the wings. Certainly, with Sutil taking a fifth place finish as early as the third round in Malaysia, the pressure started to be exerted on Vitantonio, with the team's third driver Paul di Resta being given outings in practice sessions, being groomed for the future. The question remained through the season as to how far into the future the much garlanded young Scot might be promoted to Force India's racing line-up.

Vitantonio talked last autumn of 'having a contract' to race on with the team in 2011, but the fact that he was still talking about rather than having signed it remained ominous. Fortunately, after failing to score since taking 10th place at the Belgian GP and then failing to finish for two races, he was able to keep out of trouble and bring his car home for his best result of the season in the wet at Yeongam. That was

Vitantonio will have to hope that he used up his career's quota of bad luck in 2010

sixth place and relieved the pressure. Of course, it was followed by his heavy shunt in Brazil. Talk about highs and lows...

Then, of course, he got into the limelight at the final round in Abu Dhabi when, unsighted, he mounted Michael Schumacher's spun Mercedes. Again, it wasn't his fault.

As Vitantonio assessed his chances of staying on with Force India, a lot hinged on whether Sutil was going to stay or whether di Resta, favoured by engine supplier Mercedes-Benz, would fill any gaps. Should Vitantonio's contract not be honoured, there was talk that he'd be placed with HRT.

Vitantonio's career has been full of ups and downs, but he'll always do his best to bounce back.

* Leading candidate at the time of going to press at the start of 2011.

TRACK NOTES

Nationality:	ITALIAN
Born:	6 APRIL, 1981, LOCOROTONDO, ITALY
Website:	www.liuzzi.com
Teams:	RED BULL 2005, TORO ROSSO 2006-2007, FORCE INDIA 2009-2010, HRT 2011

CAREER RECORD

First Grand Prix:	2005 SAN MARINO GP
Grand Prix starts:	63
Grand Prix wins:	0
(best result: sixth, 2007 Chinese GP, 2010 Korean GP)	
Poles:	0
Fastest laps:	0
Points:	26
Honours:	2004 FORMULA 3000 CHAMPION, 2001 WORLD KART CHAMPION, 2000 WORLD KART CUP RUNNER-UP, 1999 EUROPEAN FORMULA SUPER A KART CHAMPION, 1997 ITALIAN FORMULA A KART RUNNER-UP, 1996 ITALIAN JICA KART CHAMPION, 1995 WORLD KART RUNNER-UP, 1994 ITALIAN KART RUNNER-UP, 1993 ITALIAN KART CHAMPION

A MAN TO BEAT IN KARTING

Vitantonio was one of the stars of the international kart racing scene, failing by one place to become World Champion in 1995. He was second again in 2000 before taking the crown in 2001. Moving up to car racing, he made a good impression in Formula Renault, but his form wasn't as strong as expected in F3 in 2002. However, Red Bull promoted him to F3000 and he ranked fourth. Then in 2004 he won six of the seven races for Christian Horner's Arden team. Vitantonio got his F1 break in 2005 with Red Bull Racing, sharing the ride with Christian Klien. After scoring his first point in 2006, at Indianapolis, for Toro Rosso, sixth place was his best result in 2007, but crashed out of fourth in Canada on debris from Robert Kubica's accident. Vitantonio missed out on a possible Williams drive for 2008 then landed a test ride for Force India for 2009, leading to a race seat when Giancarlo Fisichella replaced the injured Felipe Massa at Ferrari.

MARUSSIA VIRGIN RACING

Virgin Racing overcame problems early in its maiden season and proved that it was staffed by people with strong racing credentials as it kept on progressing through the year. The second season in F1 is often tougher, but backing from Marussia will help the team move forwards.

Timo Glock and the team will be expecting to take firm strides forward in 2011 if their reliance on CFD can be made to pay dividends.

Such was the performance gap between the established Formula One teams and last year's three newcomers that even serious F1 fans will struggle to recall how Lotus, Virgin Racing or HRT fared in any particular grand prix. There were moments when they attracted the TV director's attention, but usually because they had caught fire, crashed or were being lapped. It required particular attention and even research to identify how they had done and whether indeed they managed to close the gap on the midfield teams.

In addition to the performance gap, there was a marked financial gap that meant these new teams were cut from different cloth from the established teams. Lotus was the best-financed, but Virgin Racing and especially HRT struggled for cash.

Added to that, there was the ban on in-season testing, so these newcomers effectively had their hands tied in their quest to catch up, but Virgin Racing and Lotus came out of the season with credit.

The key, though, is whether they can take another step with their second cars.

Virgin Racing has a very different business model from its rival teams, with its

structure being aimed squarely at keeping its cost base down, by subcontracting if needed, to limit the capital investment.

The team is also unusual in being divided

KEY MOMENTS AND KEY PEOPLE

TEAM HISTORY
The team was formed for 2010 from Manor Motorsport, a British team that had enjoyed success in F3 and Formula Renault under the leadership of former Formula Ford racer John Booth. It was a major step up to F1, but Booth's pedigree as a team boss had certainly helped two top drivers on their route to greater things, namely Kimi Raikkonen and Lewis Hamilton. On his promotion to run Virgin's new team, Booth handed over the reins of Manor Motorsport to others.

NICK WIRTH
The youngest Fellow of the Royal Institute of Mechanical Engineers, Nick specialises in aerodynamics. His first job was with March in 1988. He then worked for a company that he founded with Max Mosley. Called Simtek Research, this specialised in wind tunnel projects and it did a lot of consultancy work. In 1994, Simtek launched its F1 team, but money ran out early in 1995. From 1996 to 1999, Nick was chief designer at Benetton, then he formed Wirth Design and designed Acura's sports car racer solely on CFD, before joining Booth to form Virgin Racing.

2010 DRIVERS & RESULTS

Driver	Nationality	Races	Wins	Pts	Pos
Lucas di Grassi	Brazilian	19	0	0	24th
Timo Glock	German	19	0	0	25th

FOR THE RECORD

Country of origin:	England
Team base:	Dinnington, England
Telephone:	(44) 01909 560331
Website:	www.virginracing.com
Active in Formula One:	From 2010
Grands Prix contested:	19
Wins:	0
Pole positions:	0
Fastest laps:	0

THE TEAM

Chief executive officer:	Graeme Lowdon
Team principal:	John Booth
Technical director:	Nick Wirth
Head of race engineering:	Mark Herd
Team manager:	Dave O'Neill
Chief engineer:	Dieter Gass
Race engineers:	Rob Jones & Scott Walker
Test driver:	tba
Chassis:	Virgin VR-02
Engine:	Cosworth V8
Tyres:	Pirelli

into the racing side and the manufacturing side. The former is headed by John Booth with Wirth Research, a company based in Bicester belonging to the team's technical director Nick Wirth, handling the latter.

Richard Branson, boss of the global Virgin group, had toyed with becoming involved in F1 in 2009 when he was courted by Brawn GP. He took his interest further when he became involved with Brawn, which submitted a bid to join the F1 circus as Manor Motorsport for last year before being rebranded as Virgin Racing. However, the team can't get by on his money alone and there's no open chequebook. Indeed, this was proved last autumn, when Branson agreed to continue to back the team through 2011 and even to reduce the space covered by Virgin logos to leave the team more space to sell to other sponsors.

Fortunately, sponsors did start to get involved, with lifestyle products company QNet signing up last autumn. Then, a few days later, it was announced that the team would be known as Marussia Virgin Racing in deference to the burgeoning Russian sports car manufacturer that already has a strong relationship with Cosworth.

Branson is cagey, but has a respect for what Wirth and Booth are doing: "The amount of money this team is spending is maybe £20 million less than Lotus. So, to be almost matching them car for car is great, and our reliability is better."

Perhaps the most memorable difference between Virgin Racing and the other teams was its decision from the outset to design its cars entirely with Computational Fluid Dynamics and use no wind tunnel work at all. This offered a huge cost saving for the new team and may be ahead of its time, but it certainly meant that the VR-01's first run-out was a real voyage of discovery. Unfortunately, there was the early-season embarrassment of the car having been designed with a fuel tank that was too small for the engine's requirements once refuelling was banned. However, this was rectified and both Timo Glock and Lucas di Grassi found improving form after the four flyaway races that set the season rolling.

For di Grassi, it was a useful season for learning the circuits; for Glock, it was a season of frustration, but his input was highly valued as the team found its feet on this most exacting of stages.

> "We had to design the 2010 car in such a short space of time from a standing start. There is an awful lot of extra knowledge that has gone into this year's car."
>
> **Graeme Lowdon**

Nick Wirth is convinced that wind tunnels are a thing of the past and now he must prove it.

TIMO GLOCK

Timo is a driver who is having a most unusual Formula One career, full of downs as well as ups, and he will be hoping that Virgin Racing can make solid progress in its second year, so that he can put his name back up in lights. He has the skill, so now he needs a car to match.

It's not often fair to compare and contrast, but the difference between the start of this German driver's 2010 campaign and the one that went before it could not have been more stark. When with Toyota in 2009, he was placed fourth in Melbourne, then finished third at a soaking Sepang. Last year, with F1 novices Virgin Racing, he qualified 19th and 21st in Sakhir, then Melbourne, and retired from both. Life was very different at the tail end of the grid, and the disparity in budget between the two teams could not have been any more obvious.

In short, despite driving his socks off, Timo's only realistic target was to try to be the highest-placed finisher among the six drivers from the three new teams. This he managed on three occasions through the 19 grands prix, at Istanbul, Hockenheim and Monza, and that was the best he could hope for.

It was clear was that there had been progress made through the year, but also that much of the focus had turned to getting the car right at the second time of asking, in 2011, as Lotus pulled away at the front of the pack in 2010.

Timo was frustrated by retirements and will be praying the new car is fast and reliable.

Timo is a popular member of the Virgin Racing team, and he really got stuck in to helping the crew overcome the inevitable problems of finding its feet at the sport's top level. However, much of his campaign will have been frustrating and he won't want to do this for ever, so only solid progress towards the midfield this year will keep him interested.

Furthermore, regardless of the progress that he and the team ought to make together this year, Timo will want his name to be mentioned when openings with even the midfield teams are in discussion. Motor racing is all about momentum and results, so a young charger may be deemed more attractive in such a situation, which would be most unfair for this solid and increasingly experienced scrapper whose first grand prix outing was as long ago as 2004.

TRACK NOTES

Nationality:	GERMAN
Born:	18 MARCH 1982, LINDENFELS, GERMANY
Website:	www.timo-glock.de
Teams:	JORDAN 2004, TOYOTA 2008-09, VIRGIN RACING 2010-11

CAREER RECORD

First Grand Prix:	2004 CANADIAN GP
Grand Prix starts:	54
Grand Prix wins:	0
(best result: second, 2008 Hungarian GP, 2009 Singapore GP)	
Poles:	0
Fastest laps:	1
Points:	51
Honours:	2007 GP2 CHAMPION, 2001 GERMAN FORMULA BMW CHAMPION, 2000 GERMAN FORMULA BMW JUNIOR CHAMPION

TWO BITES AT THE CHERRY

Timo is a rarity, for he stepped back from F1 to GP2 and won the title at his second attempt in 2007, thus earning a second shot at F1. His early career suggested that he had the talents to stay in F1 once he'd got there with Jordan in 2004, as Timo had collected titles in Formula BMW Junior and Formula BMW. Racing in F3 in 2002, he ranked third in the German series. Then, in 2003, Timo ended up fifth in the European F3 series, three places ahead of Nico Rosberg, after winning three races. Having started 2004 as Jordan's third driver, he replaced Giorgio Pantano and scored on his debut in Canada. However, there was no ride in 2005, so he raced in Champ Cars, making a considerable impression. To ensure that he made it back to F1, he elected to contest GP2 in 2006. He ranked only fourth, but won the title in 2007. Toyota helped him back to F1 in 2008 and he stayed with the Japanese team until it quit at the end of the 2009 season.

JEROME D'AMBROSIO

Having appeared four times in Friday practice sessions for Virgin Racing in last year's end-of-season grands prix, this likeable 25-year-old Belgian has stepped up from GP2 to the big time by replacing Lucas di Grassi in the team's second car for its second year in F1.

The second seat with a tail-end team lies prey to being filled by a driver with money as these teams need the finance to try to advance to the midfield, and so it is that Jerome d'Ambrosio steps up from the fringes of Formula One into one of the coveted race seats.

Jerome thus becomes the first Belgian driver in F1 since Bertrand Gachot in 1995. Belgium's most recent grand prix winner is Thierry Boutsen in 1990, with Williams, and it was Boutsen who helped him in his first steps in single-seater racing. After that, Jerome made it to GP2 and spent three years trying to land the title, albeit never ranking higher than ninth, which he achieved in 2009.

However, when Genii Capital bought a controlling share of the Renault F1 team midway through December 2009, it was a considerable boost for the drivers on the roster of its Gravity Driver Management programme, with Jerome and Chinese racer Ho-Pin Tung both moving into the frame for the team's number two seat for 2010. By dint of greater experience and success at GP2 level, Jerome was adjudged the more likely of the duo to land the ride. However, Tung's nationality had strong

In joining Virgin, Jerome becomes the first Belgian F1 driver since Thierry Boutsen.

marketing possibilities in the Far East that could tip the balance in his favour. Then, of course, Vitaly Petrov brought money from Russia and the promise of great exposure should the country land a grand prix and that left Jerome on the sidelines to contest his third year of GP2

while waiting for another opening.

Jerome's perseverance paid off, though, and his pursuit of Virgin Racing for the occasional outing in a practice session on a grand prix meeting Friday kept his name in the frame for a race seat for 2011.

Then, in the week before Christmas, he edged out di Grassi and will now have to prove to those who don't know his reputation that he can bring more than just money. The team is already impressed, though, not just with his personable demeanour but also his intelligent feedback when he drove its car.

TRACK NOTES

Nationality:	BELGIAN
Born: 27 DECEMBER 1985, ETTERBEEK, BELGIUM	
Website:	www.jeromedambrosio.com
Teams:	2011 VIRGIN RACING

CAREER RECORD	
First Grand Prix:	2011 BAHRAIN GP
Grand Prix starts:	0
Grand Prix wins:	0
Poles:	0
Fastest laps:	0
Points:	0
Honours:	2008 GP2 ASIA RUNNER-UP, 2007 FORMULA MASTER CHAMPION, 2003 BELGIAN FORMULA RENAULT 1600 CHAMPION, 2001 FORMULA A KART WORLD CHAMPION, 2000 MONACO JUNIOR KART CUP WINNER

HE COMES WITH F1 EXPERIENCE

Inspired to try karting when eight, Jerome went on to become World Champion by 15. He then tried cars with ex-F1 racer Thierry Boutsen's team and won the Belgian Formula Renault 1600 series. Two years of Formula Renault followed and he raced in Italian F3000 in 2006 to learn more about powerful single-seaters. Stepping down the power band in 2007, Jerome won the inaugural Formula Master title. He truly moved onto the international stage in GP2 in 2008. Having warmed up in the GP2 Asia series, he stayed on with DAMS in the main GP2 series and ranked 11th, with second place finishes at Valencia and Spa-Francorchamps helping him to beat team-mate Kamui Kobayashi. Contesting the second GP2 Asia series, he finished as runner-up to Kobayashi. Jerome improved only to ninth in 2009, but his form was patchier in 2010 and he was even dropped so that Romain Grosjean could try the car, but he never equalled his win at Monaco and fell to 12th.

TALKING POINT: THE NEW PITS AT SILVERSTONE

The drivers raced on a comprehensively revised Silverstone track layout last year and this time they'll be faced with new pits and the start line being in a different location.

The British GP felt different last year but, from most vantage points, it looked the same. What had changed was the new circuit loop that took the circuit right at Abbey instead of left, then twisted its way around the Arena infield loop before sending the drivers down the new Wellington Straight to Brooklands, where it rejoined the old circuit. Gone were Bridge (removed as it was thought too dangerous for the MotoGP racing that had just been landed following the demise of Donington Park) and Priory, but this was more than made up for by the twists and turns of the new £5m section.

This was only the first stage in the circuit's ambitious redevelopment plans, changes that had been pushed for by Formula One promoter Bernie Ecclestone. The changes that Ecclestone really wanted, though, are the far more major ones being introduced for this summer: the new pits, pit buildings and paddock, with a bill closer to £30m, which is something that could only be contemplated once a 10-year

contract to host the British Grand Prix was signed by the various parties.

Located just over half a lap away from the long-standing start line between Woodcote and Copse, the new start line is on the stretch of track between Club Corner and Abbey, with the magnificent new pits and paddock to the right of this short straight. They offer considerably more modern facilities than before and thus match anything offered by the often government-funded circuits that have been built around the globe to entice F1 to their nations.

Of government funding for Silverstone, despite years of pitching, there is none, leaving circuit owners, the British Racing Drivers' Club, to foot the entire bill.

Designed by the world-famous sports architecture practice Populous, the company behind the Emirates and Wembley stadiums, plus the new grandstands at Ascot, the concrete and glass pit buildings house more than just superior pit garages with a larger

paddock apron behind, as the pit lane is far wider than the one that it is replacing and the new pit wall more capacious.

The pits building, topped by a new race control building, is cutting edge in shape, its roofline rising and falling in a sharp pattern of ridges above lofty, glass-fronted hospitality dining and spectating areas that sit atop the media centre, which in turn looks down across the pit lane and pit wall to the track and the new grandstands beyond.

The largest change to many spectators, though, will be the fact that the rush to the first corner at the start of the race won't be to Copse – a fearsome seventh-gear right-hand bend. Instead, there will be a shorter blast to the Abbey kink, where cars will jostle not just for line through this corner but track position into the left-hander at Farm Curve that follows almost immediately after it. Expect some side-by-side action through both of these corners before the drivers have to brake hard for Village Corner, then double back

for the Loop. Don't expect everyone to get through unscathed.

Copse will of course still be a tricky corner, but never again will spectators there hold their breath as the entire pack of cars rushes towards it on the opening lap. By the time the cars reach Copse this summer, the field will be strung out.

So, 63 summers after the circuit opened, Silverstone has merely undergone yet another of its intermittent transformations. What will stay the same, though, is that this is a circuit with a high-speed flow surrounded by some of the world's most knowledgeable F1 fans.

The British Racing Drivers' Club aren't stopping at this, as other elements of their redevelopment plans already include a manufacturer test centre with hospitality facilities on the revamped Stowe circuit, a new hospitality building to serve the Southern Circuit – one of five tracks at Silverstone. In the pipeline are an extended business park near Luffield, two hotels, an extreme sport and leisure complex and even a university campus for the study of automotive technology and engineering. When finished, it will clearly live up to its slogan of "more than just a circuit", acting as even more of a focus for Britain's world-leading motorsport industry, and it certainly won't feel like the Second World War airfield from which it was created.

Above: The pits in 1958 didn't even have a pit wall separating them from the track and the crew had to clamber over a wall to attend to the cars. This is Jo Bonnier's Maserati.

Below: This architectural drawing of the new pits shows the position of the new start line between Club Corner and Abbey.

TALKING POINT: THOSE WHO JUST MISSED OUT ON BEING CHAMPION

Success can be achieved by the smallest of margins, but history masks this, as when you're a champion, you're a champion for good. Conversely, the runner-up is usually forgotten. To redress the balance, this is a celebration of the men who came up short.

Imagine the sheer gut-wrenching pain of disappointment when, after a season of toil and turmoil, of avoiding crashes, of nursing home a sick car and yet gathering wins and points wherever possible, the end has been reached and you're not World Champion. You're the driver whose endeavours will soon be forgotten. You're the runner-up... All such a driver can do is look to the following year, while the new champion basks in the glow of their success all winter and enjoys the accolade for the rest of their life.

Over the years, there have been some incredibly close calls. Take the narrowest losing margin, just half a point, which is the amount by which Alain Prost lost out to his McLaren team-mate Niki Lauda in 1984. He had also been runner-up the year before, losing out to Nelson Piquet by just two points when Renault failed to continue its development to the season's end. Thank goodness that Prost could forget this at the end of 1985, when he landed the first of his four F1 titles.

Lauda himself had been deprived of the 1976 title by just a point by James Hunt in a year that witnessed his near-fatal crash at the Nurburgring and his astonishing comeback just two races later.

There have been spectacular final-round trip-ups, most notably Nigel Mansell's spectacular tyre blow-out in Adelaide in 1986, when he headed off up the escape road, wrestling his Williams to a standstill as Prost nipped by to take the second of his crowns. The same circuit also witnessed another British driver being denied. This was Damon Hill in 1994, when Michael Schumacher had clipped the wall and damaged his Benetton. Hill spotted the gap and pounced, only for Schumacher to drive across at him and put his Williams out of the race in one of the German's earlier examples of "win at all costs driving".

Perhaps one of the most dramatic trip-ups came in the Brazilian GP of 2007 when Lewis Hamilton went to the final round of his rookie season with a four-point lead but got overexcited on the opening lap and lost position, then his McLaren fell into neutral for 30 seconds and dropped him to 18th and his desperate drive back through the field left him one place and just one point short as Kimi Raikkonen won the race and the title for Ferrari. Hamilton's team-mate Fernando Alonso finished that race third and was also one point short in the final reckoning. Thank goodness Hamilton reversed this disappointment there the following year.

However, the drivers for whom one feels most sorry are those who came up short and then never went on to be World Champion to ease the disappointment.

Take the most dramatic of recent failures. This was in 2008, when Felipe Massa won a see-sawing race at his home track, Interlagos, and his family and the Ferrari team started to celebrate, only for Hamilton to manage to pass Timo Glock's slick-shod Toyota as it slid around on an increasingly wet track to take the place he needed with just one corner to go.

Stirling Moss is heralded as the best driver never to be World Champion and, having fallen three points short in 1956, he went closer still in 1958, when he won four of the 10 rounds for Vanwall but ended one point short of Ferrari's Mike Hawthorn, who won but once. Had Moss not been such a sportsman in the Portuguese GP, where he defended Hawthorn, denying that he had had his Ferrari push-started against the direction of the circuit flow after spinning and thus getting him reinstated, he would have been champion. Moss, though, didn't want to win that way.

Three years later, Wolfgang von Trips also ended up a point short, with the German aristocrat having been killed in an accident in the penultimate race in Italy, leaving the title to be taken by his Ferrari team-mate Phil Hill, who triumphed that day at Monza.

When it comes to "choking", to falling apart under pressure, Carlos Reutemann takes the prize. In 1981, he travelled to Las Vegas for the final round with a one-point lead over Brabham's Nelson Piquet, but fell from first to fourth by the first turn and faded to an eventual eighth and so Piquet pipped him.

Most recently, there's Mark Webber's tail-off in 2010. Having led the title race comfortably, he'll have nightmares about crashing out of the Korean GP, then qualifying only fifth for the finale in Abu Dhabi, when a front-row slot was essential if he wanted to have a crack at Fernando Alonso. History will relate that he didn't even end the year as runner-up, dropping to third overall after the final race.

Left: If it hadn't been for his triumphant 1992 campaign, Nigel Mansell would still be feeling the pain of this last-race blow-out in 1986.

Below: Mike Hawthorn, with pipe, was World Champion, but Stirling Moss (left) never was.

Bottom: Mark Webber lost out in Abu Dhabi last year, then revealed that he'd been racing with a broken shoulder.

Below: Felipe Massa was World Champion for about 10 seconds in 2008 before Lewis Hamilton gained the position he wanted.

KNOW THE TRACKS 2011

Another new year, another new circuit seems to have been the mantra of the Formula One World Championship in recent years, and 2011 will be no exception. Last year, it was South Korea's turn to join the grand prix circus, with Yeongam. This year, it's India's, adding another flavour to the overall mixture as F1 spreads its message into ever more countries around the world, giving yet further global exposure to the world's most exciting sporting spectacle.

There are 20 grands prix on the calendar for 2011, the largest number yet. While the teams have felt increasingly stretched in recent years as this number has risen from 16, the banning of in-season testing has at least meant that the engineers and mechanics get to spend some time at home between March and November, but the time that they spend sitting in airports and on aeroplanes continues to rise.

Not so long ago, there were a few "flyaway" races at the start of the season and a few more at the end. In between was the meat of the season, the European races. They're still there, albeit without a French GP and with Spa-Francorchamps and the Nurburgring even

talking about sharing a slot on alternate years due to ongoing financial difficulties. However, they number only nine, and thus are in the minority, while F1 supremo Bernie Ecclestone's desire to establish grands prix on every continent bar Antarctica has turned to a reality, as shown by the locations of the six races at the 'business end' of the season, in Singapore, Japan, Korea, India, Brazil and Abu Dhabi. As recently as 2007, only Japan and Brazil of these hosted grands prix.

The front end of the season, visiting Bahrain, Australia, Malaysia and China, is as it was in 2010. And, after the dire opening race in Bahrain last year, when a loop was added to the Sakhir circuit

and contributed nothing to the spectacle while at the same time removing one of the circuit's best overtaking spots, one has to hope for a better race this time around.

The first hint of something new on the calendar comes at the fifth round, with Turkey's race being brought yet further forward, taking over Spain's traditional slot of holding the first leg of F1's European tour. Yes, the Istanbul Park circuit is sited on the eastern (Asia Minor) side of the Bosporus, but it feels like a European race after the transcontinental tour to the first four grands prix, with its time zone far more in line with those of F1's main TV viewing audience: Europe. While the race is sure to attract a huge TV audience, it really craves tens of thousands of fans flocking in to fill the grandstands, as it has yet to draw a decent crowd.

After the varied delights of the Spanish and Monaco GPs, neither of which offers much scope for overtaking, it's off to Canada. This grand prix was long twinned with the United States GP, but that remains shelved until the proposed circuit near Austin in Texas comes on stream in 2012.

Then the teams will return to their European bases for rounds on the street circuit around Valencia's docks before a run of five races in a row on classic tracks at Silverstone, the Nurburgring, the Hungaroring (the novice in this company as its first grand prix was only back in 1986), Spa-Francorchamps and Monza.

Silverstone offered a revised layout last year, with a new loop between Abbey and Brooklands. This year the difference will be greater still, as the start line will no longer be between Woodcote and Copse, but moved adjacent to a new pits and paddock complex between Club Corner and Abbey.

With the teams' transporters parked up at the team headquarters and the gear loaded onto specially chartered flights, F1 hits the road again for those vital final six rounds.

The night race in Singapore has only been around since 2008 but already feels like part of F1's furniture, with the comparison to the venue for the following race, Japan's flowing Suzuka, offering challenges from the opposite end of the spectrum. Korea's Yeongam circuit will hopefully be completely finished this October after the 11th-hour scramble even to get its tarmac surface in place last year. Then comes F1's newest new track, in India, the latest from the pen of circuit architect Hermann Tilke. There is obviously massive pressure to get this finished on time, particularly after India didn't enjoy the world watching its rush to complete the stadia and facilities for last year's Commonwealth Games.

If the World Championship proves as tight as it was in 2010, there will still be plenty to play for at the final two rounds, with Brazil taking over the drama of holding the final round again from Abu Dhabi, meaning that the shootout will be held on a bumpy, dipping circuit prone to rain storms rather than on a billiard-table-smooth twister by a marina in a desert.

So, you'd think that F1 is in rude health and that this expansion is a sign that it's surviving the economic recession, but the true sign will be when the newer races aren't contested in front of grandstands with row upon row of empty seats.

SAKHIR

Changes to the Bahrain circuit last year lengthened the lap but did nothing to make the racing more exciting and it's now the poor relation of the Middle East's two races.

The drivers faced a new challenge in 2010 as the circuit was modified for the first time since its introduction in 2004, with the lap gaining an extra loop.

This loop was inserted into the layout after Turn 4. Instead of running out of this right-hand hairpin down to a left-right kink, the track swung left and snaked through an additional seven corners before rejoining the original circuit just before that set of esses. This changed the flow and gave the engineers problems as they sought the best set-up for both this and the fast-sweeping corners elsewhere on the lap.

However, they'll have to dig out their old data, as the event organisers have decided that the experiment wasn't a hit and have reverted to the original layout for 2011.

Whatever grip the engineers can achieve as they find a compromise that suits both tight and open will be welcomed by the drivers, as the circuit is famously affected by sand blown in from the surrounding rocky desert.

There are two constants: the weather is invariably bright and hot, thus eliminating the chance for rain to spice up proceedings, and the crowds are sparse, the grandstands populated by expatriate workers rather than Bahrainis, who continue to love high-performance road cars but have yet to be coaxed out into the heat to watch racing live.

"Bahrain is a circuit that requires really good braking stability and traction. There are no real high-speed corners so the set-up work focuses more on the mechanical side." **Robert Kubica**

64

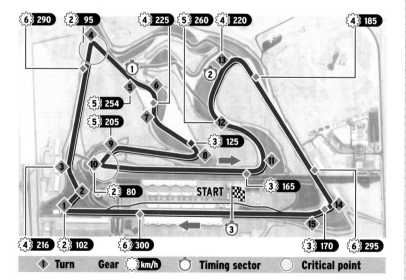

◆ Turn	Gear	☼ km/h	◯ Timing sector	◯ Critical point

2010 POLE TIME: **VETTEL (RED BULL)**, 1M54.101S, 123.491MPH/198.739KPH
2010 WINNER'S AVERAGE SPEED: 115.744MPH/186.272KPH

2010 FASTEST LAP: **ALONSO (FERRARI)**, 1M58.287S, 119.126MPH/191.715KPH
LAP RECORD: **M SCHUMACHER (FERRARI)**, 1M30.252S, 134.26MPH/216.061KPH, 2004

INSIDE TRACK
BAHRAIN GRAND PRIX

Date:	**13 March**
Circuit name:	**Bahrain International Circuit**
Circuit length:	**3.363 miles/5.412km**
Number of laps:	**57**
Telephone:	**00 973 406222**
Website:	**www.bahraingp.com.bh**

PREVIOUS WINNERS	
2004	**Michael Schumacher** FERRARI
2005	**Fernando Alonso** RENAULT
2006	**Fernando Alonso** RENAULT
2007	**Felipe Massa** FERRARI
2008	**Felipe Massa** FERRARI
2009	**Jenson Button** BRAWN
2010	**Fernando Alonso** FERRARI

First race: Michael Schumacher brought his road show to Bahrain in 2004 and gave a demonstration in his Ferrari of why he had six world titles to his name, leading from pole position, with only team-mate Rubens Barrichello for company as they pulled ever further clear. They finished one-two, with Jenson Button's BAR the best of the rest, almost half a minute behind.

Best race: Ferrari was at the forefront in the best Bahrain GP to date when Felipe Massa led the way in 2007. However, he didn't have it as easy as Schumacher had, as he had McLaren rookie Lewis Hamilton snapping at his heels all race, anxious to secure his first win as they outperformed their supposed team leaders, Kimi Raikkonen and Fernando Alonso, finishing just 2 seconds apart.

Best corner: Turn 1 is where the action is most likely to happen as the drivers brake from almost 200mph into this right-hand hairpin. Go in too fast, though, and a driver will be on the wrong line for Turn 2. Obviously, the first corner is also a scene of considerable action on the opening lap.

Local hero: Bahrain is still waiting for its first racing star, although that's not so surprising from a country with a population of less than a million and no circuit within its borders until 2004.

Australia waited a long time to host a grand prix but is now an established event on the championship calendar, with a circuit that almost always produces thrills and spills.

The Formula One circus loves visiting city circuits, as proximity to large numbers of people, to say nothing of a wide choice of hotels, bars and restaurants, makes for a more enjoyable visit than to a circuit deep in the countryside. Think Montreal and Monaco.

Melbourne is thus a popular race for all concerned, as the city has all of these in abundance, as well as weather that's normally warm and sunny and so a far cry from the tail end of the northern hemisphere winter left behind.

The circuit around the lake in downtown Albert Park, with the cityscape in the background, is neither fast nor slow, although any driver hanging on around the long, long left at the back of the lake between Turns 10 and 11 might beg to differ, especially as the esses of Turns 11 and 12 are all but hidden until the drivers arrive there.

The Australian GP always has a great atmosphere, with low grandstands lining nearly the entire length of the circuit, all located almost right next to the track to give it an intimate feel. Furthermore, with a packed programme of support races and aerial displays, this is one of the year's top events. Then again, with Melbourne cornering top events in tennis and cricket, too, the citizens expect a show.

INSIDE TRACK
AUSTRALIAN GRAND PRIX

Date:	**27 March**
Circuit name:	**Albert Park**
Circuit length:	**3.295 miles/5.3km**
Number of laps:	**58**
Telephone:	**00 61 3 92587100**
Website:	**www.grandprix.com.au**

PREVIOUS WINNERS	
2002	**Michael Schumacher** FERRARI
2003	**David Coulthard** McLAREN
2004	**Michael Schumacher** FERRARI
2005	**Giancarlo Fisichella** RENAULT
2006	**Fernando Alonso** RENAULT
2007	**Kimi Raikkonen** FERRARI
2008	**Lewis Hamilton** McLAREN
2009	**Jenson Button** BRAWN
2010	**Jenson Button** McLAREN

First race: F1 insiders were impressed when F1 made its first modern-times visit to Melbourne and Damon Hill won on the lake-circling circuit for Williams. However, had his car not suffered from falling oil pressure, victory would have gone to his team-mate Jacques Villeneuve on his debut.

Best race: The 2008 Australian GP was the best enjoyed in Albert Park to date, with Kimi Raikkonen coming out on top for Ferrari in a race that marked Lewis Hamilton's F1 debut and he showed instant attack as he drove around the outside of team-mate Fernando Alonso at the first corner.

Best corner: Turn 1 offers the most action on the opening lap, but it's Turn 3 that keeps the fans excited all race long. This tight right is at a point where the wall-lined track bursts out into the open from under the trees and where many a great overtaking move is attempted, but not always pulled off, as ambitions exceed traction and the car arriving fast often runs across the grass.

Local hero: Well, that will be Mark Webber, who came right to the forefront in 2010 and showed his sense of occasion by placing his unfancied Minardi fifth on his F1 debut here in 2002, which for the tail-end Minardi team was as good as a win, particularly to the team's Australian boss, Paul Stoddart.

65

"I like the Albert Park circuit a lot. It doesn't really feel like a street circuit, as it is very challenging and has some interesting corners to negotiate." **Rubens Barrichello**

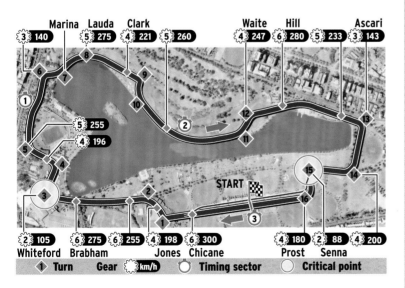

Marina	Lauda	Clark		Waite	Hill		Ascari
3 140	5 275	4 221	5 260	4 247	6 280	5 233	3 143

5 255
4 196

START

Whiteford	Brabham		Jones	Chicane		Prost	Senna	
2 105	6 275	6 255	4 198	6 300		4 180	2 88	4 200

◆ Turn   Gear   km/h   ○ Timing sector   ○ Critical point

2010 POLE TIME: **VETTEL (RED BULL),**
1M23.919S, 141.351MPH/227.482KPH
2010 WINNER'S AVERAGE SPEED:
121.649MPH/195.775KPH

2010 FASTEST LAP: : **WEBBER (RED BULL),**
1M28.358S, 134.282MPH/216.106KPH
LAP RECORD: **M SCHUMACHER (FERRARI),**
1M24.125S, 141.016MPH/226.933KPH, 2004

SEPANG

The home of the Malaysian GP is that rare thing: a modern circuit that encourages side-by-side racing. With a high chance of rain, drivers know not to predict anything.

On the evidence of this sinuous and tricky circuit, architect Hermann Tilke showed a great understanding of what a modern circuit should be all about. Wide with long straights out of slow corners that feed into slow corners, it gives the drivers a real chance to line up and complete overtaking moves at several points around the lap.

The run to the first corner on the opening lap is always one of intense excitement, as the cars can arrive three abreast into this hairpin. Then the drivers have to sort themselves out to see who will back off as they jockey for position not just for this first turn but also for dipping Turn 2, which makes them double back again immediately. Go in tight or hang around out wide, that's the question...

Some of Sepang's corners offer a real challenge, such as fifth-gear Turn 5, fourth-gear Turn 7 and, most notably, the flat-out left at Turn 12.

With two notable straights, up to the final corner and then down to Turn 1, the drivers at least have time to check all the functions on their steering wheels.

There is one element against which they have no control: rain can arrive in the tropics at this time of year at any minute. And, in April, it can come down both suddenly and very heavily, as has been experienced in the past.

"The Malaysian GP is always a good event. It's very tough physically, but there is a variety of corners and also some overtaking spots, so it's an event I look forward to." **Adrian Sutil**

INSIDE TRACK
MALAYSIAN GRAND PRIX

Date:	**10 April**
Circuit name:	**Sepang Circuit**
Circuit length:	**3.444 miles/5.542km**
Number of laps:	**56**
Telephone:	**00 60 3 85262000**
Website:	**www.malaysiangp.com.my**

PREVIOUS WINNERS	
2001	**Michael Schumacher** FERRARI
2002	**Ralf Schumacher** WILLIAMS
2003	**Kimi Raikkonen** McLAREN
2004	**Michael Schumacher** FERRARI
2005	**Fernando Alonso** RENAULT
2006	**Giancarlo Fisichella** RENAULT
2007	**Fernando Alonso** McLAREN
2008	**Kimi Raikkonen** FERRARI
2009	**Jenson Button** BRAWN
2010	**Sebastian Vettel** RED BULL

First race: Long held as one of the early races of the championship, the first Malaysian GP was held as the penultimate race in 1999, when the title battle was being fought between McLaren's Mika Hakkinen and Ferrari's Eddie Irvine. Returning from a broken leg, Michael Schumacher protected Irvine and enabled him to win before they were disqualified, then reinstated.

Best race: The 2001 race stands out for being won by an inspired tyre call. Ferrari led away but both slid off on lap 3 as rain hit. Their race was saved by a decision to fit intermediates when those ahead went for full wets. Michael Schumacher then came through to win from Rubens Barrichello.

Best corner: To get a clue as to which car is handling well, the Turn 5 and 6 sequence is a great guide, for it shows whether a car has the ability to stay on line through the fifth-gear left, then be able to be in position for the right-hander that follows. Sadly, you'll see precious little overtaking here.

Local hero: Alex Yoong remains the only Malaysian driver to have raced in F1, with Minardi in 2001 and then staying on for a full season in 2002. Fairuz Fauzy was third driver for Lotus in 2010.

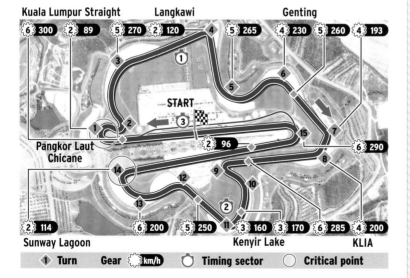

Kuala Lumpur Straight — **Langkawi** — **Genting**

6 300 | 2 89 | 5 270 | 2 120 | 5 265 | 4 230 | 5 260 | 4 193

START

Pangkor Laut Chicane

2 96 | 6 290

Sunway Lagoon — **Kenyir Lake** — **KLIA**

2 114 | 6 200 | 5 250 | 3 160 | 3 170 | 6 285 | 4 200

◆ **Turn**   **Gear** km/h   ○ **Timing sector**   ○ **Critical point**

2010 POLE TIME: **WEBBER (RED BULL),** 1M49.327S, 113.407MPH/182.511KPH
2010 WINNER'S AVERAGE SPEED: **123.367MPH/198.540KPH**

2010 FASTEST LAP: **WEBBER (RED BULL),** 1M37.054S, 127.763MPH/205.615KPH
LAP RECORD: **MONTOYA (WILLIAMS),** 1M34.223S, 131.595MPH/211.772KPH, 2004

SHANGHAI

Formula One was hugely excited when it held a grand prix for the first time in China in 2004, but the world's most populous nation has yet to return the same level of passion.

Pound signs were large in the eyes of the teams' commercial directors in the early 21st century when it was announced that the world's fastest-growing market had opened its doors to F1. They were convinced that this would produce a huge financial return and boost the awareness of their sponsors' brands.

Combine this with the truly stunning circuit that the Chinese government bankrolled to rise from a swampy area outside Shanghai and all was looking good. But their ambitious construction is now coming back to haunt them, as the enormous grandstands have never been filled, with the seats in the giant ones outside Turns 12

and 13 now covered to prevent worldwide TV audiences from noting that they're empty.

The circuit itself is interesting, and very much a Hermann Tilke design, with the first four corners similar to the opening sequence at his earlier work, Sepang. They are then echoed at the end of the back straight, albeit turning left, then right rather than the other way around. Exit speed from here is crucial as Turn 13 feeds onto the ultra-long back straight to the lap's best overtaking spot: Turn 14. This hairpin is wide on entry but its kinked exit can force those on the outside line to lift.

The track's good, the weather can be mixed, but the crowd's too small.

"The Shanghai circuit is not one of my favourite ones, as it's very impersonal, but it does have a very long back straight which is always a good place for overtaking." **Nico Hulkenberg**

INSIDE TRACK
CHINESE GRAND PRIX

Date:	**17 April**
Circuit name:	**Shanghai International Circuit**
Circuit length:	**3.390 miles/5.450km**
Number of laps:	**56**
Telephone:	**00 86 2162520000**
Website:	**www.f1china.com.cn**

PREVIOUS WINNERS

2004	**Rubens Barrichello** FERRARI
2005	**Fernando Alonso** RENAULT
2006	**Michael Schumacher** FERRARI
2007	**Kimi Raikkonen** FERRARI
2008	**Lewis Hamilton** McLAREN
2009	**Sebastian Vettel** RED BULL
2010	**Jenson Button** McLAREN

First race: F1's first taste of China came in 2004 and newly crowned champion Michael Schumacher was expected to be a pace-setter for Ferrari. However, he spun out of control qualifying, clipped a car, then finished a lapped 12th. Luckily for Ferrari, team-mate Rubens Barrichello held off stern challenges from BAR's Jenson Button and McLaren's Kimi Raikkonen.

Best race: Michael Schumacher's wet-weather ability and conditions suiting his Bridgestone intermediate tyres were required for him to score his 91st grand prix win in 2006. He'd started sixth, with Fernando Alonso on pole for Renault, but his Bridgestone inters were better than his rival's Michelins, so he hit the front and resisted Alonso's charge.

Best corner: Turns 1-4 are a handful as they rise and fall and keep on twisting, but Turn 14 is the favourite as it's where most passing moves are tried. If a driver gets a tow down the straight, there's enough width to line up a move, but many a driver simply brakes too late and goes straight on.

Local hero: Last year, China took a step closer to having its first F1 driver as Ho-Pin Tung was test driver for Renault. However, with testing all but non-existent, there's still a way to go before the GP2 racer is ready for a race seat.

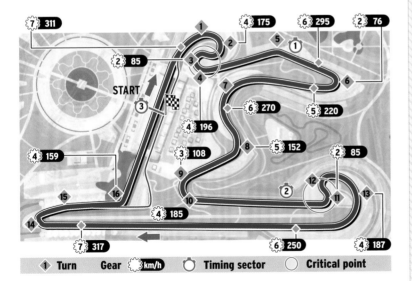

🔹 **Turn**   **Gear**   ❄️ **km/h**   ⭕ **Timing sector**   ⚪ **Critical point**

2010 POLE TIME: **VETTEL (RED BULL)**, 1M34.558S, 129.064MPH/207.708KPH
2010 WINNER'S AVERAGE SPEED: 106.590MPH/171.541KPH

FASTEST LAP: **HAMILTON (McLAREN)**, 1M42.061S, 119.478MPH/192.282KPH
LAP RECORD: **M SCHUMACHER (FERRARI)**, 1M32.238S, 132.202MPH/212.759KPH, 2004

ISTANBUL

Turkey and F1 never seemed likely partners as the country had no racing history. The track built for 2005 is great, but the event lacks fans and atmosphere.

As a race circuit, this is magnificent. Built on the Asia Minor side of Istanbul, it has gradient, it has flow and it offers a stern challenge to the drivers. For this very reason, they love it, reckoning that it will offer just what they are looking for to sort the men from the boys, maximising their sheer driving talent.

Istanbul Park's grandstands have never got near to being full since this Hermann Tilke-designed circuit made its debut in 2005, but the racing has inevitably been good, with incident aplenty to spice it up. Take 2009's race here, when Sebastian Vettel clattered the kerbs at Turn 10 and lost the lead to Brawn GP's Jenson

Button on the opening lap, or last year, when Vettel pulled across on team-mate Mark Webber and took both off to make Lewis Hamilton's job easier.

The beauty of a lap here is that it starts with an awkward, off-camber corner at Turn 1, teases the drivers with the downhill, treble-apex Turn 8 and throws in Turn 12, a heavy-braking, turn-in-and-hope left-hander at the end of the back straight, all different and all challenging.

This is the sort of circuit that a driver can really attack. It might destroy his tyres in the process, but just a few laps of banzai attack can reap dividends.

> "You can overtake there, the circuit is wide and I enjoy the many different kinds of corners – not just the well-known Turn 8, but the rest of the lap too." **Vitaly Petrov**

68

INSIDE TRACK
TURKISH GRAND PRIX

Date:	8 May
Circuit name:	**Istanbul Park Circuit**
Circuit length:	**3.317 miles/5.338km**
Number of laps:	**58**
Telephone:	**00 90 216 418 5222**
Website:	**www.formula1-istanbul.com**

PREVIOUS WINNERS	
2005	**Kimi Raikkonen** McLAREN
2006	**Felipe Massa** FERRARI
2007	**Felipe Massa** FERRARI
2008	**Felipe Massa** FERRARI
2009	**Jenson Button** BRAWN
2010	**Lewis Hamilton** McLAREN

First race: Kimi Raikkonen was on a mission in 2005, arriving at the new circuit shooting for Renault's points leader Fernando Alonso. The Finn led all the way for McLaren and needed team-mate Juan Pablo Montoya to keep Alonso back, but the Colombian slipped up at Turn 8 with two laps to go and let the Spaniard through.

Best race: The 2006 Turkish GP was the most exciting to date as the deployment of a safety car after Scuderia Toro Rosso's Vitantonio Liuzzi crashed, threatening to upset the order. However, Ferrari's pole-sitter Felipe Massa was able to benefit as team-mate Michael Schumacher had to queue in the pits behind him, and this was enough to give him victory.

Best corner: Although there are plenty of great corners at Istanbul Park, the best has got to be Turn 8. It's not only difficult but visually engrossing as the drivers can be seen trying to get the correct turn-in point through its three downhill apexes, with any loss of line leaving them to attempt to wrestle the car back under control or risk a bumpy ride across the outfield, as Juan Pablo Montoya endured so embarrassingly in 2005.

Local hero: Turkey remains on the sidelines in terms of up-and-coming talent, held back by the country's lack of a racing infrastructure, with its highest-level racer Jason Tahinci, who raced in GP2 in 2008, but has since quit the sport.

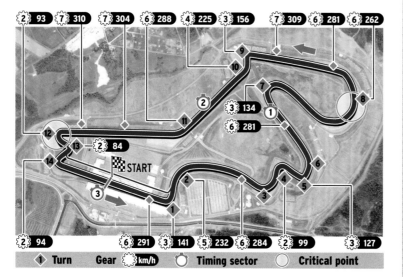

93 310 304 288 225 156 309 281 262

94 291 141 232 284 99 127

◆ **Turn** **Gear** ❀km/h ○ **Timing sector** ○ **Critical point**

2010 POLE TIME: **WEBBER (RED BULL)**, 1M26.295S, 138.376MPH/222.696KPH
2010 WINNER'S AVERAGE SPEED: 129.907MPH/209.066KPH

2010 FASTEST LAP: **PETROV (RENAULT)**, 1M29.165S, 133.924MPH/215.530KPH
LAP RECORD: **MONTOYA (McLAREN)**, 1M24.770S, 138.096MPH/222.167KPH, 2005

Fernando Alonso's presence always fills the grandstands, but this is a circuit crying out for reinvention with passing possibilities if it is to excite a new generation of fans.

Spain had had a grand prix for decades, but it was desperately seeking a venue that felt like a permanent home. Then along came the Circuit de Catalunya, just a short drive from Barcelona, in 1991. At a stroke, thoughts of tired Jarama and crowd-light Jerez were extinguished. Fifteen years later, the trouble is that the crowds might be large, but the racing is almost never better than processional here.

The format of a long main straight into a tight corner, a right-left esse actually ought to produce overtaking aplenty. But, lap 1 aside, Turn 1 just doesn't produce the goods often enough. The lap from there twists and dips and climbs and twists again, but lacks one key ingredient: anywhere else to attempt to overtake.

Matters improved in 2007 when the Turn 14/15 esses were added. It slightly increased the chance of a car getting under the wing of a car it is chasing onto the downhill main straight. But only slightly, which is a shame, as the fans thronging the hillsides and filling the grandstands deserve better, deserve the sight of a driver catching a tow past the pits before deciding whether to pull out and dive for the inside or brave it out around the outside to take the line into Turn 2.

"There are some fast corners, like Turn 9 and the final corner, but the majority of the track is made up of pretty long corners where you really need the car to do all the work." **Jenson Button**

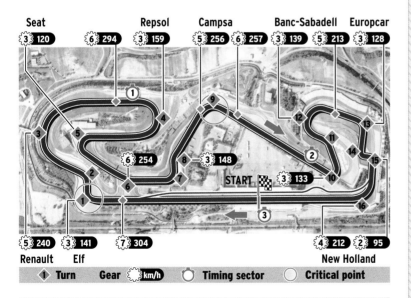

Seat
3 120   6 294   Repsol 3 159   Campsa 5 256   6 257   Banc-Sabadell 3 139   5 213   Europcar 3 128

6 254   8   3 148
6
START   3 133

3

5 240   3 141   7 304   Renault   Elf   New Holland   4 212   2 95

◆ Turn   Gear ⚙km/h   ○ Timing sector   ○ Critical point

2010 POLE TIME: **WEBBER (RED BULL),**
1M19.995S, 130.148MPH/209.454KPH
2010 WINNER'S AVERAGE SPEED:
119.596MPH/192.471KPH

2010 FASTEST LAP: **HAMILTON (McLAREN),**
1M24.357S, 123.444MPH/198.664KPH
LAP RECORD: **RAIKKONEN (FERRARI),**
1M21.670S, 127.5MPH/205.192KPH, 2008

INSIDE TRACK
SPANISH GRAND PRIX

Date:	**22 May**
Circuit name:	**Circuit de Catalunya**
Circuit length:	**2.892 miles/4.654km**
Number of laps:	**66**
Telephone:	**00 34 93 5719771**
Website:	**www.circuitcat.com**

PREVIOUS WINNERS

2001	**Michael Schumacher** FERRARI
2002	**Michael Schumacher** FERRARI
2003	**Michael Schumacher** FERRARI
2004	**Michael Schumacher** FERRARI
2005	**Kimi Raikkonen** McLAREN
2006	**Fernando Alonso** RENAULT
2007	**Felipe Massa** FERRARI
2008	**Kimi Raikkonen** FERRARI
2009	**Jenson Button** BRAWN
2010	**Mark Webber** RED BULL

First race: The Circuit de Catalunya had a dream debut in 1991 as its first World Championship round was spiced up by a duel between two of F1's steeliest characters: Nigel Mansell and Ayrton Senna. The sight of them all but rubbing wheels at 190mph past the pits still stands out in many a memory.

Best race: As 1991 is mentioned above, the next best race at Barcelona came in 1996, when Michael Schumacher ignored the fact that the sun doesn't always shine in Spain and put on a masterclass in handling torrential rain to take his first win for Ferrari. His closest rival, Benetton's Jean Alesi, finished 45 seconds behind.

Best corner: Added in 2007, Turns 14 and 15 offer extra interest to the lap, not so much in terms of overtaking, as there's never much of that at this Spanish circuit, but in terms of positioning, as a good exit from here will allow a driver to have the power down through Turn 16, then superior speed down the main straight to hopefully pull off a pass into Turn 1.

Local hero: Fernando Alonso continues to rule the roost, but he has support from Jaime Alguersuari, who will endeavour, like post-Michael Schumacher German drivers, to come out from the double World Champion's enormous shadow.

MONACO

There's no circuit more famous or so fêted, but also none so ridiculous. It's like trying to fit a quart into a pint pot. It ought not to work at all, but it very much does.

Trying to fit the Monaco street circuit into a regular category doesn't work. It's narrow, it's bumpy, it has precious few places to overtake and abysmal paddock facilities to boot, yet the teams wouldn't hear of dropping it to make way for another race. Monaco is special, you see, as it might not be a great place to go racing but it's a great place for a team's sponsors to go and watch racing cars.

Yachts in the harbour and a casino in the square, Monaco has all the trappings of fortune that so many aspire to. It's dreamland, and every sport ought to have a venue like that.

The lap starts on a curving "straight", feeds into a tight right, climbs a steep hill, then crests it and works its way back down to the seafront, only to dive into a curving tunnel under a hotel. After bursting back out into the light, next up is a left-right-left chicane, then the drivers blast past the harbour full of multi-million-pound yachts to complete the lap. If a driver does this consistently better than anyone else, then he will be climbing the steps to receive his trophy from Prince Albert and the rest of the royal family.

From almost every angle, the Monaco GP really is a grand prix like no other.

"For me, this is the most difficult circuit raced on during the season, as it is very challenging. You have to really concentrate in order to avoid the slightest mistake." **Pedro de la Rosa**

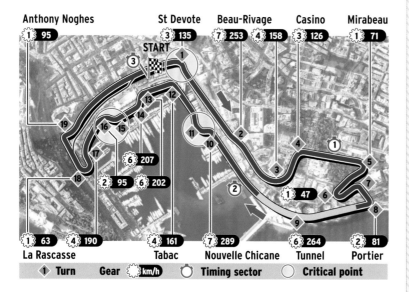

Anthony Noghes · St Devote · Beau-Rivage · Casino · Mirabeau

La Rascasse · Tabac · Nouvelle Chicane · Tunnel · Portier

◆ Turn   Gear ⚙ ▮km/h   ⏱ Timing sector   ○ Critical point

2010 POLE TIME: **WEBBER (RED BULL)**, 1M13.826S, 101.184MPH/162.84KPH
2010 WINNER'S AVERAGE SPEED: 88.119MPH/141.814KPH

2010 FASTEST LAP: **VETTEL (RED BULL)**, 1M15.192S, 99.368MPH/159.918KPH
LAP RECORD: M SCHUMACHER (FERRARI), 1M14.439S, 100.373MPH/161.527KPH, 2004

INSIDE TRACK
MONACO GRAND PRIX

Date:	**29 May**
Circuit name:	**Monte Carlo Circuit**
Circuit length:	**2.075 miles/3.339km**
Number of laps:	**78**
Telephone:	**00 377 93152600**
Website:	**www.acm.mc**

PREVIOUS WINNERS

2001	**Michael Schumacher** FERRARI
2002	**David Coulthard** McLAREN
2003	**Juan Pablo Montoya** WILLIAMS
2004	**Jarno Trulli** RENAULT
2005	**Kimi Raikkonen** McLAREN
2006	**Fernando Alonso** RENAULT
2007	**Fernando Alonso** McLAREN
2008	**Lewis Hamilton** McLAREN
2009	**Jenson Button** BRAWN
2010	**Mark Webber** RED BULL

First race: The first Monaco GP was in 1929, but the first one in the World Championship came in 1950 and it was all but stopped when there was a mass pile-up on the first lap, with Juan Manuel Fangio managing to squeeze past the blockage early on the second lap to continue to an all but unchallenged win for Alfa Romeo.

Best race: The 1982 Monaco GP stands out as one of the most astonishing races ever as rain hit with three laps to go and leader Alain Prost slid off. After this, Riccardo Patrese, Didier Pironi and Andrea de Cesaris all held the lead and lost it before Patrese recovered from a spin in his Brabham to get going again and triumph in a race that left the commentators breathless.

Best corner: St Devote, the first corner, is a challenge as drivers want to carry as much speed as possible up the hill but have to balance that against the risk of going in too fast and clipping the barriers.

Local hero: Monegasque drivers have been few and far between, but Louis Chiron secured the best result in their home race when he was placed third in 1950 in his Maserati, two laps down on Juan Manuel Fangio's Alfa Romeo, delayed by the first lap pile-up.

MONTREAL

The sun almost always seems to shine on the Canadian GP, blessed with a spectacular setting, a great city as a backdrop and perpetual race action spiced up with incident.

Named after Canada's most famous racing son, the Circuit Gilles Villeneuve is actually not the sort of circuit of which the flamboyant Ferrari driver approved. He was more of a Spa-Francorchamps sort of driver. For, although there are tricky sections on the circuit built on an island in the St Lawrence River, it's not the full-blooded challenge he adored.

The racing is always good, however, with the right kink into sharp left into long right sequence at the start of the lap guaranteed to produce excitement on the opening lap, as shown last year.

The back section has a tantalising sequence of esses, with walls lining the track on both sides, so they're great for a driver trying to take a sinuous line, but terrible for a driver trying to pass a slower car. This means that almost all of the overtaking attempts are made into the L'Epingle hairpin at the far end of the circuit or into the final corner, the chicane onto the start/finish straight, a corner that draws more than its share of cars into the wall on its exit.

If the walls don't catch the drivers out, the circuit's car-breaking nature leaves cars on the sidelines, as a lot of time is spent at full throttle and the braking required is some of the heaviest on the F1 calendar.

"As it's a temporary circuit, it's a major challenge the whole way around the lap. There's the constant threat of the walls and it's critical not to make any mistakes here." **Jarno Trulli**

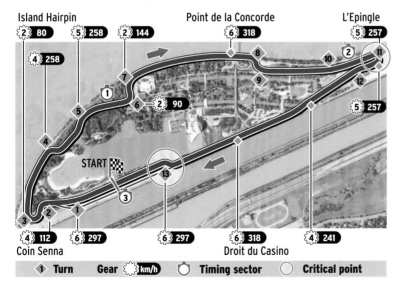

Island Hairpin — ⟲2 80 — ⟲5 258 — ⟲2 144 — Point de la Concorde — ⟲6 318 — L'Epingle — ⟲5 257

⟲4 258

START

⟲4 112 — ⟲6 297 — ⟲6 297 — ⟲6 318 — ⟲4 241
Coin Senna — Droit du Casino

⟲5 257

⟲2 90

↑ Turn   Gear ⟲ km/h   ◯ Timing sector   ◯ Critical point

2010 POLE TIME: HAMILTON (McLAREN), 1M15.105S, 129.898MPH/209.035KPH
2010 WINNER'S AVERAGE SPEED: 121.216MPH/195.079KPH
2010 FASTEST LAP: KUBICA (RENAULT), 1M16.972S, 126.738MPH/203.965KPH
LAP RECORD: BARRICHELLO (FERRARI), 1M13.622S, 132.511MPH/213.246KPH, 2004

INSIDE TRACK
CANADIAN GRAND PRIX

Date:	**12 June**
Circuit name:	**Circuit Gilles Villeneuve**
Circuit length:	**2.71 miles/4.361km**
Number of laps:	**70**
Telephone:	**001 514 350 0000**
Website:	**www.grandprix.ca**

PREVIOUS WINNERS

2000	**Michael Schumacher** FERRARI
2001	**Ralf Schumacher** WILLIAMS
2002	**Michael Schumacher** FERRARI
2003	**Michael Schumacher** FERRARI
2004	**Michael Schumacher** FERRARI
2005	**Kimi Raikkonen** McLAREN
2006	**Fernando Alonso** RENAULT
2007	**Lewis Hamilton** McLAREN
2008	**Robert Kubica** BMW SAUBER
2010	**Lewis Hamilton** McLAREN

First race: There was good luck and bad on display in the first Canadian GP held in Montreal in 1978. Suffering the bad luck was Jean-Pierre Jarier, called up by Lotus after Ronnie Peterson was killed at Monza. He shocked everyone when he qualified on pole and then streaked off towards his first win, only to be thwarted by an oil leak. The good luck belonged to Gilles Villeneuve, who inherited the win in his Ferrari.

Best race: Nothing makes a great race stand out like a surprise finish and this is what Nigel Mansell produced in 1991, when he waved to the fans as he rounded L'Epingle for the final time, confident that he was so far clear that nothing would stand between him and victory. But then his Williams glided to a halt and wouldn't restart, letting Benetton's Nelson Piquet snatch victory. He blamed the gearbox. The team said he'd let the revs drop too low and stalled.

Best corner: From the drivers' point of view, the twisting esses from Turns 4 to 7 demand the utmost precision but can bite.

Local hero: Canada is waiting for its next star and Robert Wickens is looking the most likely, having won races in A1GP, F2 and GP3 in the past two seasons.

VALENCIA

Here's a circuit that might be maturing into a place of interest. Certainly, Mark Webber made it spectacular last year as he flipped his Red Bull off Heikki Kovalainen's Lotus.

A complaint thrown at street circuits is always that they're slow and full of fiddly corners, lacking anywhere for the drivers to give the cars their head. This can't be levelled at Valencia's harbour-framing circuit, for it has four decent straights and cars can all but hit 200mph down the longest of these.

The European GP was brought to Valencia in 2008, as the port city was anxious to find an event to fill the sporting vacuum left by the departure of yachting's America's Cup, which had been based there. The circuit, whose layout was produced by Hermann Tilke's design office, was shaped around the outside of the yacht harbour, next to the container ship docks. But, unlike Monaco, there were open spaces and no steep inclines to fight against. In this way Tilke made sure that there were straights worthy of the name. A bridge over the entry channel to the harbour provides a photogenic backdrop.

The facilities were drab and the harbour all but empty of yachts for the debut event in 2008, so it lacked the necessary glamour to endear it to people, but the atmosphere has been improving each year and the high-up TV cameras angles reveal that the circuit is just a hop and a skip away from a sandy beach.

"At Valenica, you really have to keep your eye on the ball – a bit like Monaco – because the fast straights together with the barriers mean that you can easily get caught out." **Timo Glock**

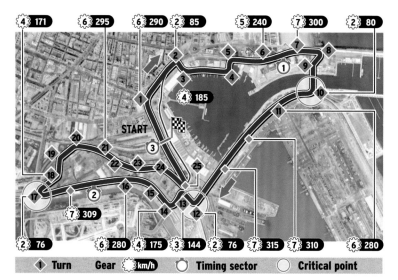

START

Turn	Gear	km/h	Timing sector	Critical point

2010 POLE TIME: **VETTEL (RED BULL)**, 1M37.587S, 125.463MPH/201.914KPH
2010 WINNER'S AVERAGE SPEED: 114.593MPH/184.42KPH

2010 FASTEST LAP: **BUTTON (McLAREN)**, 1M38.766S, 122.74MPH/197.531KPH
LAP RECORD: **GLOCK (TOYOTA)**, 1M38.683S, 122.837MPH/197.687KPH, 2009

INSIDE TRACK
EUROPEAN GRAND PRIX

Date:	**26 June**
Circuit name:	**Valencia Circuit**
Circuit length:	**3.401 miles/5.474km**
Number of laps:	**57**
Telephone:	**00 34 963164007**
Website:	**www.valenciastreetcircuit.co**

PREVIOUS WINNERS	
2008	**Felipe Massa** FERRARI
2009	**Rubens Barrichello** BRAWN
2010	**Sebastian Vettel** RED BULL

First race: The teams didn't know what to expect of the circuit when they turned up for the first time in 2008. However, Ferrari guessed best for set-up and Felipe Massa did the rest, winning as he pleased from pole position, finishing clear of Lewis Hamilton's McLaren. However, he escaped without a time penalty for pulling out of his pit stop into the path of another car, so it could all have been very different.

Best race: It was a case of third time lucky for Valencia, as the 2010 European GP proved the best so far. Victory went to Red Bull Racing's Sebastian Vettel, but he was pressed hard by Lewis Hamilton into Turn 2 before escaping. Mark Webber made a poor start and was playing catch-up when he was sent skywards by hitting Heikki Kovalainen's Lotus. He was lucky to survive that, and team-mate Vettel was lucky that the safety car period didn't cost him the lead, winning by 5 seconds from Hamilton.

Best corner: Turn 12 is where it happens. It's not the trickiest corner of the lap, merely a 90-degree right. What makes it important, though, is the fact that it's at the end of the circuit's longest straight, thus a place for defending or for having a go at overtaking.

Local hero: Fernando Alonso comes from Asturias in northern Spain, but the locals in Valencia are more than happy to focus on the fact that he's Spanish and were aghast when he was eliminated on lap 1 in 2008.

SILVERSTONE

Last year there was the new loop at Silverstone, this year there will be the new pit lane and the start/finish line half a lap away from the old one. Things are a-changin'.

Look through its history, ever since racing was first held there in 1948, and Silverstone has not been averse to change. The nature of the circuit has remained pretty constant though, as a fast, flowing lap that keeps the drivers on their toes.

The most comprehensive change for years was revealed in 2010, with a new loop cutting across the infield before joining the old Club straight and bypassing the Bridge section entirely. It took a bit of getting used to, but it was quick and, although bumpy in places, in some ways augmented the old place.

Now the new pit lane is in place and the start line moved from after Woodcote to after Club Corner. So, although the drivers will be racing here for a second time, it will feel very different on the opening lap as they vie for position into Abbey rather than the more open Copse. A few might come unstuck, especially if the worst bump of all is still mid-corner.

F1 ringmaster Bernie Ecclestone spent years badmouthing Silverstone when it was superior to many circuits that escaped censure. However, his jibes have borne fruit. Not in the investment of government money, but circuit owners, the British Racing Drivers' Club, have pushed Silverstone back to the forefront of world circuits, with 305,000 fans last year proving that they like it.

INSIDE TRACK
BRITISH GRAND PRIX

Date:	**10 July**
Circuit name:	**Silverstone**
Circuit length:	**3.666 miles/5.900km**
Number of laps:	**52**
Telephone:	**01327 857271**
Website:	**www.silverstone.co.uk**

PREVIOUS WINNERS	
2001	**Mika Hakkinen** McLAREN
2002	**Michael Schumacher** FERRARI
2003	**Rubens Barrichello** FERRARI
2004	**Michael Schumacher** FERRARI
2005	**Juan Pablo Montoya** McLAREN
2006	**Fernando Alonso** RENAULT
2007	**Kimi Raikkonen** FERRARI
2008	**Lewis Hamilton** McLAREN
2009	**Sebastian Vettel** RED BULL
2010	**Mark Webber** RED BULL

First race: The British GP of 1950 was the first World Championship round and there was no likelihood that Alfa Romeo wouldn't win, as its cars filled all the places on the four-car front row. One retired, but poleman Giuseppe Farina won, with the next fastest cars behind the lead trio finishing two laps down.

Best race: Rubens Barrichello's victory for Ferrari in 2003 was one of the great British GPs, as it produced overtaking almost every lap, survived a lunatic running on the track and allowed Barrichello to race side by side with Kimi Raikkonen for a third of the lap before nailing a move.

Best corner: Becketts has been the best corner ever since Maggots fed right into Becketts rather than left in 1991. Drivers have to commit here, turning in seventh gear and hanging on before flicking the car left into the second part of the esse. It's one of those corners where the laws of physics seem not to apply.

Local hero: Are you a Lewis Hamilton fan or a Jenson Button fan? World Champions both, they're producing golden years for British F1 fans, who have, for periods in the past, been known to cheer for their favourite teams when no British driver is shining.

> "Through the opening seven corners of Silverstone's lap, the speed of an F1 car never drops below 200kph (125mph) and there are some very fast changes of direction." **Mark Webber**

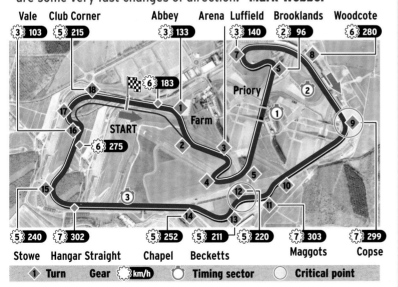

Vale	Club Corner		Abbey	Arena	Luffield	Brooklands	Woodcote

START

Priory

Farm

Stowe	Hangar Straight	Chapel	Becketts	Maggots	Copse

◆ **Turn** **Gear** km/h ○ **Timing sector** ○ **Critical point**

2010 POLE TIME: **VETTEL (RED BULL)**, 1M29.615S, 147.27MPH/237.009KPH
2010 WINNER'S AVERAGE SPEED: 134.892MPH/217.088KPH

2010 FASTEST LAP: **ALONSO (FERRARI)**, 1M30.874S, 145.018MPH/233.384KP
LAP RECORD: **ALONSO (FERRARI)**, 1M30.874S, 145.018MPH/233.384KPH, 2010

It's the turn of the Nuburgring to stage the 2011 German Grand Prix and drivers will be only too aware of the tight first corner that catches them out year after year.

Working to a one year on, one year off pattern with Hockenheim since 2007, whereas previously they each hosted a grand prix every year, the Nurburgring feels like an old friend who has been missing for a while.

Back for 2011, the Nurburgring will be a circuit that Mark Webber relishes returning to, as it was here that the Australian Red Bull Racing driver finally scored his first grand prix win in 2009.

The circuit is a modern mixture of corners sitting astride the pits and paddock of the original circuit, but it very much has an identity of its own, having been used by F1 most years since 1984. The first part of the lap was transformed considerably in 2002 when the original right-left ess backed by a huge, car-catching gravel trap was replaced by a right-hand hairpin feeding into a long and lightly banked left into a tighter left-right. On the opening lap, drivers have to opt for their line into Turn 1, Castrol-S, and pray that they're not torpedoed by a rival and then be in the right position to get into Turn 2.

Thereafter, the track drops away down to the Dunlop Kehre, climbs again to Michelin, then drops from Bit Kurve before bottoming out halfway to the NGK Schikane, a wonderful left-right flick on the face of the slope.

"The Nurburgring is a really fun track. A lot of the corners are cambered, both positively and negatively, which is unusual."
Jenson Button

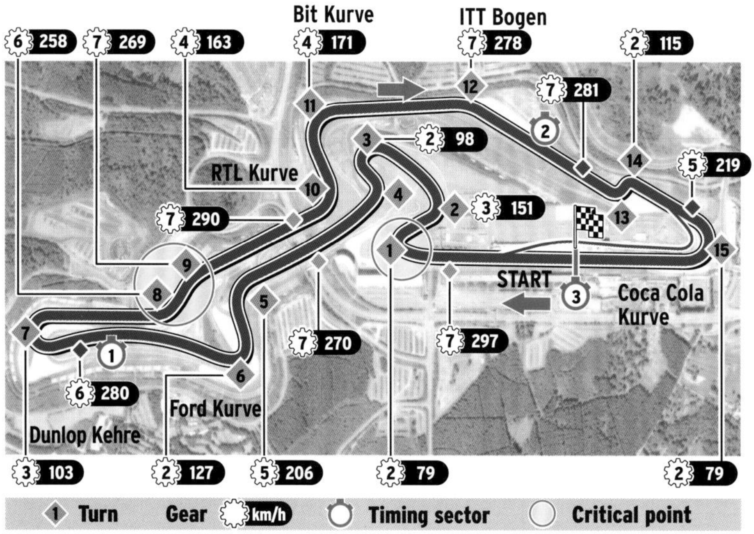

74

Track map labels

Bit Kurve — ITT Bogen — RTL Kurve — START — Coca Cola Kurve — Ford Kurve — Dunlop Kehre

6	258	7	269	4	163	4	171	7	278	2	115
7	281
11	3	2	98	2
7	290	10	4	2	3	151	14	5	219
13	15
9	1	3
8	5
7	1	6	7	270	7	297
6	280
3	103	2	127	5	206	2	79	2	79

◆ Turn   Gear ⚙ km/h   ○ Timing sector   ○ Critical point

2009 POLE TIME: **WEBBER (RED BULL)**, 1M32.230S, 124.866MPH/200.953KPH
2009 WINNER'S AVERAGE SPEED: 119.053MPH/191.598KPH

2009 FASTEST LAP: **ALONSO (RENAULT)**, 1M33.365S, 123.341MPH/198.498KPH
LAP RECORD: **M SCHUMACHER (FERRARI)**, 1M29.468S, 128.721MPH/207.157KPH, 2004

INSIDE TRACK
GERMAN GRAND PRIX

Date:	**24 July**
Circuit name:	**Nurburgring**
Circuit length:	**3.199 miles/5.148km**
Number of laps:	**60**
Telephone:	**00 49 2691 923060**
Website:	**www.nuerburgring.de**

PREVIOUS WINNERS

1999*	**Johnny Herbert** STEWART
2000*	**Michael Schumacher** FERRARI
2001*	**Michael Schumacher** FERRARI
2002*	**Rubens Barrichello** FERRARI
2003*	**Ralf Schumcher** WILLIAMS
2004*	**Michael Schumacher** FERRARI
2005*	**Fernando Alonso** RENAULT
2006*	**Michael Schumacher** FERRARI
2007*	**Fernando Alonso** McLAREN
2009	**Mark Webber** RED BULL

* AS THE EUROPEAN GP

First race: Treating the current circuit as having a separate history from the 14-mile Nordschleife, its first grand prix was the 1984 European GP, which was the penultimate race of the season and was dominated by McLaren's Alain Prost as he attempted to reel in his team-mate Niki Lauda for the title.

Best race: Nothing has matched the drama of the 1999 European GP here in which changing weather conditions led to Heinz-Harald Frentzen, David Coulthard, Ralf Schumacher and Giancarlo Fisichella all leading before Johnny Herbert gave Stewart its only win.

Best corner: For overtaking and incident, nothing comes close to the first corner. For late-race surprise attacks, the uphill NGK Schikane has always provided its share of overtaking attempts, particularly if the chasing driver has made a good exit to Bit Kurve and caught a tow along the kinked straight. Then, it's usually a case of aim and pray.

Local hero: Sebastian Vettel had to play second fiddle to his Red Bull team-mate Mark Webber on F1's most recent visit in 2009 and you can be sure that neither he nor his fans will accept anything other than victory this time. He has a considerable way to go to match compatriot Michael Schumacher's five wins.

HUNGARORING

The sun normally shines on the Hungaroring, but not on the racing, as this mid-European circuit is one of the hardest on which to pull off an overtaking manoeuvre.

When one thinks of the Hungarian GP, one thinks of a mad dash away from the starting grid down to the first corner, a little bit of jostling for position both into Turn 1 and out of it, then down towards Turn 2. After that, it's queues of cars running in line astern, sometimes with one all but climbing over the car ahead but unable to find a way past. Place-changing tends to happen in the pit lane. So, although the track dips and climbs around an attractive setting and the grandstands are usually full, the Hungarian GP is almost never an exciting one. Also, temperatures are normally high and it can prove a real sweat for the drivers and crews.

The lap starts on one side of a valley, dips into Turn 1, drops to Turn 2 and on down through Turn 3 to the valley floor halfway to Turn 4 before rising again, with the ascent up the far side of the valley continuing until the chicane at Turn 6. After a run of sweepers through to Turn 11, the track drops into the valley again before climbing through Turn 12, the hairpin at Turn 13 and up onto the level again out of the final corner.

The timing of a safety car period has plenty of ramifications at this circuit, as fighting past slower cars is tricky and a team's tactics about when to pit are thus more crucial than usual.

> "The Hungaroring has acquired something of a reputation for being a slow track on which it's impossible to overtake, but I don't really agree with that." **Lewis Hamilton**

INSIDE TRACK
HUNGARIAN GRAND PRIX

Date:	**31 July**
Circuit name:	**Hungaroring Circuit**
Circuit length:	**2.722 miles/4.381km**
Number of laps:	**70**
Telephone:	**00 36 2 844 1861**
Website:	**www.hungaroring.hu**

PREVIOUS WINNERS	
2001	**Michael Schumacher** FERRARI
2002	**Rubens Barrichello** FERRARI
2003	**Fernando Alonso** RENAULT
2004	**Michael Schumacher** FERRARI
2005	**Kimi Raikkonen** McLAREN
2006	**Jenson Button** HONDA
2007	**Lewis Hamilton** McLAREN
2008	**Heikki Kovalainen** McLAREN
2009	**Lewis Hamilton** McLAREN
2010	**Mark Webber** RED BULL

First race: It seemed like a revolution in 1986 when F1 went behind the Iron Curtain. A move away from communist politics has since made this mean nothing and what is left is a race in which Nelson Piquet caught and passed pole-sitter Ayrton Senna's Lotus to win for Williams in front of 200,000 fans.

Best race: There haven't been many great races here, as passing is so hard, but the Nigel Mansell/Ayrton Senna tussle in 1989 stands out, for the Brazilian couldn't stop the Ferrari driver's climb from 12th to first.

Best corner: It has to be Turn 1. There's a dipping entry and there are fireworks here on the opening lap on almost every visit, with drivers more desperate to make up places than on almost any other circuit, as passing is so hard to come by any later in the race.

Local hero: Hungary still awaits its first grand prix winner. Zsolt Baumgartner entertained the home fans when he stood in for Ralph Firman in two races in 2003 after the British driver was injured, starting at the Hungaroring. Then, after a season with Minardi in 2004, he ran out of money.

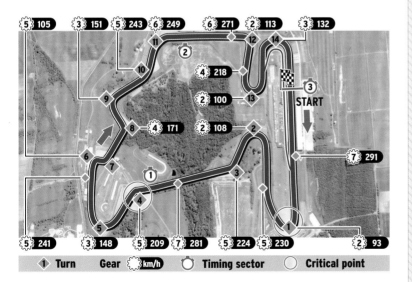

| 5 105 | 3 151 | 5 243 | 6 249 | 6 271 | 2 113 | 3 132 |

START

| 4 218 |
| 2 100 |
| 4 171 | 2 108 |
| 7 291 |

| 5 241 | 3 148 | 5 209 | 7 281 | 5 224 | 5 230 | 2 93 |

◆ **Turn**   **Gear**   ⚙ **km/h**   ○ **Timing sector**   ○ **Critical point**

2010 POLE TIME: **VETTEL (RED BULL),**
1M18.773S, 124.408MPH/200.215KPH
2010 WINNER'S AVERAGE SPEED:
113.083MPH/181.989KPH

2010 FASTEST LAP: **VETTEL (RED BULL),**
1M22.362S, 118.993MPH/191.501KPH
LAP RECORD: **M SCHUMACHER (FERRARI),**
19.071S, 123.828MPH/199.461KPH, 2004

This is the one circuit above all others that true F1 fans should visit, as it has it all, from dips to climbs, to twists and flat-out blasts. And it has plenty of weather...

Ask Formula One drivers for their favourite circuit and the majority will say Spa-Francorchamps. One visit will convince any fan that they are right, for the fast corners are fearsome. There's reward for the brave and even more so for a driver who can combine being gung-ho with the ability to be accurate enough to keep his momentum going.

For years, there was talk of one corner above all others: Eau Rouge. Only the best of the best would consider trying to take it without a lift off the throttle as the cars hit the compression where the downhill run from the La Source hairpin bucked into a steep climb, the drivers having to

twist left and right as they did so. It must have been hard, as even the great Ayrton Senna had to build up to it. Now, though, it's taken flat in top by everyone after being resurfaced. It still makes a great spectacle, though.

Indeed, spectacle is what it's all about at Spa-Francorchamps and admiring the artistic flow that a driver really in control of a car can paint around the dramatic topography.

It's nowhere near as tough as it was, with even Blanchimont now flat out in top, but even that was a pale shadow of how the track was 40 years ago, when it ran into the next valley and was fast, fast, fast.

INSIDE TRACK
BELGIAN GRAND PRIX

Date:	**28 August**
Circuit name:	**Spa-Francorchamps Circuit**
Circuit length:	**4.352 miles/7.004km**
Number of laps:	**44**
Telephone:	**00 32 8727 5138**
Website:	**www.spa-francorchamps.be**

PREVIOUS WINNERS	
1999	**David Coulthard** McLAREN
2000	**Mika Hakkinen** McLAREN
2001	**Michael Schumacher** FERRARI
2002	**Michael Schumacher** FERRARI
2004	**Kimi Raikkonen** McLAREN
2005	**Kimi Raikkonen** McLAREN
2007	**Kimi Raikkonen** FERRARI
2008	**Felipe Massa** FERRARI
2009	**Kimi Raikkonen** FERRARI
2010	**Lewis Hamilton** McLAREN

First race: Spa hosted the fourth round of the 1950 World Championship, and it was won by one of that year's dominant Alfa Romeos. This time, it was Juan Manuel Fangio's turn and he swapped the lead with team-mate Giuseppe Farina before the latter slowed with transmission trouble.

Best race: The 1992 Belgian GP was great, but the 2009 encounter stands out as a weird one that seemed determined to produce a surprise, as there was a Force India on pole and its driver, Giancarlo Fisichella, led for the first four laps. Then Kimi Raikkonen took over for Ferrari and did enough to resist Fisichella by less than a second.

Best corner: Overtaking happens into Bus Stop, but the right-left esses at Les Combes are the best bet, as these are approached up the very long straight from Raidillon, a corner through which drivers are known to get it wrong and so compromise their momentum up the hill. Then, with late braking, a passing manoeuvre is often on.

Local hero: Belgium has produced great F1 drivers, with Jacky Ickx the best. However, 21 years have passed since Thierry Boutsen became the last Belgian to win a grand prix. For 2011, GP2 race winner Jerome d'Ambrosio will be carrying the nation's hopes.

"Sectors 1 and 3 require low drag, while sector 2 requires maximum downforce, so a well-compromised set-up is crucial for a quick lap time." **Sam Michael, Williams technical director**

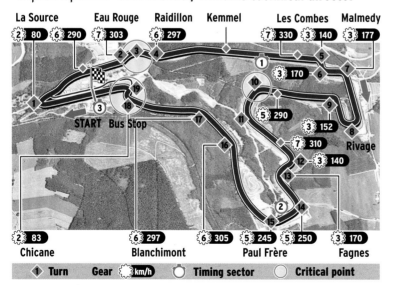

2010 POLE TIME: **WEBBER (RED BULL)**, 1M45.778S, 148.116MPH/238.370KPH
2010 WINNER'S AVERAGE SPEED: 128.940MPH/207.509KPH

2010 FASTEST LAP: **HAMILTON (MCLAREN)**, 1M49.069S, 143.647MPH/231.178KPH
LAP RECORD: **VETTEL (RED BULL)**, 1M47.263S, 146.065MPH/235.070KPH, 2009

MONZA

This circuit has history in its every atom, as its age is more than matched by the sheer number of enthralling races that it has hosted since opening its gates back in 1922.

Few circuits have changed as little as Monza has since it opened in 1922. Monaco's changes have been limited by being in a townscape. Monza's changes, with space available, have been limited by the fact that it simply works as a circuit.

The banked section that was last used in a grand prix in 1961 lies gathering moss on the infield to the right of the track as the drivers rush into the first chicane but, the insertion of chicanes apart, this circuit has a footprint that even the drivers from the 1940s would recognise.

The nature of Monza is still flat out for much of the lap, with the circuit split into the open area near the pits and huge grandstands, and the section through the woods in this royal park. The flow has been interrupted by chicanes at three points around the lap since 1972, sadly breaking up the epic dices between packs of drivers slipstreaming each other.

For all this, and all the wonderful history it contributes to the sport, there's still the less than classic spectacle of the drivers tripping over each other as they reach the first chicane on the opening lap. One feels it would be better bypassed at the start and used from the second lap onwards.

INSIDE TRACK
ITALIAN GRAND PRIX

Date:	**11 September**
Circuit name:	**Monza Circuit**
Circuit length:	**3.6miles/5.793km**
Number of laps:	**53**
Telephone:	**00 39 39 24821**
Website:	**www.monzanet.it**

PREVIOUS WINNERS	
2001	**Juan Pablo Montoya** WILLIAMS
2002	**Rubens Barrichello** FERRARI
2003	**Michael Schumacher** FERRARI
2004	**Rubens Barrichello** FERRARI
2005	**Juan Pablo Montoya** McLAREN
2006	**Michael Schumacher** FERRARI
2007	**Fernando Alonso** McLAREN
2008	**Sebastian Vettel** TORO ROSSO
2009	**Rubens Barrichello** BRAWN
2010	**Fernando Alonso** FERRARI

"Monza is a track that is technically not as easy as you would expect, even though it looks as though it's simply a question of going flat-out all the way around." **Rubens Barrichello**

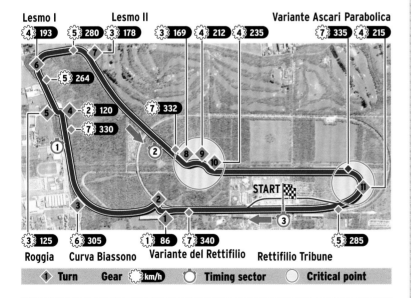

Lesmo I   4 193   5 280   3 178   **Lesmo II**   3 169   4 212   4 235   **Variante Ascari**   7 335   4 215   **Parabolica**

6   5 264   5   4   2 120   7 332   7 330   1   2   8 9 10   11   **START**

3 125   6 305   1 86   7 340   5 285

Roggia   **Curva Biassono**   **Variante del Rettifilio**   **Rettifilio Tribune**

◆ **Turn**   **Gear**   km/h   ○ **Timing sector**   ○ **Critical point**

2010 POLE TIME: **ALONSO (FERRARI),** 1M21.962S, 158.104MPH/254.444KPH
2010 WINNER'S AVERAGE SPEED: **149.656MPH/240.849KPH**

2010 FASTEST LAP: **ALONSO (FERRARI),** 1M24.139S, 154.013MPH/247.861KPH
LAP RECORD: **BARRICHELLO (FERRARI),** 1M21.046S, 159.909MPH/257.349KPH 2004

First race: As one of the six circuits to host a round of the 1950 World Championship, Monza goes back to the start of F1. Giuseppe Farina rounded out that first year by winning for Alfa Romeo and overcoming the challenge of Ferrari's Alberto Ascari after he went out with a gearbox problem and his own team-mate Juan Manuel Fangio retired.

Best race: There was a great finish in 1971. But, for action all the way, 1965 stands out with 42 lead changes. Jim Clark led the early laps for Lotus, but was passed and repassed by the BRM duo of Graham Hill and Jackie Stewart, plus Ferrari's John Surtees. But both Surtees and Clark retired before Stewart led the final two laps to take his maiden grand prix win.

Best corner: Parabolica, the fourth-gear, 180-degree right-hander that completes the lap, is far from easy. The line is so notably particular that drivers seldom try to overtake into it. However, if they get a good run through here and carry speed out of its exit onto the main straight, it's a huge help.

Local hero: For all its passion for racing, Italy has provided but two World Champions, with Giuseppe Farina winning the 1950 title for Alfa Romeo, then Alberto Ascari being crowned in 1952 and 1953 for Ferrari. Until its next ace turns up, the fans will cheer for Ferrari.

SINGAPORE

Racing around city streets is one thing, but Singapore adds a dramatic extra dimension as the racing is held in the dark when the heat of the day backs off after nightfall.

It's hot and humid in the tropics and this near-equatorial venue is no place to go racing unless teams, drivers and their cars can cope with the conditions. So, in a step to overcome this, and to fit in with European TV scheduling, it was decided from the outset that Singapore would host its race after nightfall. Not only would conditions be less extreme, but the television images of a floodlit circuit with an illuminated cityscape in the background were welcomed too as something different.

Monaco's grand prix is held downtown and Montreal's on an island in its river, but this is far more metropolitan, as the skyscrapers rise above it.

Starting its lap alongside a seafront park, the track then runs along a series of short straights past the bank headquarters before turning left through Turn 9 and along the sides of the cricket pitches in front of the famed Raffles Hotel. The most notable landmark is the Andersen Bridge that it crosses just after this, before the cars blast back across a causeway to snake through a park, even under a grandstand, to turn left onto the start/finish straight once more.

There are bumps, the light isn't consistent around the circuit and drivers have to acclimatise themselves to be racing when they would normally be having dinner, but the difference is refreshing.

 "You can't make mistakes in Monaco, but in Singapore you often get a second chance if you do stumble as there is so much run-off area at the tighter corners." **Vitantonio Liuzzi**

78

INSIDE TRACK
SINGAPORE GRAND PRIX

Date:	**25 September**
Circuit name:	**Singapore Circuit**
Circuit length:	**3.152 miles/5.073km**
Number of laps:	**61**
Telephone:	**00 65 67315900**
Website:	**www.singaporegp.sg**

PREVIOUS WINNERS		
2008	**Fernando Alonso** RENAULT	
2009	**Lewis Hamilton** McLAREN	
2010	**Fernando Alonso** FERRARI	

First race: The records show that Fernando Alonso won the inaugural Singapore GP, but allegations of race-fixing levelled at his Renault team have besmirched this. It all went wrong for the Spaniard in qualifying when a fuel hose came off, leaving him 15th. He made little progress as Felipe Massa led for Ferrari, but pitted early and benefited when team-mate Nelson Piquet Jr spun into the wall, bringing out the safety car. This left him fifth and Nico Rosberg ahead of him had to serve a drive-through and he advanced to victory.

Best race: Singapore's 2009 race was a pure one, with a result not tainted by allegations of race fixing, unlike in 2008. This was Lewis Hamilton's race from start to finish after he'd started his McLaren from pole and was followed through Turn 1 after a blast of KERS power by Nico Rosberg. Behind them, Mark Webber attacked Fernando Alonso and both ran wide, allowing Timo Glock through to fourth behind Sebastian Vettel. Rosberg then ruined his race by running over the white line at pit exit, collecting a drive-through, and the timing of a safety car spell meant that he had to delay pitting and fell to 14th. No one, though, could touch Hamilton.

Best corner: Turn 7 remains the best for drivers looking to pass. It's approached down a kinked straight and the 90-degree left has walls close at hand but, on a circuit offering few options, it has to be considered.

Local hero: No Singaporean driver has reached F1 yet, so local fans will have to pin their colours to teams rather than drivers.

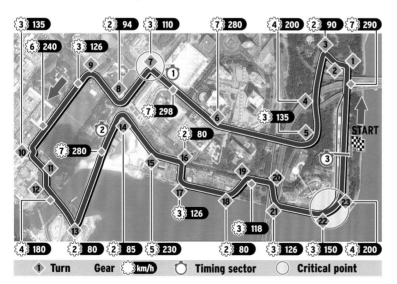

Turn　**Gear**　**km/h**　**Timing sector**　**Critical point**

2010 POLE TIME: **ALONSO (FERRARI)**, 1M45.390S, 107.675MPH/173.287KPH	2010 FASTEST LAP: **ALONSO (FERRARI)**, 1M47.976S, 105.097MPH/169.138KPH
2010 WINNER'S AVERAGE SPEED: 97.817MPH/157.422KPH	LAP RECORD: **RAIKKONEN (FERRARI)**, 1M45.599S, 107.358MPH/172.776KPH 2008

SUZUKA

> There's prestige in winning at Monza, but victory at Suzuka isn't something that tends to fall into the hands of anyone but the greats. It's the most demanding of all.

There was widespread disappointment a few years ago when the Japanese GP turned its back on Suzuka and headed to a revived Fuji Speedway. Was F1 making a mistake and dropping one of its greatest tracks? Then, after finding Toyota-funded Fuji less than brilliant for racing, the circus came back to Honda-owned Suzuka for 2008.

The reason Suzuka is revered is that it offers a challenge to drivers and engineers alike, thanks to its combination of corners, inclines and often severe wet weather.

The lap starts benignly, with a gentle downhill entry into the first corner - famous for Ayrton Senna spearing Alain Prost off in 1990 - and its equivalent Turn 2. However, the uphill double set of esses that follows is impossible on a computer game, so must be tantalising in real life.

With straights being a rarity at Suzuka, the drivers are fighting constantly to bring their car into line to position it for the next corner and it's only when they have got their cars through the second Degner that they can relax momentarily.

Spoon Curve, at the far end of the circuit, seems to go on for ever before the cars fire out onto the back straight, through the once awesome 130R, and head for the main trouble spot: the Casio Triangle, with its heavy braking, blind entry over a brow and off-camber exit.

> "Suzuka is technically very challenging, really quick and a real drivers' circuit that demands the very best both out of you and out of the car." **Nico Rosberg**

INSIDE TRACK
JAPANESE GRAND PRIX

Date:	**9 October**
Circuit name:	**Suzuka**
Circuit length:	**3.608 miles/5.806km**
Number of laps:	**53**
Telephone:	**00 81 593 783620**
Website:	**www.suzukacircuit.co.jp**

PREVIOUS WINNERS	
1999	**Mika Hakkinen** McLAREN
2000	**Michael Schumacher** FERRARI
2001	**Michael Schumacher** FERRARI
2002	**Michael Schumacher** FERRARI
2003	**Rubens Barrichello** FERRARI
2004	**Michael Schumacher** FERRARI
2005	**Kimi Raikkonen** McLAREN
2006	**Fernando Alonso** RENAULT
2009	**Sebastian Vettel** RED BULL
2010	**Sebastian Vettel** RED BULL

First race: Suzuka's first World Championship grand prix was in 1987 and title-shot Nigel Mansell eliminated himself with an accident in practice. Then Gerhard Berger produced Ferrari's first win in over two years after Alain Prost's McLaren had a puncture.

Best race: The 1994 race was a game of chess between title protagonists Michael Schumacher and Damon Hill. Schumacher led away in his Benetton in monsoon conditions, but the safety car had to be deployed after cars aquaplaned off the circuit. Then Martin Brundle spun off and hit a marshal, breaking his leg, and the race was halted. On the restart, Hill knew that he had to overcome an 8.6-second deficit and did so. Schumacher fought back and claimed the lead on aggregate but had to pit for more fuel. Rejoining 14.5 seconds down, he attacked, but ended up just seconds short.

Best corner: The exit of Casio Triangle at the end of the lap is really tricky, as drivers have to get onto the right line to get on the throttle early through the final corner to carry speed onto the pit straight.

Local hero: Kamui Kobayashi did his early racing here and he appears set to be Japan's next hero after years spent with their drivers not hitting the heights hoped of them.

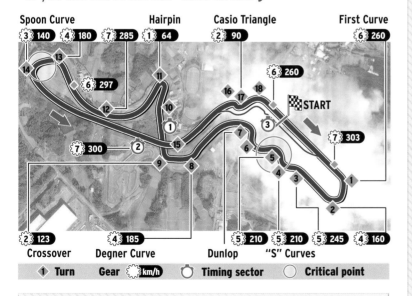

Spoon Curve | Hairpin | Casio Triangle | First Curve

Crossover | Degner Curve | Dunlop | "S" Curves

◆ Turn   Gear   km/h   ◯ Timing sector   ◯ Critical point

2010 POLE TIME: VETTEL (RED BULL), 1M30.785S, 143.083MPH/230.271KPH
2010 WINNER'S AVERAGE SPEED: 126.727MPH/203.948KPH

2010 FASTEST LAP: WEBBER (RED BULL), 1M33.474S, 138.968MPH/223.647KPH
LAP RECORD: RAIKKONEN (McLAREN), 1M31.540S, 141.904MPH/228.373KPH 2005

YEONGAM

This Asian economic powerhouse wanted to impress with its new circuit in 2010 and it certainly did that. Now South Korea needs a top driver to cement the nation's interest.

Formula One fans have become used to the arrival of new circuits in countries that were once considered the far side of the sporting globe. Indeed, as F1's European heartland lost its pre-eminence, so grands prix started to be held in Malaysia, China and Bahrain.

Then, South Korea wanted to get in on the act and the Korea Auto Valley Organisation announced that it would be building a state-of-the-art circuit for its inaugural race in 2010, almost 200 miles from capital Seoul.

The plans for the Korean International Circuit looked great, but there was concern in July that it simply wasn't going to be ready on time, as the track had yet to be laid. Then the KAVO said that the track would be given its debut 50 days ahead of the inaugural Korean GP, in an event on 5 September, with deposed HRT driver Karun Chandhok demonstrating a Red Bull F1 car.

The track was indeed ready just in time and the first race at the KIC revealed a circuit with an unusual anticlockwise direction that fed into a hairpin away from the grid, causing all sorts of problems on the opening lap, then F1's longest straight, all 0.74 miles of it, down to another hairpin. From there, the circuit is endlessly twisty, all the way around to the constant radius Turn 17 that arcs through almost 180 degrees as it brings the cars to a left kink that feeds them back onto the start straight again.

"I like the part from Turn 4 to Turn 6, with very different lines and the possibility to overtake." **Fernando Alonso**

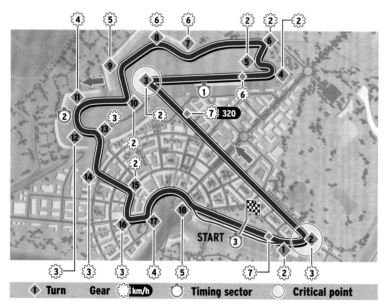

2010 POLE TIME: **VETTEL (RED BULL)**, 1M35.585S, 127.677MPH/205.476KPH
2010 WINNER'S AVERAGE SPEED: 68.349MPH/109.997KPH

2010 FASTEST LAP: **ALONSO (FERRARI)**, 1M50.257S, 113.919MPH/183.335KPH
LAP RECORD: **ALONSO (FERRARI)**, 1M50.257S, 113.919MPH/183.335KPH, 2010

INSIDE TRACK
SOUTH KOREA GRAND PRIX

Date:	**16 October**
Circuit name:	**Korea International Circuit**
Circuit length:	**3.489 miles/5.615km**
Number of laps:	**57**
Telephone:	**00 82 7154646061**
Website:	**www.koreangp.kr**

PREVIOUS WINNERS

2010	**Fernando Alonso** FERRARI

First race: Last October's inaugural South Korean GP was almost brought to a halt by torrential rain that left the track flooded and only three laps were run before the race was red-flagged. It was restarted after an hour, though, and Fernando Alonso won when Sebastian Vettel's engine failed.

Best race: Well, it had to be last year's, as that was the only grand prix held at the KIC so far. It was certainly enthralling, though.

Best corner: Turn 3 is the pick of the pack, as circuit designer Hermann Tilke wanted a place where overtaking was likely rather than just possible and so designed F1's longest straight into one of its tightest corners. Better still, the straight is turned on to through a slow corner, allowing for a driver making a better exit to pull into the slipstream of the car ahead, then use the tow to gather the speed required to attempt to dive past under braking. When drivers get it wrong here, though, they wreck their speed down the straight to Turn 4, so it's a make as well as a break corner.

Local hero: Korean drivers are thin on the ground at the top level. The establishment of their own grand prix is sure to bring on some for the future. Leading the way is Keisuke Kunimoto, a 22-year-old Japanese driver with Korean heritage who spent 2010 competing in the Europe-based Formula Renault 3.5 series after winning the Macau F3 GP in 2008. Jin-Woo Hwang also has experience of powerful single-seaters after he was hauled from GT racing in Japan to compete in A1GP for the Korean team in 2008, but he struggled, as you'd expect.

JAYPEE GROUP CIRCUIT

India has a long history of motor racing, but this is its first crack at the sport's top level. The race might even get the nation to watch a sport other than cricket.

Built on a complex known as the Jaypee Greens Sports City, the circuit is located at Greater Noida, some 35 miles south of Delhi. The home of the new Indian GP is located right alongside the Yamuna Expressway, the main motorway between the capital city and the tourist capital, Agra, home of the world-famous Taj Mahal.

Running clockwise, the Hermann Tilke-desgined lap starts with a blast to a sharp right-hand corner. It's not a hairpin, but a 100-degree turn that has its exit feeding directly into an arcing left-hander down to a right-hand hairpin. The exit from here is crucial, as it feeds out onto the circuit's longest straight.

At the end of this is another tight corner, turning about 145 degrees to the right. There's then a decent length straight into a fast left kink, then an esse, a short straight and another esse, rather like the opening stretch of the TI Circuit used to host the Pacific GP in 1994 and 1995.

After rounding a long, long right, the circuit doubles back through an esse to a fastish right, a short straight and a tight left to feed the cars back onto the start/finish straight.

The aim is for the circuit to be completed by this February, and certainly not for it to have the race against time faced by South Korea's circuit last year.

"The most exciting corner is going to be Turns 10 and 11, an uphill, long, long right-hander that won't be unlike Spoon Curve at Suzuka even or Turn 8 at Istanbul." **Karun Chandhok**

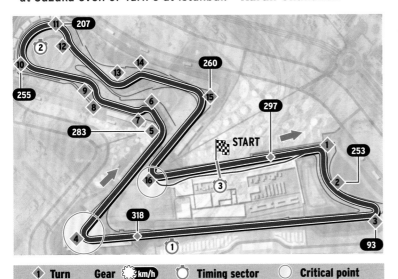

◆ Turn   Gear ✿km/h   ◯ Timing sector   ◯ Critical point

2010 POLE TIME:	2010 FASTEST LAP:
NOT APPLICABLE	**NOT APPLICABLE**
2010 WINNER'S AVERAGE SPEED:	LAP RECORD:
NOT APPLICABLE	**NOT APPLICABLE**

INSIDE TRACK
INDIAN GRAND PRIX

Date:	**30 October**
Circuit name:	**Jaypee Group Circuit**
Circuit length:	**3.418 miles/5.500km**
Number of laps:	**56**
Telephone:	**tba**
Website:	**www.indiangrandprix.net**

PREVIOUS WINNERS
Not applicable

Racing in India: There has been no F1 in India until this year, but the country has long had a grand prix. Held on a couple of circuits near Chennai (formerly Madras) from the 1980s until the 1990s, it was for cars from the Formula Atlantic and later F3 categories, with overseas drivers tending to take the spoils. Plans for a circuit near Calcutta to host a World Championship round surfaced in the late 1990s, the Hyderabad staking its claim. But neither landed a deal to bring F1 to India. Then Mumbai (formerly Bombay) put its name into the hat, but that deal was scuppered by a change in tobacco advertising legislation and also overriding public opinion, which felt that India had more pressing matters for investment than welcoming F1.

Best corner: Turn 4, the right-hand hairpin at the end of the back straight, ought to provide the best of the overtaking action under braking, particularly on the opening lap, when the field is still bunched.

Local hero: Thus far, India has had just two F1 drivers. Narain Karthikeyan was the first, racing for Jordan in 2005. However, he lost his ride at the end of the season and became a test driver for Williams, before starring in the now defunct A1GP series for India, winning races at Zhuhai and Brands Hatch. He then headed to the United States, where he's breaking into NASCAR. Karun Chandhok followed in his tracks and was showing ever-improving form for HRT last year, without the benefit of any testing, before he was dropped to make way for Sakon Yamamoto with a much-needed injection of funds for this struggling team.

YAS MARINA

Having spared no expense in building this remarkable circuit, the Abu Dhabi race organisers raised the bar in 2009 in terms of standards and gave F1 an opulent new image.

The Yas Marina circuit is out of this world, an ultra-modern racing circuit located amid an extravagant sports and entertainment complex. With money no object, the circuit was built not only to show the world Abu Dhabi in an opulent and confident light, but to trump the Sakhir circuit in neighbouring Bahrain. In both aims, it succeeded.

The complex contains a marina full of superyachts, a Ferrari World indoor theme park, a golf course, apartments and a stunning shopping mall, all elements of a complex constructed to add glamour to Abu Dhabi and to attract tourists. Should they want to stay, there is the super-stylish Yas Hotel and six others.

The first sector of the lap is the fast part, including quick corners and the long back straight that is also used as a drag strip. Then comes the street circuit section, with tighter corners. The lap is completed by the marina section, with a series of 90-degree bends around the marina and under the bridge between the two parts of the Yas Hotel.

As a circuit, there are shortcomings to be ironed out if overtaking is to be more plentiful, but it is for now a thing of beauty, a circuit that causes every first-time visitor's jaw to drop, leaving them in no doubt that this sheikhdom certainly isn't facing the financial woes of nearby Dubai.

"The track has a bit of everything, with high-speed and low-speed corners, positive and negative camber, and the walls are pretty close most of the way around." **Jenson Button**

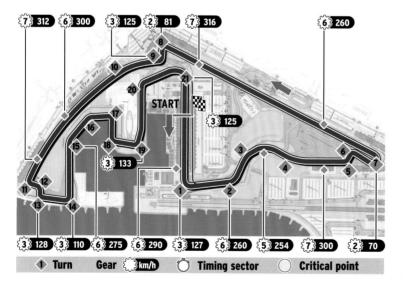

◆ **Turn**   **Gear** 🔆 **km/h**   ⭕ **Timing sector**   ⚪ **Critical point**

2010 POLE TIME: **VETTEL (RED BULL)**, 1M39.394S, 124.997MPH/201.163KPH
2010 WINNER'S AVERAGE SPEED: **118.012MPH/189.923KPH**

2010 FASTEST LAP: **HAMILTON (MCLAREN)**, 1M41.274S, 122.676MPH/197.428KPH
LAP RECORD: **VETTEL (RED BULL)**, 1M40.279S, 123.89MPH/199.383KPH 2009

INSIDE TRACK
ABU DHABI GRAND PRIX

Date:	**13 November**
Circuit name:	**Yas Marina**
Circuit length:	**3.429 miles/5.518km**
Number of laps:	**56**
Telephone:	**00 971 4366 2125**
Website:	**www.yasmarinacircuit.com**

PREVIOUS WINNERS		
2009	**Sebastian Vettel**	RED BULL
2010	**Sebastian Vettel**	RED BULL

First race: The inaugural race in 2009 looked set to mark McLaren's late-season comeback as Lewis Hamilton set the pace, but it didn't turn out that way. He led, but a brake problem made him park up, leaving the way clear for Red Bull's Sebastian Vettel to win as he pleased. He was helped as team-mate Mark Webber's car didn't take in enough fuel at its second stop and so he had to switch to economy mode and try to hang on as Jenson Button closed in. Already crowned champion at the previous race in Brazil, Button had nothing to gain, but the Brawn driver gave it a mighty go.

Best race: Last year's race was a better sporting spectacle than that inaugural race at the Yas Marina circuit, but, after the first-lap safety car deployment, it was more like a game of chess and Webber and Alonso got it wrong, ending their title hopes as Vettel reigned supreme at the front.

Best corner: Overtaking has proved remarkably difficult on this Hermann Tilke-designed circuit, but the chicane at Turns 5 and 6 is a place where a few try their luck, often with the move being settled going into Turn 7, which follows almost immediately. Conversely, the worst corner is the tight left-right as the pit exit jinks its way under the circuit before rising and re-emerging on the opposite side of the circuit.

Local hero: There are still no Abu Dhabian drivers at the top level of international single-seater racing, with Porsche Supercup competitor Khaled Al Qubaisi the highest-ranked in any form of motorsport.

INTERLAGOS

Interlagos has been given the wake-up call for its facilities being scruffy, but its twisting stretch of tarmac delivers the goods in terms of exciting racing year in, year out.

The circuit came under fire last August from Bernie Ecclestone when the F1 supremo said it was the "worst circuit" on the F1 calendar and that its future "depended on significant improvements".

There are still five more years on its contract, but the scope is there for much to be modernised to ensure contract extension after 2015, with its cramped, aged paddock certainly the area with the most pressing need for modernisation.

Opened for racing in 1940, this wonderful circuit wraps itself around the curving hillscape in the outer suburbs of sprawling Sao Paulo, taking its character from the crests and dips. The original circuit was longer, running further down the slopes to the lakes beyond, but it took a chopping back of the lap length from just under five miles to less than three miles when F1 visited in 1980 for the World Championship to return in 1990.

The first corner was turned into a sharply falling left with a blind entry. Momentum out of here and through Curva do Sol is critical for a good run down the hill to Descida do Lago, at which point the track starts feeding back up the hill to Ferradura before traversing the face of the slope with drops and climbs until it reaches Junção, the point where it starts the long climb back to the start/finish straight.

INSIDE TRACK
BRAZILIAN GRAND PRIX

Date:	**27 November**
Circuit name:	**Interlagos**
Circuit length:	**2.667 miles/4.292km**
Number of laps:	**71**
Telephone:	**00 55 11 813 5775**
Website:	**www.interlagos.com**

PREVIOUS WINNERS	
2001	**David Coulthard** McLAREN
2002	**Michael Schumacher** FERRARI
2003	**Giancarlo Fisichella** JORDAN
2004	**Juan Pablo Montoya** WILLIAMS
2005	**Juan Pablo Montoya** McLAREN
2006	**Felipe Massa** FERRARI
2007	**Kimi Raikkonen** FERRARI
2008	**Felipe Massa** FERRARI
2009	**Mark Webber** RED BULL
2010	**Sebastian Vettel** RED BULL

First race: After hosting a non-championship grand prix in 1972, Interlagos welcomed the World Championship in 1973 and local hero Emerson Fittipaldi produced the perfect result, passing his Lotus team-mate Ronnie Peterson at the start and winning by 13 seconds from Jackie Stewart's Tyrrell.

Best race: It will take years before the 2008 title shoot-out is bettered, as it had the plot of Felipe Massa hunting for glory at home and Lewis Hamilton tasked with the job of landing a first world title there for the second year running. Rain added to the mix and it took Hamilton until the final few corners to regain the position he required to land the crown.

Best corner: The Senna "S" that follows immediately after the first corner is always the scene of action as drivers attempt to complete a passing move that started at the crest of the hill and is made difficult by the need to get into position for the second part of the esse as the track bends left.

Local hero: On paper, this is still Felipe Massa, but his stock plummeted at home in Brazil last year when he acceded to team orders and let Ferrari team-mate Fernando Alonso through to win the German GP. At a stroke, this dissipated the sympathy accorded him after he was pipped to the 2008 title.

"Interlagos is a good fun track. It's good for overtaking as well, especially with the long straight past the pit lane going into the Senna 'S'." **Nico Rosberg**

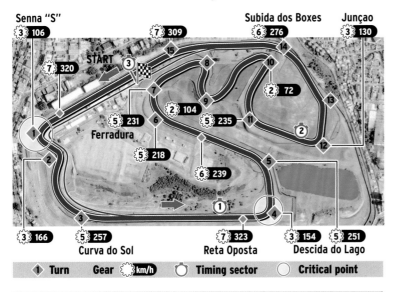

	Turn		Gear	km/h		Timing sector		Critical point

2010 POLE TIME: **HULKENBERG (WILLIAMS),** 1M14.470S, 129.434MPH/208.304KPH

2010 WINNER'S AVERAGE SPEED: 122.375MPH/196.944KPH

2010 FASTEST LAP: **HAMILTON (MCLAREN),** 1M13.851S, 130.518MPH/210.049KPH

LAP RECORD: **MONTOYA (WILLIAMS),** 1M11.473S, 134.837MPH/217KPH 2004

Whichever circuit is visited in any of the countries hosting the World Championship, eyes are always drawn to Ferraris and especially to the one driven by Fernando Alonso.

REVIEW OF THE 2010 SEASON

Whatever turned the 2010 World Championship into the thriller it was ought to be bottled, as the combination of the top drivers with the top three teams and an ebbing and flowing of form and fortune made this the most enthralling season in living memory, with plots and subplots at every turn as the months went by.

This was a campaign that started with the least exciting race in years in Bahrain as Formula One experienced a race without refuelling for the first time since 1994 and this appeared to tally with a race stripped of overtaking or even the need to overtake. Yet, all talk of gloom and doom was soon dismissed as the racing got better and better from there.

It wasn't all nip and tuck, and passing at every corner. But what made the 2010 World Championship such a great one was the fact that the very top drivers were with the top teams, offering intra-team battles as well as inter-team ones. Undoubtedly, Ferrari did its bit to alter this, with its clumsy use of banned team orders at the German GP, for which it picked up a nominal fine. However, Red Bull Racing and McLaren stood steadfastly by the tenets of fair play and their honesty

in letting both of their pairs of drivers gun for ultimate glory added another layer of intrigue to what was a fabulous season.

Another factor that made this such a great championship was the ebbing and flowing of form between the top three teams, making it hard to predict with any certainty just who would be challenging at the front on any given weekend.

The Adrian Newey-inspired Red Bull RB6 was the pick of the pack, but assorted clashes and mechanical failures let Ferrari's Fernando Alonso and McLaren's Lewis Hamilton and Jenson Button stay in the hunt. The most embarrassing gaffe came at the Turkish GP, when Webber didn't want to let team-mate Vettel past after he had been told to turn his engine down a bit. They clashed and were out, leaving Hamilton to hold off Button for a McLaren one-two.

What arose from this, especially after Red Bull's Helmut Marko blamed Webber, was the Australian letting people know that he felt as though he was being treated as number two in a team that supposedly offered its drivers equal opportunities. Indeed, while McLaren chuckled as it too races with this intention, the whole matter came to a head with Ferrari's clumsy place-changing at Hockenheim.

Webber's dogged attack took him into the points lead. But, incredibly, after Webber crashed on F1's first visit to Korea and Vettel had his Renault engine blow when leading, Alonso produced a run of three wins and a third between Monza and Yeongam to put himself at the top of the pile. When Red Bull Racing scored a one-two in the penultimate race, in Brazil, that could have restored Webber to within a point of the lead, but Red Bull refused to countenance dropping Vettel from the lead to Webber's advantage with a slow pit stop. Many considered this to be madness, as their result clinched the team its first constructors' title but left Alonso eight points clear before the Abu Dhabi finale.

Their decision to leave Vettel to win was made to work when he won the race at the Yas Marina from pole and both Alonso and Webber got caught out, firstly by qualifying poorly and then by a couple of midfield runners getting ahead of them after pitting under safety car conditions at the end of the opening lap, then delaying their progress.

Both Ferrari and McLaren had moments when their cars were as fast as the Red Bulls, but their form was erratic and so they couldn't capitalise sufficiently when the Red Bulls or their drivers stumbled.

Behind this trio of teams, Mercedes GP was the best of the rest. This was a rebranded version of the stop-gap Brawn GP outfit that waltzed off with both titles in 2009. Nico Rosberg must have fancied his chances when he signed from Williams, but all attention was then turned on the team's second signing, Michael Schumacher. However, the seven-time world champion took until the closing races to get up to speed, and the driver who claimed the best results outside the six drivers racing for Red Bull, McLaren and Ferrari was Renault's Robert Kubica, who took a second and two thirds to Rosberg's three thirds.

As with the top three teams, the next two - Mercedes and Renault - endured fluctuating form. Then Williams came on strong as the year advanced, to the extent that veteran signing Rubens Barrichello scored in four races in a row towards the season's end, then rookie Nico Hulkenberg scooped a surprise pole for the Brazilian GP. This late push for points moved Sir Frank Williams's once dominant team past Force India with only one race to go and they stayed a point ahead at the final round to claim sixth place overall.

Sauber was able to mix it with the best of the midfield on occasion, most notably with the entertaining Kamui Kobayashi at the wheel. Languishing behind was Scuderia Toro Rosso, as having to build its own chassis for the first time left its drivers far from the pace.

There were three new teams, but their relatively low budgets and the banning of in-season testing meant that all they could hope to do was to close the gap between themselves and the slowest of the established teams. Lotus proved best at this, but Virgin Racing's CFD-only designed chassis was almost its match. HRT's Dallara-built was perhaps not competitive out of the box, but an almost total lack of development left its drivers lapping at the tail of the field.

Fernando Alonso made a dream debut for Ferrari as he opened his campaign with a win, but it was a race that belonged to Sebastian Vettel until his Red Bull was hit by an electrical problem that dropped him down the order. Felipe Massa made it a Ferrari one-two finish.

After great excitement in the build-up to the season, with many top drivers having swapped teams and the arrival of three new teams at the back of the grid, the first race of 2010 proved to be intensely disappointing.

Continuing the form that Red Bull Racing showed at the end of 2009, it claimed pole, with Sebastian Vettel lining up ahead of the Ferraris of Felipe Massa and Fernando Alonso and Lewis Hamilton's McLaren.

Many eyes were focused on the return of seven-time world champion Michael Schumacher, but he still had work to do as he would line up seventh, two places behind his Mercedes team-mate Nico Rosberg.

Vettel powered into the lead. Behind him, Massa made a poor getaway to his first race since suffering head injuries in 2009 and Alonso pounced, lining himself up to be on the inside line into Turn 2.

There was nothing that Alonso could do about Vettel, though. Well, not until they had all completed their single pit stop, for tyres only now that refuelling had been banned. The German was controlling the race, with Alonso having given up trying to pass him when, with 15 laps remaining, the Red Bull lost power and the Ferrari flashed into the lead. A corner later, Massa was by him too.

Vettel was able to continue, but Hamilton caught and passed him too. Fortunately, a conversation with his pit crew led to an engine setting change that enabled him to speed up again and so fourth was saved.

The Mercedes duo claimed fifth and sixth places, Rosberg ahead of Schumacher, with reigning champion Jenson Button chasing them to the finish after taking seventh from Mark Webber when the Australian had a slow pit stop. With points awarded down to 10th for the first time, Vitantonio Liuzzi and Rubens Barrichello also took home points for Force India and Williams respectively.

When people look back at this race, two elements will stand out. There was a near total lack of overtaking, suggesting that

SAKHIR ROUND 1

Date: **14 March 2010**

Laps: **49** • Distance: **191.786 miles/308.651km** • Weather: **Hot and dry**

Pos	Driver	Team	Result	Stops	Qualifying Time	Grid
1	Fernando Alonso	Ferrari	1h39m20.396s	1	1m54.608s	3
2	Felipe Massa	Ferrari	1h39m36.495s	1	1m54.242s	2
3	Lewis Hamilton	McLaren	1h39m43.578s	1	1m55.217s	4
4	Sebastian Vettel	Red Bull	1h39m59.195s	1	1m54.101s	1
5	Nico Rosberg	Mercedes	1h40m00.609s	1	1m55.241s	5
6	Michael Schumacher	Mercedes	1h40m04.559s	1	1m55.524s	7
7	Jenson Button	McLaren	1h40m05.676s	1	1m55.672s	8
8	Mark Webber	Red Bull	1h40m06.756s	1	1m55.284s	6
9	Vitantonio Liuzzi	Force India	1h40m13.404s	1	1m55.653s	12
10	Rubens Barrichello	Williams	1h40m22.885s	1	1m55.33s	11
11	Robert Kubica	Renault	1h40m29.489s	1	1m55.885s	9
12	Adrian Sutil	Force India	1h40m43.454s	1	1m56.309s	10
13	Jaime Alguersuari	Toro Rosso	1h40m53.052s	1	1m57.071s	18
14	Nico Hulkenberg	Williams	48 laps	2	1m55.857s	13
15	Heikki Kovalainen	Lotus	47 laps	1	2m00.313s	21
16	Sebastien Buemi	Toro Rosso	46 laps	1	1m56.265s	17
17	Jarno Trulli	Lotus	46 laps	1	1m59.852s	20
R	Pedro de la Rosa	BMW Sauber	28 laps/hydraulics	1	1m56.237s	14
R	Bruno Senna	HRT	17 laps/overheating	0	2m03.24s	23
R	Timo Glock	Virgin	16 laps/gearbox	0	1m59.728s	19
R	Vitaly Petrov	Renault	13 laps/suspension	0	1m56.619s	17
R	Kamui Kobayashi	BMW Sauber	11 laps/hydraulics	0	1m56.27s	16
R	Lucas di Grassi	Virgin	2 laps/hydraulics	0	2m00.587s	22
R	Karun Chandhok	HRT	1 lap/spun off	0	2m04.904s	24

FASTEST LAP: ALONSO, 1M58.287S, 119.120MPH/191.706PH ON LAP 45 • RACE LEADERS: VETTEL 1-33; ALONSO 34-49

Alonso had a dream result to start his Ferrari career, but it should have been Vettel's race.

the recommendations of F1's Overtaking Working Group had failed. Secondly, the new teams - Lotus, Virgin Racing and HRT - were far from the pace and were unlikely to catch the slowest of the established teams during their maiden season. The best-placed of their finishers was Heikki Kovalainen in 15th place for Lotus.

AUSTRALIAN GP

After the dull opening race in Bahrain, a sprinkle of drizzle before the start in Melbourne tilted this race to the other end of the spectrum with overtaking galore. Jenson Button triumphed for McLaren, helped by Sebastian Vettel's Red Bull suffering a loose wheel.

This race ought to have been a Red Bull Racing benefit, as Sebastian Vettel and Mark Webber lined up on the front row. What threatened to make it more difficult was the arrival of light rain as the cars assembled on the grid. Intermediate tyres were fitted, but an extra element had been added to the mix.

Vettel had no trouble powering away from pole, but Webber got too much wheelspin, as did Fernando Alonso from third. Best start of all came from Felipe Massa, from fifth on the grid, and he rocketed past Jenson Button into second place before Turn 1.

It was there that Alonso's race came unstuck, as he turned into Button and was pitched into a spin. The order was shuffled as drivers sought to avoid him and Michael Schumacher failed, his Mercedes receiving a clout that required a pit visit.

What triggered the safety car, though, happened further around the lap when Kamui Kobayashi lost his Sauber's nose against Sebastien Buemi's Toro Rosso, into Turn 6, then took out Buemi and Nico Hulkenberg's Williams as they turned in.

As racing resumed, Button used his special feel for conditions by deciding to pit on lap 6 for slicks. Others thought that he was mad, and so did he to start with as he slid off at Turn 3. However, his pace picked up and two laps later most followed his lead. When all was done and Webber had been made to wait an extra lap so that Red Bull didn't have both its cars in together, Vettel still led, but Button was up to second. Webber, on the other hand, had fallen to fifth when he emerged from the pits, but slid off at Turn 1 and Massa dived by.

Vettel's better fortune lasted only until lap 26, when his front left wheel worked loose, so likely victory turned to nothing. Button assumed a lead he wouldn't lose.

Another driver displaying excellent touch was Robert Kubica who jumped Massa during the scramble into the pits.

Smiles all round as Robert Kubica, Jenson Button and Felipe Massa celebrate on the podium.

MELBOURNE ROUND 2

Date: **28 March 2010**

Laps: **58** • Distance: **191.11 miles/307.562km** • Weather: **Damp with drizzle**

Pos	Driver	Team	Result	Stops	Qualifying Time	Grid
1	**Jenson Button**	McLaren	1h33m36.531s	1	1m24.675s	4
2	**Robert Kubica**	Renault	1h33m48.565s	1	1m25.372s	9
3	**Felipe Massa**	Ferrari	1h33m51.019s	1	1m24.837s	5
4	**Fernando Alonso**	Ferrari	1h33m52.835s	1	1m24.111s	3
5	**Nico Rosberg**	Mercedes	1h33m53.214s	2	1m24.884s	6
6	**Lewis Hamilton**	McLaren	1h34m06.429s	2	1m25.184s	11
7	**Vitantonio Liuzzi**	Force India	1h34m36.378s	1	1m25.743s	13
8	**Rubens Barrichello**	Williams	1h34m37.067s	2	1m25.217s	8
9	**Mark Webber**	Red Bull	1h34m43.85s	3	1m24.035s	2
10	**Michael Schumacher**	Mercedes	1h34m45.922s	3	1m24.927s	9
11	**Jaime Alguersuari**	Toro Rosso	1h34m47.832s	2	1m26.089s	17
12	**Pedro de la Rosa**	BMW Sauber	1h34m50.615s	1	1m25.747s	14
13	**Heikki Kovalainen**	Lotus	56 laps	1	1m28.797s	19
14	**Karun Chandhok**	HRT	53 laps	2	1m30.613s	22
R	**Timo Glock**	Virgin	41 laps/suspension	1	1m29.592s	23*
R	**Lucas di Grassi**	Virgin	26 laps/hydraulics	2	1m30.185s	24*
R	**Sebastian Vettel**	Red Bull	25 laps/wheel	1	1m23.919s	1
R	**Adrian Sutil**	Force India	9 laps/engine	0	1m26.036s	10
R	**Vitaly Petrov**	Renault	9 laps/spun off	1	1m26.471s	18
R	**Bruno Senna**	HRT	4 laps/hydraulics	0	1m30.185s	21
R	**Sebastien Buemi**	Toro Rosso	0 laps/accident	0	1m25.638s	12
R	**Nico Hulkenberg**	Williams	0 laps/accident	0	1m25.748s	15
R	**Kamui Kobayashi**	BMW Sauber	0 laps/accident	0	1m25.777s	16
NS	**Jarno Trulli**	Lotus	0 laps/hydraulics	0	1m29.111s	20

FASTEST LAP: WEBBER, 1M28.358S, 134.282MPH/216.106KPH ON LAP 47 • RACE LEADERS: VETTEL 1-8, 11-25; WEBBER 9-10; BUTTON 26-58
* STARTED FROM THE PIT LANE

Despite having the pace to qualify only ninth, he held on to finish second. Hamilton caught him, but McLaren brought him in for fresh tyres, a decision that Lewis thought was wrong. His subsequent charge back to challenge Alonso for fourth was scuppered when Webber, right on his tail, slid into him and pitched both off the track.

This was a grand prix that was won on the run down to the first corner on the opening lap as Sebastian Vettel outdragged his pole-sitting team-mate Mark Webber and then stayed ahead to lead home a Red Bull Racing one-two as Nico Rosberg proved the best of the rest.

Rain or the imminent arrival of rain is an ever-present factor at Sepang and so it shaped the Malaysian GP. Such was Mark Webber's pace that he would have claimed pole come what may. Indeed, his margin over second fastest qualifier, Nico Rosberg, was 1.3 seconds in the wet. However, he didn't have to face a challenge from McLaren's and Ferrari's drivers, as their teams left them in the pits in the first qualifying session instead of sending them out in the wet conditions to set a "banker" lap. Their decision to wait for it to dry, which it didn't, left Jenson Button 17th, Fernando Alonso 19th, Lewis Hamilton 20th and Felipe Massa 21st.

So it was that Webber started with few potential frontrunners around him. Yet it was Sebastian Vettel, starting from third, who made the best start. He passed Rosberg, then got a tow from Webber to Turn 1, where he dived down the inside into the lead. Webber said afterwards that he hadn't seen him in his blindspot and there was sympathy as the sidepod-mounted mirrors, later banned, offered a limited view.

Once behind, and with no sign of rain approaching, Webber realised that his excellent qualifying lap was to count for nothing. With no refuelling and just a simple tyre stop ahead of him, the Australian knew that the race would belong to his team-mate. Indeed, Vettel didn't put a foot wrong, and so it was, with Webber snapping around in his wake and setting the race's fastest lap late on just to prove what could have been.

Rosberg came in in third, for Mercedes GP's first podium finish, while Robert Kubica showed again that he will collect any points on offer, finishing fourth for Renault.

Adrian Sutil collected a good result for Force India, fifth, but had to survive a great deal of pressure from Hamilton, who was the most effective of the poorly qualified quartet. However, Hamilton's McLaren's tyres were past their best by the time he caught Sutil and so he had to settle for sixth.

SEPANG ROUND 3

Date: **4 April 2010**

Laps: **56** • Distance: **192.864 miles/310.385km** • Weather: **Hot and sunny**

Pos	Driver	Team	Result	Stops	Qualifying Time	Grid
1	Sebastian Vettel	Red Bull	1h33m48.412s	1	1m50.789s	3
2	Mark Webber	Red Bull	1h33m53.261s	1	1m49.327s	1
3	Nico Rosberg	Mercedes	1h34m01.916s	1	1m50.673s	2
4	Robert Kubica	Renault	1h34m07.001s	1	1m51.051s	6
5	Adrian Sutil	Force India	1h34m09.471s	1	1m50.914s	4
6	Lewis Hamilton	McLaren	1h34m11.883s	1	1m53.05s	20
7	Felipe Massa	Ferrari	1h34m15.48s	1	1m53.283s	21
8	Jenson Button	McLaren	1h34m26.33s	1	No time	17
9	Jaime Alguersuari	Toro Rosso	1h34m59.014s	1	1m49.464s	14
10	Nico Hulkenberg	Williams	1h35m01.811s	1	1m51.001s	5
11	Sebastien Buemi	Toro Rosso	1h35m07.35s	2	1m49.207s	13
12	Rubens Barrichello	Williams	55 laps	2	1m51.511s	7
13	Fernando Alonso	Ferrari	54 laps/engine	1	1m53.044s	19
14	Lucas di Grassi	Virgin	53 laps	1	1m59.977s	24
15	Karun Chandhok	HRT	53 laps	1	1m56.299s	22
16	Bruno Senna	HRT	52 laps	1	1m57.269s	23
17	Jarno Trulli	Lotus	51 laps	1	1m52.884s	18
NC	Heikki Kovalainen	Lotus	46 laps	2	1m52.27s	15
R	Vitaly Petrov	Renault	32 laps/gearbox	1	1m48.76s	11
R	Vitantonio Liuzzi	Force India	12 laps/throttle	0	1m52.254s	10
R	Michael Schumacher	Mercedes	9 laps/wheelnut	0	1m51.717s	8
R	Kamui Kobayashi	BMW Sauber	8 laps/engine	0	1m51.767s	9
R	Timo Glock	Virgin	2 laps/spun off	0	1m52.52s	16
NS	Pedro de la Rosa	BMW Sauber	0 laps/engine	–	1m48.771s	12

FASTEST LAP: WEBBER, 1M37.054S, 127.763MPH/205.615KPH ON LAP 53 • RACE LEADERS: VETTEL 1–22, 25–56; WEBBER 23–24

Red Bulls to the fore as Sebastian Vettel dives past Mark Webber to take the lead into Turn 1.

Massa advanced to seventh, Button to eighth and Alonso to ninth, but the Spaniard's engine failed with two laps to go and so, some way behind, Jaime Alguersuari and Nico Hulkenberg completed the scorers in ninth and 10th, with Lucas di Grassi the best-placed finisher from the three new teams, in 14th place.

If you had wanted to pick a driver to take control of a race held in mixed weather conditions in 2010, that driver would have been Jenson Button and the 2009 World Champion did it again in Shanghai to make it two wins from four starts to mark the beginning of his new life at McLaren.

With two Red Bulls on the front row and rain due on race day, everyone expected a repeat of their domination of the race in similar conditions in 2009. Yet, that wasn't what happened. Indeed, both pole-starter Sebastian Vettel and Mark Webber left China with long faces, having slid back to sixth and eighth places respectively.

Instead, Jenson Button and Lewis Hamilton collected a one-two for McLaren.

There had been drizzle before the start, but not the heavy rain that had left the track flooded 12 months earlier. However, Fernando Alonso appeared to get perfect traction at the start and vaulted from third to go second behind Vettel, then passed him as well as they powered from the grid. His start had been too soon, though, and the Spaniard would be hit with a drive-through penalty and his aspirations dented.

Webber also nipped by Vettel, but all were slowed when the safety car was brought out by an accident between Vitantonio Liuzzi, Sebastien Buemi and Kamui Kobayashi.

Most teams took this as an opportunity to change from slicks to intermediates, but Webber slid into his jack, costing both himself and Vettel, who was queuing behind him. So Felipe Massa, Michael Schumacher and Lewis Hamilton all gained places.

By staying out, Nico Rosberg led, followed by Jenson Button and then the Renaults. Their decision to stay out looked all the better when those who'd had inters fitted pitted again for slicks a lap or two later.

Button hunted down Rosberg and took the lead on lap 19, when rain started to fall and Rosberg made a mistake going onto the back straight, allowing Button to get a run on the approach to the hairpin. Then they both pitted for inters.

All this pair's hard work was undone when the safety car came out for a second time after Jaime Alguersuari clipped Bruno Senna's HRT. Alonso was laughing the most, as this wiped out much of the time he had

Button leads Hamilton and Massa early on, but rose to first by staying out when others pitted.

SHANGHAI ROUND 4

Date: **18 April 2010**

Laps: **56** • Distance: **189.84 miles/305.518km** • Weather: **Overcast then rain**

Pos	Driver	Team	Result	Stops	Qualifying Time	Grid
1	**Jenson Button**	McLaren	1h46m42.163s	2	1m34.979s	5
2	**Lewis Hamilton**	McLaren	1h46m43.693s	4	1m35.034s	6
3	**Nico Rosberg**	Mercedes	1h46m51.647s	2	1m34.923s	4
4	**Fernando Alonso**	Ferrari	1h46m54.032s	5	1m34.913s	3
5	**Robert Kubica**	Renault	1h47m04.376s	2	1m35.364s	8
6	**Sebastian Vettel**	Red Bull	1h47m15.473s	4	1m34.558s	1
7	**Vitaly Petrov**	Renault	1h47m29.763s	2	1m36.311s	14
8	**Mark Webber**	Red Bull	1h47m34.335s	4	1m34.806s	2
9	**Felipe Massa**	Ferrari	1h47m39.959s	4	1m35.18s	7
10	**Michael Schumacher**	Mercedes	1h47m43.912s	4	1m35.646s	9
11	**Adrian Sutil**	Force India	1h47m45.037s	4	1m35.963s	10
12	**Rubens Barrichello**	Williams	1h47m45.828s	4	1m35.748s	11
13	**Jaime Alguersuari**	Toro Rosso	1h47m53.579s	6	1m36.047s	12
14	**Heikki Kovalainen**	Lotus	55 laps	2	1m39.52s	21
15	**Nico Hulkenberg**	Williams	55 laps	6	1m36.647s	14
16	**Bruno Senna**	HRT	54 laps	4	1m40.469s	23
17	**Karun Chandhok**	HRT	52 laps	4	1m40.578s	24*
R	**Jarno Trulli**	Lotus	26 laps/hydraulics	4	1m39.399s	20
R	**Lucas di Grassi**	Virgin	8 laps/clutch	0	1m39.783s	22*
R	**Pedro de la Rosa**	BMW Sauber	7 laps/engine	0	1m37.02s	17
R	**Sebastien Buemi**	Toro Rosso	0 laps/accident	0	1m36.149s	13
R	**Kamui Kobayashi**	BMW Sauber	0 laps/accident	0	1m36.422s	15
R	**Vitantonio Liuzzi**	Force India	0 laps/accident	0	1m37.161s	18
NS	**Timo Glock**	Virgin	0 laps/engine	-	1m39.278s	19*

FASTEST LAP: HAMILTON, 1M42.061S, 119.478MPH/192.282PH ON LAP 13 • **RACE LEADERS:** ALONSO 1-2; ROSBERG 3-18; BUTTON 19-56
* •STARTED FROM THE PIT LANE

lost with his drive-through penalty.

After the field was released again, Button broke clear and the man on the move was Hamilton, who made it past Rosberg to claim second at the pit stops. Rosberg held on for third, with Alonso relieved to have got back up to fourth. As ever, Kubica did all he could for Renault, enjoying beating both Red Bulls.

SPANISH GP

Red Bull Racing's Mark Webber produced a near-perfect performance to claim the first win of his 2010 campaign, having used pole position to good effect, while Lewis Hamilton was denied second place by wheel failure with two laps to go, promoting Fernando Alonso to second.

Pole position didn't bring Mark Webber any joy in Malaysia, but an FIA-enforced change in the positioning of cars' mirrors offered him greater protection from a surprise attack into the first corner. However, he didn't need this and made a good enough start to be in front by the time the field reached the right-hander. Thereafter, the race was his.

Getting in front on the Circuit de Catalunya invariably means staying in front, as passing is so difficult around this twisting circuit. And so it proved. The Red Bulls' margin of superiority in qualifying was so vast – Webber was 0.834s faster around the lap than Lewis Hamilton's third-placed McLaren – that his escape at the front wasn't a surprise.

Vettel tucked in behind, but Hamilton was close enough when they came in for their one planned pit stop to take advantage of a slow stop for Vettel when a sticking front right delayed the German. A lap later, Hamilton's stop was also flawed, but his crew had done just enough for him to emerge fractionally ahead of Vettel in second place. Webber was 9s clear.

At the same time, Jenson Button lost a position to Michael Schumacher when a dragging clutch delayed him and caused a mechanic to drop a wheel nut. He came out just in front, but Schumacher, who stopped a lap earlier, motored past into Turn 1 then delayed him for the remainder of the race, all 50 laps of it.

As Webber continued in peerless form at the front, Vettel's slim hopes of retaking second from Hamilton were wrecked when a braking problem hit his RB6 and he ran through a gravel trap. This necessitated a second pit stop for investigation, on lap 54, but the team sent him back out again, now in fourth place behind Fernando Alonso.

However, Alonso would get to climb one step higher on the podium and Vettel would actually get onto the podium when, with two laps to go, Hamilton's MP4-25 suffered

BARCELONA ROUND 5
Date: **9 May 2010**

Laps: **66** • Distance: **189.75 miles/305.374km** • Weather: **Dry and bright**

Pos	Driver	Team	Result	Stops	Qualifying Time	Grid
1	**Mark Webber**	Red Bull	1h35m44.101s	1	1m19.995s	1
2	**Fernando Alonso**	Ferrari	1h36m08.166s	1	1m20.937s	4
3	**Sebastian Vettel**	Red Bull	1h36m35.439s	2	1m20.101s	2
4	**Michael Schumacher**	Mercedes	1h36m46.296s	1	1m21.294s	6
5	**Jenson Button**	McLaren	1h36m47.829s	1	1m20.991s	5
6	**Felipe Massa**	Ferrari	1h36m49.868s	1	1m21.585s	9
7	**Adrian Sutil**	Force India	1h36m57.042s	1	1m21.985s	11
8	**Robert Kubica**	Renault	1h36m57.778s	1	1m21.353s	7
9	**Rubens Barrichello**	Williams	65 laps	1	1m23.125s	17
10	**Jaime Alguersuari**	Toro Rosso	65 laps	1	1m22.207s	15
11	**Vitaly Petrov**	Renault	65 laps	1	1m22.139s	19*
12	**Kamui Kobayashi**	BMW Sauber	65 laps	1	1m21.984s	10
13	**Nico Rosberg**	Mercedes	65 laps	2	1m21.408s	8
14	**Lewis Hamilton**	McLaren	64 laps	1	1m20.829s	3
15	**Vitantonio Liuzzi**	Force India	64 laps	1	1m22.854s	16
16	**Nico Hulkenberg**	Williams	64 laps	2	1m22.131s	13
17	**Jarno Trulli**	Lotus	63 laps	1	1m24.674s	18
18	**Timo Glock**	Virgin	63 laps	1	1m25.475s	22*
19	**Lucas di Grassi**	Virgin	62 laps	1	1m25.556s	23*
R	**Sebastien Buemi**	Toro Rosso	42 laps/hydraulics	2	1m22.191s	14
R	**Karun Chandhok**	HRT	27 laps/suspension	1	1m26.75s	24*
R	**Pedro de la Rosa**	BMW Sauber	18 laps/accident damage	1	1m22.026s	12
R	**Bruno Senna**	HRT	0 laps/accident	0	1m27.122s	21
NS	**Heikki Kovalainen**	Lotus	0 laps/gearbox	0	24.748s	20

FASTEST LAP: HAMILTON, 1M24.357S, 123.444MPH/198.664PH ON LAP 59 • RACE LEADER: WEBBER 1–66
* 5-PLACE GRID PENALTY

Mark Webber took the lead at the start, but Sebastian Vettel wasn't able to remain second!

wheel failure and pitched him into the wall in Turn 3.

The other drivers to gain extra points because of this included his own team-mate Button, who rose to fifth, even though still stuck behind Schumacher, with Felipe Massa following close behind, with Adrian Sutil and Robert Kubica the other unlapped runners.

MONACO GP

In winning the Monaco GP from pole position, Mark Webber not only displayed consummate skill with his dominant victory but also laid down a clear marker to his Red Bull Racing team-mate Sebastian Vettel in their battle for supremacy.

With his second win in a row, Mark Webber moved into equal first position in the World Championship with team-mate Sebastian Vettel. However, the intensity of the Australian's post-race celebrations, as he somersaulted into the Red Bull swimming pool, revealed just how much this meant to him, how he believed it proved that he was now the main man in the team.

That the team then extended Webber's contract by a year to include 2011 extinguished rumours that he might lose his ride to Kimi Raikkonen as the Finn was discussing a return from rallying.

The hardest job at Monaco is to land pole and Webber stuck his RB6 on that vital grid slot by 0.294 seconds, not from Vettel but from Renault's Robert Kubica after Vettel slipped up.

Vettel exonerated himself by getting past Kubica before they reached St Devote. Felipe Massa slotted into fourth ahead of Lewis Hamilton, with Rubens Barrichello gaining three places to run sixth. Jenson Button would pull off soon afterwards, his engine failing because a radiator cover had been left on.

The car that led onto lap 2 wasn't Webber's, though, but the safety car, as debris had been strewn in the tunnel when Nico Hulkenberg dumped his Williams into the barriers after incurring wing damage.

Vettel might have had a chance of taking a dive at Webber when the safety car withdrew, but Webber judged his acceleration to perfection, pulling clear.

Hamilton was the first frontrunner to make his pit stop. This dropped him to 15th, but he'd work his way back to the position from which he'd pitted: fifth.

Webber made his pit stop six laps later, rejoining still in the lead, which is where he stayed, enduring three further safety car periods to take his second win of 2010.

In fact, the final safety car period took the drivers to the end of the race, this being triggered after Jarno Trulli crashed over the

Jarno Trulli managed to drive his Lotus over Karun Chandhok's HRT at the end of the race.

MONACO ROUND 6
Date: **16 May 2010**

Laps: **78** • Distance: **161.85 miles/260.489km** • Weather: **Sunny and dry**

Pos	Driver	Team	Result	Stops	Qualifying Time	Grid
1	Mark Webber	Red Bull	1h50m13.355s	1	1m13.826s	1
2	Sebastian Vettel	Red Bull	1h50m13.803s	1	1m14.227s	3
3	Robert Kubica	Renault	1h50m15.03s	1	1m14.12s	2
4	Felipe Massa	Ferrari	1h50m16.021s	1	1m14.283s	4
5	Lewis Hamilton	McLaren	1h50m17.728s	1	1m14.432s	5
6	Fernando Alonso	Ferrari	1h50m19.696s	1	No time	24*
7	Nico Rosberg	Mercedes	1h50m20.006s	1	1m14.544s	6
8	Adrian Sutil	Force India	1h50m20.325s	1	1m15.318s	12
9	Vitantonio Liuzzi	Force India	1h50m20.66s	1	1m15.17s	10
10	Sebastien Buemi	Toro Rosso	1h50m21.554s	1	1m15.413s	13
11	Jaime Alguersuari	Toro Rosso	1h50m22.49s	1	1m16.176s	17
12	Michael Schumacher	Mercedes	1h50m39.067s**	1	1m14.59s	7
13	Vitaly Petrov	Renault	73 laps/suspension	2	1m15.576s	14
14	Karun Chandhok	HRT	70 laps/accident	1	1m19.559s	23
15	Jarno Trulli	Lotus	70 laps/accident	1	1m17.134s	19
R	Heikki Kovalainen	Lotus	58 laps/steering	1	1m17.094s	18
R	Bruno Senna	HRT	58 laps/hydraulics	1	1m18.509s	22
R	Rubens Barrichello	Williams	30 laps/suspension	1	1m14.91s	9
R	Kamui Kobayashi	BMW Sauber	26 laps/gearbox	0	1m15.922s	16
R	Lucas di Grassi	Virgin	26 laps/wheel	1	1m17.864s	21
R	Timo Glock	Virgin	22 laps/suspension	0	1m17.377s	20
R	Pedro de la Rosa	BMW Sauber	21 laps/hydraulics	0	1m15.692s	15
R	Jenson Button	McLaren	2 laps/engine fire	0	1m14.637s	8
R	Nico Hulkenberg	Williams	0 laps/wing failure	0	1m15.317s	11

FASTEST LAP: VETTEL 1M15.192S 99.368MPH/159.918PH ON LAP 71 • **RACE LEADER:** WEBBER 1–78
*STARTED FROM THE PIT LANE ** INCLUDING 20S PENALTY

top of Karun Chandhok's HRT, but the drama didn't stop there, as the Mercedes team decided that as the safety car had withdrawn, so as not to be in shot across the finish line, that the race was "go" again for the final two corners. Michael Schumacher pounced and demoted Fernando Alonso, but he was given a 20s penalty for his initiative.

Losing a team one-two finish through mechanical failure would be disappointing enough, but to lose it because a driver clashed with a team-mate has to top it all. And so Red Bull Racing handed the mantle to a much-improved McLaren, with Lewis Hamilton taking the win.

Round seven resulted in pole number seven for Red Bull, and Mark Webber's third in a row. However, McLaren had new front and rear wings and Lewis Hamilton joined Webber on the front row after lapping just 0.138s slower. Sebastian Vettel and Jenson Button filled the second row ahead of the Mercedes after Vettel was hit by a roll bar problem.

Webber took the lead, while Vettel got into second into Turn 1, only to be demoted as Hamilton fought back out of Turn 2. Michael Schumacher passed Button but, mercifully for the reigning World Champion, he got back ahead into Turn 12, preventing himself from losing touch with the lead battle.

The McLarens continued to mix it with the Red Bulls up to the pit stops, when Vettel was the first of the fast four to call in, and this was enough to help him jump Hamilton for second when the Englishman pitted the following lap, at the same time as Webber. Button stayed out longer, thus taking the lead, but reverted to fourth when he rejoined.

Webber was told on lap 38 to turn his engine down as consumption had been more than expected. Vettel knew this was his chance, and attacked. A lap later, Webber's race engineer was asked to tell Webber to let Vettel by as Hamilton was too close for comfort. The message was never sent on.

Then, on lap 40, Vettel went around the outside of Webber through the flick at Turn 11 and kept coming across. Webber didn't know he was supposed to cede and probably wouldn't have agreed, so didn't make way. The two cars clashed and Vettel's was too damaged to continue, leaving him to gesture that Webber was crazy.

Then, amazingly, we had a near-repeat scenario between the McLarens as both were told to back their engines off and Button dived past Hamilton in Turn 13. Hamilton got the place back into Turn 1 but, importantly, they respected each other's space and lived to finish one and two.

ISTANBUL ROUND 7

Date: **30 May 2010**

Laps: **58** • Distance: **192.386 miles/309.616km** • Weather: **Sunny and dry**

Pos	Driver	Team	Result	Stops	Qualifying Time	Grid
1	Lewis Hamilton	McLaren	1h28m47.62s	1	1m26.433s	2
2	Jenson Button	McLaren	1h28m50.265s	1	1m26.781s	4
3	Mark Webber	Red Bull	1h29m11.905s	2	1m26.295s	1
4	Michael Schumacher	Mercedes	1h29m18.73s	1	1m26.857s	5
5	Nico Rosberg	Mercedes	1h29m19.886s	1	1m26.952s	6
6	Robert Kubica	Renault	1h29m20.444s	1	1m27.039s	7
7	Felipe Massa	Ferrari	1h29m24.255s	1	1m27.082s	8
8	Fernando Alonso	Ferrari	1h29m34.164s	1	1m27.612s	12
9	Adrian Sutil	Force India	1h29m36.649s	1	1m27.525s	11
10	Kamui Kobayashi	BMW Sauber	1h29m53.27s	1	1m28.122s	10
11	Pedro de la Rosa	BMW Sauber	1h29m53.564s	1	1m27.879s	13
12	Jaime Alguersuari	Toro Rosso	1h29m55.42s	2	1m28.54s	16
13	Vitantonio Liuzzi	Force India	57 laps	1	1m28.958s	18
14	Rubens Barrichello	Williams	57 laps	1	1m28.392s	15
15	Vitaly Petrov	Renault	57 laps	2	1m27.43s	9
16	Sebastien Buemi	Toro Rosso	57 laps	2	1m28.273s	14
17	Nico Hulkenberg	Williams	57 laps	2	1m28.841s	17
18	Timo Glock	Virgin	55 laps	1	1m30.744s	21
19	Lucas di Grassi	Virgin	55 laps	1	1m31.989s	23*
20	Karun Chandhok	HRT	52 laps	1	1m32.06s	24
R	Bruno Senna	HRT	46 laps/fuel pressure	1	1m31.266s	22
R	Sebastian Vettel	Red Bull	39 laps/accident	1	1m26.76s	3
R	Heikki Kovalainen	Lotus	33 laps/hydraulics	0	1m30.519s	20
R	Jarno Trulli	Lotus	32 laps/hydraulics	0	1m30.237s	19

FASTEST LAP: PETROV, 1M29.165S, 133.924MPH/215.530PH ON LAP 57 • RACE LEADERS: WEBBER 1-15, 18-39; BUTTON 16-17, 48; HAMILTON 40-47, 49-58 * STARTED FROM THE PIT LANE

Lewis Hamilton was close to the Red Bulls, but their fratricide turned a podium into a win.

After pitting for a new nose, Webber salvaged third place. But one thing remains clear in this complex encounter and that is Red Bull Racing handled it poorly by attempting to blame Webber, showing an oft-suspected bias to Vettel, and would feel the waves within the team for the next month and more.

CANADIAN GP

Lewis Hamilton enjoyed winning in Turkey so much that he did it again in Montreal. Only this time he didn't need any help from warring Red Bull Racing drivers and earned the result through superior craft and strategy. Jenson Button made it a doubly good day for McLaren.

For the first time in 2010, Red Bull didn't claim pole. This time, it was Lewis Hamilton. The Red Bulls should have been next up, despite setting their times on the medium tyre, but a grid penalty for changing the gearbox dropped Mark Webber to seventh, promoting Sebastian Vettel, Fernando Alonso, Jenson Button, a galvanised Vitantonio Liuzzi and Felipe Massa.

There was contact at Turns 2 and 3, as Liuzzi was hit by Massa, thus wasting his best grid position, as he had to pit for a new nose. Behind them, Vitaly Petrov assaulted Pedro de la Rosa's Sauber,

Vettel was soon closing in on Hamilton, while Webber, who gained two places on lap 1, turned fifth place into fourth on lap 5 by passing Button into Turn 8.

Button's exceptional feel convinced him that the super-soft tyres weren't going to last and was first in for mediums. A lap later, just as Vettel shaped to pass him, Hamilton pitted to do the same. Alonso pitted too, but had a faster stop and was on the right as they left the pits, moving ahead into Turn 3.

Having started on mediums, the Red Bulls raced on in first and second, with Robert Kubica staying out and rising to third. Unexpectedly, their pace started to slow and Alonso and the McLarens were on the move, picking off the cars ahead.

Red Bull called Webber in on lap 13 for more mediums and Vettel a lap later for his super-softs, wisely splitting their strategy. Toro Rosso's Sebastien Buemi led for a lap, thanks to being among the last to pit, but then Hamilton took over, having just passed Alonso into the final corner after Buemi had delayed the Spaniard out of the far hairpin.

Things were starting to look good for McLaren, with Button closing in on the Hamilton-Alonso battle, typically saving his tyres as they duelled, especially as the Red Bulls appeared to have no answer.

Then, just before his second stop, Alonso was blocked by Jarno Trulli and lost the

Lewis Hamilton leads into Turn 1, with trouble due to strike before the field reached Turn 2.

MONTREAL ROUND 8

Date: **13 June 2010**

Laps: **70** • Distance: **189.7 miles/305.293km** • Weather: **Sunny and dry**

Pos	Driver	Team	Result	Stops	Qualifying Time	Grid
1	**Lewis Hamilton**	McLaren	1h33m53.456s	2	1m15.105s	1
2	**Jenson Button**	McLaren	1h33m55.71s	2	1m15.52s	4
3	**Fernando Alonso**	Ferrari	1h34m02.67s	2	1m15.435s	3
4	**Sebastian Vettel**	Red Bull	1h34m31.273s	2	1m15.42s	2
5	**Mark Webber**	Red Bull	1h34m32.747s	2	1m15.373s	7*
6	**Nico Rosberg**	Mercedes	1h34m49.540s	2	1m16.071s	10
7	**Robert Kubica**	Renault	1h34m50.756s	3	1m15.715s	8
8	**Sebastien Buemi**	Toro Rosso	69 laps	3	1m16.928s	15
9	**Vitantonio Liuzzi**	Force India	69 laps	2	1m15.648s	5
10	**Adrian Sutil**	Force India	69 laps	2	1m15.881s	9
11	**Michael Schumacher**	Mercedes	69 laps	3	1m16.492s	13
12	**Jaime Alguersuari**	Toro Rosso	69 laps	3	117.029s	16
13	**Nico Hulkenberg**	Williams	69 laps	3	1m16.438s	12
14	**Rubens Barrichello**	Williams	69 laps	3	1m16.434s	11
15	**Felipe Massa**	Ferrari	69 laps	4	1m15.688s	6
16	**Heikki Kovalainen**	Lotus	68 laps	3	1m18.237s	19
17	**Vitaly Petrov**	Renault	68 laps	2	1m16.844s	14
18	**Karun Chandhok**	HRT	66 laps	2	1m27.757s	24*
19	**Lucas di Grassi**	Virgin	65 laps	3	1m19.675s	23
R	**Timo Glock**	Virgin	50 laps/crash damage	4	1m18.941s	21
R	**Jarno Trulli**	Lotus	42 laps/vibration	4	1m18.698s	20
R	**Pedro de la Rosa**	BMW Sauber	30 laps/engine	1	1m17.384s	17
R	**Bruno Senna**	HRT	13 laps/gearbox	0	1m19.484s	22
R	**Kamui Kobayashi**	BMW Sauber	1 lap/spun off	0	1m18.019s	18

FASTEST LAP: KUBICA, 1M16.972S, 126.738MPH/203.965PH ON LAP 67 • RACE LEADERS: HAMILTON 1-6, 15-25, 50-70; VETTEL 7-13; BUEMI 14; ALONSO 26-27; WEBBER 28-49 * 5-PLACE GRID PENALTY

chance to swap places with Hamilton, who'd pitted two laps earlier.

Webber led from lap 28 to 49, but was fifth on rejoining, with Hamilton leading from Alonso, Button and Vettel. This order changed on lap 56, when Karun Chandhok blocked Alonso at Turn 6 and Button moved into second place at Turn 8.

EUROPEAN GP

Red Bull Racing bounced back on the streets of Valencia, with Sebastian Vettel holding off Lewis Hamilton to win, but it wasn't all glory as team-mate Mark Webber had been extremely lucky to walk away from an aerial accident when he clashed with Heikki Kovalainen's Lotus.

Taking his first pole since April was a fillip for Sebastian Vettel, especially as overtaking is all but unheard of at this harbourside track.

Behind Vettel, Mark Webber was slow away and Lewis Hamilton pounced. He then dived into Turn 2, but Vettel defended the position and there was a touch that damaged the McLaren's front wing.

Fernando Alonso had also got past Webber and he looked at trying to demote Hamilton to third, but was rebuffed. Webber lost further ground as Felipe Massa passed him, but it went from bad to worse, as running wide had left his tyres dirty and Jenson Button and Robert Kubica passed him at Turn 8, with Rubens Barrichello also seizing the moment and Williams team-mate Nico Hulkenberg taking advantage of the Australian losing momentum. Amazingly, Webber's day would only get worse...

The team brought Webber in early for his pit stop, but even this delayed him as his RB6 had a sticking wheel and he came back out in 19th. Then, attempting to pass Heikki Kovalainen, he was caught out when the Lotus driver braked earlier than expected for Turn 12 and he hit its rear, sending Webber skywards. After flipping, then landing upside down, the car righted itself and slid up an escape road. Concern turned to relief when Webber climbed out.

The deployment of the safety car was to prove crucial. A light comes on the dashboard, but it was too late for Vettel, Hamilton and Alonso to dive for the pits. It could and should have handed the advantage to Massa, but he didn't notice it, and so Kubica and Button were the first in.

The arrival of the safety car from the pit exit was also crucial, as Vettel was able to get past and keep going at full racing speed. Hamilton ought to have been able to follow suit, but he hesitated, then went back on the throttle just too late, and his passing of the safety car was adjudged illegal. He was hit with a drive-through penalty.

VALENCIA ROUND 9

Date: **27 June 2010**

Laps: **57** • Distance: **191.919 miles/308.864km** • Weather: **Sunny and dry**

Pos	Driver	Team	Result	Stops	Qualifying Time	Grid
1	**Sebastian Vettel**	Red Bull	1h40m29.571s	1	1m37.587s	1
2	**Lewis Hamilton**	McLaren	1h40m34.613s	2	1m37.969s	3
3	**Jenson Button**	McLaren	1h40m42.229s	1	1m38.210s	7
4	**Rubens Barrichello**	Williams	1h40m55.198s	1	1m38.428s	9
5	**Robert Kubica**	Renault	1h40m56.693s	1	1m38.137s	6
6	**Adrian Sutil**	Force India	1h40m59.739s	1	1m38.851s	13
7	**Kamui Kobayashi**	BMW Sauber	1h41m00.536s	1	1m39.343s	18
8	**Fernando Alonso**	Ferrari	1h41m02.380s	1	1m38.075s	4
9	**Sebastien Buemi**	Toro Rosso	1h41m05.870s	1	1m38.586s	11
10	**Nico Rosberg**	Mercedes	1h41m13.953s	1	1m38.627s	12
11	**Felipe Massa**	Ferrari	1h41m16.192s	1	1m38.127s	5
12	**Pedro de la Rosa**	BMW Sauber	1h41m16.985s	1	1m39.264s	16
13	**Jaime Alguersuari**	Toro Rosso	1m41m17.810s	1	1m39.458s	17
14	**Vitaly Petrov**	Renault	1h41m17.858s	1	1m38.523s	10
15	**Michael Schumacher**	Mercedes	1h41m18.397s	3	1m39.234s	15
16	**Vitantonio Liuzzi**	Force India	1h41m20.461s	1	1m38.884s	14
17	**Lucas di Grassi**	Virgin	56 laps	1	1m42.086s	21
18	**Karun Chandhok**	HRT	56 laps	1	1m42.600s	23
19	**Timo Glock**	Virgin	55 laps**	2	1m42.140s	22
20	**Bruno Senna**	HRT	55 laps	2	1m42.851s	24
21	**Jarno Trulli**	Lotus	53 laps	2	1m40.658s	19
R	**Nico Hulkenberg**	Williams	49 laps*/exhaust	1	1m38.428s	8
R	**Heikki Kovalainen**	Lotus	8 laps/accident	0	1m40.882s	20
R	**Mark Webber**	Red Bull	8 laps/accident	1	1m37.662s	2

FASTEST LAP: BUTTON, 1M38.766S, 122.740MPH/197.531PH ON LAP 54 • RACE LEADERS: VETTEL 1-57
** POST-RACE 20S PENALTY * POST-RACE 5S PENALTY.

McLaren duo Hamilton and Button are sort of happy, but Vettel had reason to be delighted.

The penalty for Ferrari was far greater, though, as Alonso and Massa were delayed by the safety car and tumbled far down the order when they pitted.

Vettel was thus able to win the race as he pleased, with Hamilton 5s behind in second after his penalty. Kamui Kobayashi pitted on lap 53, allowing Button through for third.

Feelings had been running high within Red Bull Racing since Mark Webber felt the team had shown its preference for Sebastian Vettel at the Turkish GP, which is why he said "Not bad for a number two driver" when he won at Silverstone.

Silverstone presented a new challenge to the drivers, as it sent them onto a new loop from Abbey to Brooklands, but this didn't stop the Red Bull duo, who claimed the first two places on the grid, Sebastian Vettel on pole ahead of Mark Webber, with a gap of two-thirds of a second back to the next fastest driver, Ferrari's Fernando Alonso.

There should have been smiles all round, but the simmering tension in the team was stirred after Vettel damaged his new-style front wing and was promptly given the one off Webber's car for qualifying. Webber was less than impressed.

Home fans came out in record numbers, but had to make do with Lewis Hamilton qualifying fourth. For Jenson Button, qualifying was a disaster and he couldn't make his MP4-25 handle, ending up 14th.

Webber forced his way onto the inside line into Copse. Vettel tried to squeeze him out but was too slow to move across and the Australian pushed Vettel to the outside as they negotiated the turn. Hamilton got in close behind, but his front wing clipped Vettel's right rear tyre and the German was forced over the kerb and his tyre started to deflate.

The Ferraris also touched, at Becketts, with Felipe Massa the one afflicted. Enjoying better fortune, Button passed four rivals off the grid and overtook the slow-moving Vettel and Massa to finish lap 1 in eighth.

Hamilton stuck to Webber, then Webber eased clear. With Robert Kubica running third but struggling for grip, Nico Rosberg and those behind were forced to reconsider their strategies. The Renault driver wouldn't last the distance, retiring with diff failure.

Webber and Hamilton were still comfortably clear after their pit stops, with the late-pitting Nico Hulkenberg reaching third before he pitted as the safety car was called out following a collision between Adrian Sutil and Pedro de la Rosa at Copse.

Webber kept Hamilton at bay at the

This win appeared to be worth more than 25 points to Mark Webber, who had a point to prove.

BRITAIN ROUND 10

Date: **11 July 2010**

Laps: **52** • Distance: **190.632 miles/306.793km** • Weather: **Warm and dry**

Pos	Driver	Team	Result	Stops	Qualifying Time	Grid
1	**Mark Webber**	Red Bull	1h24m38.2s	1	1m29.758s	2
2	**Lewis Hamilton**	McLaren	1h24m39.56s	1	1m30.556s	4
3	**Nico Rosberg**	Mercedes	1h24m59.507s	1	1m30.625s	5
4	**Jenson Button**	McLaren	1h25m00.186s	1	1m31.699s	14
5	**Rubens Barrichello**	Williams	1h25m09.656s	1	1m31.175s	8
6	**Kamui Kobayashi**	BMW Sauber	1h25m10.371s	1	1m31.421s	12
7	**Sebastian Vettel**	Red Bull	1h25m14.934s	1	1m29.615s	1
8	**Adrian Sutil**	Force India	1h25m19.132s	1	1m31.399s	11
9	**Michael Schumacher**	Mercedes	1h25m19.799s	1	1m31.43s	10
10	**Nico Hulkenberg**	Williams	1h25m20.212s	1	1m31.635s	13
11	**Vitantonio Liuzzi**	Force India	1h25m20.659s	1	1m31.708s	20*
12	**Sebastien Buemi**	Toro Rosso	1h25m25.827s	1	1m32.012s	16
13	**Vitaly Petrov**	Renault	1h25m37.574s	2	1m31.796s	15
14	**Fernando Alonso**	Ferrari	1h25m40.585s	3	1m30.426s	3
15	**Felipe Massa**	Ferrari	1h25m45.689s	2	1m31.172s	7
16	**Jarno Trulli**	Lotus	51 laps	1	1m34.864s	21
17	**Heikki Kovalainen**	Lotus	51 laps	1	1m34.405s	18
18	**Timo Glock**	Virgin	50 laps	1	1m34.775s	19
19	**Karun Chandhok**	HRT	50 laps	1	1m36.576s	23
20	**Sakon Yamamoto**	HRT	50 laps	1	1m36.968s	24
R	**Jaime Alguersuari**	Toro Rosso	44 laps/spun off	1	1m32.43s	17
R	**Pedro de la Rosa**	BMW Sauber	29 laps/crash damage	2	1m31.274s	9
R	**Robert Kubica**	Renault	19 laps/driveshaft	1	1m31.04s	6
R	**Lucas di Grassi**	Virgin	9 laps/hydraulics	0	1m35.212s	22

FASTEST LAP: ALONSO, 1M30.874S, 145.011MPH/233.37KPH ON LAP 52 • RACE LEADER: WEBBER 1–52
* 5-PLACE GRID PENALTY FOR IMPEDING

restart, then controlled the race. Even with the safety car period wiping out their disadvantage, Rosberg and Button were 20s down by flag-fall for third and fourth, but

10s up on Barrichello and Kobayashi.

Behind them, remarkably, was Vettel, who had tigered back from 24th place after his puncture to finish in seventh place.

GERMAN GP

Fans all over the world used to cheer a Ferrari one-two result, but this one at Hockenheim was tainted even before the chequered flag fell, as the team had effected a very clumsy piece of order-changing to move Fernando Alonso past Felipe Massa to finish the race in front.

The order at the front of the grid has a slightly new look in Germany as it was Ferrari that stepped up to the mark to challenge Red Bull Racing rather than McLaren. The reason for this gain was that the Italian team had got its exhaust-blown diffuser to work better and Fernando Alonso came within 0.003s of taking pole instead of Sebastian Vettel.

Felipe Massa qualified third but he made an excellent start and passed not only Vettel whose RB6 got bogged down but also team-mate Alonso, who had been squeezed towards the pit wall by Vettel as they sped to Turn 1, with Massa going around the outside into the opening right-hander.

Making matters worse for Red Bull, Mark Webber was also slow away from fourth on the grid and was deposed by Jenson Button, but he was forced to lift to avoid the warring Alonso and Vettel and Webber moved back into fourth, only to have Lewis Hamilton power past him on the run to the hairpin.

So, Ferrari was first and second, but the team wanted the order to be Alonso then Massa rather than the other way around, as Alonso started the race ranked fifth in the points table on 98, whereas Massa was only eighth, with 67 points, fully 78 behind points leader Hamilton. So they wanted the order at the front swapped. But how?

After they had both made their one pit stop to change from super-soft tyres to hards, Massa started to struggle and Alonso was soon all over him and on the radio to the team, requesting that he be allowed past. It was at this point that Massa pulled clear, only for Alonso catch him a few laps later, with their pace enough to drop Vettel.

Now they were out on their own and through came the message to Massa: "OK Felipe, Fernando is faster than you. Can you confirm that you have received that information?"

Massa let Alonso by and 25 laps later they finished in that order with Vettel third.

HOCKENHEIM ROUND 11

Date: **25 July 2010**

Laps: **67** • Distance: **190.414 miles/306.442km** • Weather: **Warm and dry**

Pos	Driver	Team	Result	Stops	Qualifying Time	Grid
1	**Fernando Alonso**	Ferrari	1h27m38.864s	1	1m13.793s	2
2	**Felipe Massa**	Ferrari	1h27m43.06s	1	1m14.29s	3
3	**Sebastian Vettel**	Red Bull	1h27m43.985s	1	1m13.791s	1
4	**Lewis Hamilton**	McLaren	1h28m05.76s	1	1m14.566s	6
5	**Jenson Button**	McLaren	1h28m08.346s	1	1m14.427s	5
6	**Mark Webber**	Red Bull	1h28m22.47s	1	1m14.347s	4
7	**Robert Kubica**	Renault	66 laps	1	1m15.079s	7
8	**Nico Rosberg**	Mercedes	66 laps	1	1m15.179s	9
9	**Michael Schumacher**	Mercedes	66 laps	1	1m15.026s	11
10	**Vitaly Petrov**	Renault	66 laps	1	1m15.307s	13
11	**Kamui Kobayashi**	BMW Sauber	66 laps	1	1m15.084s	12
12	**Rubens Barrichello**	Williams	66 laps	1	1m15.109s	8
13	**Nico Hulkenberg**	Williams	66 laps	1	1m15.339s	10
14	**Pedro de la Rosa**	BMW Sauber	66 laps	2	1m15.55s	14
15	**Jaime Alguersuari**	Toro Rosso	66 laps	2	1m15.588s	15
16	**Vitantonio Liuzzi**	Force India	65 laps	3	1m18.952s	21
17	**Adrian Sutil**	Force India	65 laps	3	1m15.467s	19*
18	**Timo Glock**	Virgin	64 laps	1	1m18.343s	23*
19	**Bruno Senna**	HRT	63 laps	2	1m18.592s	20
R	**Heikki Kovalainen**	Lotus	56 laps/accident	1	1m18.3s	18
R	**Lucas di Grassi**	Virgin	50 laps/spun	0	No time	24*
R	**Sakon Yamamoto**	HRT	19 laps/gearbox	1	1m19.844s	22
R	**Jarno Trulli**	Lotus	3 laps/gearbox	1	1m17.583s	17
R	**Sebastien Buemi**	Toro Rosso	1 lap/crash damage	0	1m15.974s	16

FASTEST LAP: VETTEL, 1M15.824S, 134.947MPH/217.177PH ON LAP 67 • RACE LEADERS: MASSA 1–14, 23–48; ALONSO 15–22, 49–67
* 5-PLACE GRID PENALTY

Felipe Massa doesn't know what to think as Fernando Alonso basks in his "rightful" win.

Then, for changing the course of the race by issuing team orders, Ferrari was found guilty no doubt as Massa's engineer said "sorry" when he thanked Massa for responding to that radio call. Then came the World Motor Sport Council decision in August and Ferrari escaped with a $100,000 fine.

HUNGARIAN GP

The 2010 F1 season just couldn't stop filling its races with intrigue, and this time it was the Red Bull Racing drivers back in the spotlight as Sebastian Vettel was hit by a time penalty and Mark Webber grabbed his fourth win of the year to take the championship lead.

Mark Webber had won only twice before 2010, so he was delighted to have extended his tally to six in Hungary. Better still, with Lewis Hamilton failing to score, he took the championship lead.

His team-mate Sebastian Vettel grabbed pole and did so in style, lapping 0.4s faster than the Australian. Yet such was the dominance of the RB6s around the twisting track, where top speed is less important than an ability to take corners, that third fastest qualifier Fernando Alonso's Ferrari was 1.2s off pole.

Vettel made a far better start than his abysmal one in Germany. However, Alonso had made a blinder and was level with Vettel as the field poured down the slope into Turn 1. He was on the outside, though, and had to back off and slot into second place the German moved across the track on the exit.

With Webber third and now sure to be delayed by Alonso's slower Ferrari, Vettel must have felt that he had this one in the bag, as the Hungaroring is fabled as a track that offers next to no overtaking opportunity.

Then, as so often here, the safety car was called out. This was for the clearing of debris on lap 15 after the front wing from Vitantonio Liuzzi's Force India collapsed following contact on lap 1.

Vettel saw the signal just in time to scramble his entry into the pits and almost everyone else followed him in. But, crucially, not Webber, as the team had decided that this was his best chance to usurp Alonso.

There was trouble in the pits for Nico Rosberg when he was signalled to pull away before a dropped wheelnut had been retrieved and his right rear wheel came off, hitting one of his old Williams mechanics, who was, fortunately, OK.

In the melee, Robert Kubica pulled into the path of Adrian Sutil.

Then, while sitting second behind Webber and without a working radio Vettel was

Vettel leads Alonso, Webber and Massa into Turn 1, but he wasn't there at the end of the race.

HUNGARY ROUND 12

Date: **1 August 2010**

Laps: **70** • Distance: **190.54 miles/306.645km** • Weather: **Hot and dry**

Pos	Driver	Team	Result	Stops	Qualifying Time	Grid
1	**Mark Webber**	Red Bull	1h41m05.571s	1	1m19.184s	2
2	**Fernando Alonso**	Ferrari	1h41m23.392s	1	1m19.987s	3
3	**Sebastien Vettel**	Red Bull	1h41m24.823s	2	1m18.773s	1
4	**Felipe Massa**	Ferrari	1h41m33.045s	1	1m20.331s	4
5	**Vitaly Petrov**	Renault	1h42m18.763s	1	1m21.229s	7
6	**Nico Hulkenberg**	Williams	1h42m22.294s	1	1m21.71s	10
7	**Pedro de la Rosa**	BMW Sauber	69 laps	1	1m21.411s	9
8	**Jenson Button**	McLaren	69 laps	1	1m21.292s	11
9	**Kamui Kobayashi**	BMW Sauber	69 laps	1	1m22.222s	18
10	**Rubens Barrichello**	Williams	69 laps	1	1m21.331s	12
11	**Michael Schumacher**	Mercedes	69 laps	1	1m21.63s	14
12	**Sebastien Buemi**	Toro Rosso	69 laps	1	1m21.897s	15
13	**Vitantonio Liuzzi**	Force India	69 laps	1	1m21.927s	16
14	**Heikki Kovalainen**	Lotus	67 laps	1	1m24.12s	20
15	**Jarno Trulli**	Lotus	67 laps	1	1m24.199s	21
16	**Timo Glock**	Virgin	67 laps	1	1m24.05s	19
17	**Bruno Senna**	HRT	67 laps	1	1m26.391s	23
18	**Lucas di Grassi**	Virgin	66 laps	2	1m25.118s	22
19	**Sakon Yamamoto**	HRT	66 laps	1	1m26.453s	24
R	**Lewis Hamilton**	McLaren	23 laps/gearbox	1	1m20.499s	5
R	**Robert Kubica**	Renault	23 laps/crash damage	2	1m21.328s	8
R	**Nico Rosberg**	Mercedes	15 laps/wheel	1	1m21.082s	6
R	**Adrian Sutil**	Force India	15 laps/collision	0	1m21.517s	13
R	**Jaime Alguersuari**	Toro Rosso	1 lap/engine	0	1m21.998s	17

FASTEST LAP: VETTEL, 1M22.362S, 118.987MPH/191.491PH ON LAP 70 • RACE LEADERS: VETTEL 1-15; WEBBER 16-70

unaware that the safety car was about to withdraw and was more than the mandatory maximum of 10 car lengths behind him at the restart. This was calamitous, as it meant

that he was given a drive-through penalty.

So, Webber won as he pleased, Alonso took second place and Vettel did well to recover third. He was gutted.

McLaren's drivers had said that this and the following race at Monza were its best bets for wins in the closing stages of the World Championship and Lewis Hamilton duly delivered, but team-mate Jenson Button was knocked out of second place, and the race, by Sebastian Vettel.

The discussion of flexible wings rumbled on as McLaren continued to seek clarification from the FIA. Their target, most notably, was Red Bull Racing and it's possible that the sport's governing body, having doubled the amount that needs to be resisted in a load-bearing test, could have started to make an impact at Spa-Francorchamps, as Lewis Hamilton was less than a tenth of a second off Mark Webber's pole time on this lengthy circuit. Then, in the race, he had the legs on the Australian.

In truth, while Hamilton made a good start, Webber handed him the lead by making a woeful one, dropping to sixth place.

Jenson Button rose from fifth to third on lap 1, passed Robert Kubica when he made a mistake at Eau Rouge on lap 2 and fought for the next 15 laps to keep McLaren running first and second.

However, Button had bent his left front wing endplate on the opening lap and was struggling. Sebastian Vettel sensed this and closed in. Just as light rain arrived on lap 17, the German got onto Button's tail, but he lost control as he tried to pass the McLaren into the Bus Stop and slammed into it. Incredibly he was able to continue, just managing to scrabble into the pit entry. After taking on a new nose, he was called back in again to serve a drive-through penalty. For Button, though, there was only anger and retirement.

It wasn't all easy going for Hamilton, as he nearly threw away all his hard work when he ran through a gravel trap at Rivage with just nine laps to go. This slashed his lead by 13s, but he recovered, regained focus and was able to stroke it home from there.

With Fernando Alonso spinning out, Vettel's drive-through penalty dropping him to 15th and Button left on the sidelines, first and second places for Hamilton and Webber gave them both a massive championship boost, putting them, they hoped, into a position where they might start to receive

SPA-FRANCORCHAMPS ROUND 13 Date: **29 August 2010**

Laps: **44** • Distance: **191.488 miles/308.171km** • Weather: **Light rain fell on lap 1 and again before half-distance**

Pos	Driver	Team	Result	Stops	Qualifying Time	Grid
1	**Lewis Hamilton**	McLaren	1h29m04.268s	2	1m45.863s	2
2	**Mark Webber**	Red Bull	1h29m05.839s	2	1m45.778s	1
3	**Robert Kubica**	Renault	1h29m07.761s	2	1m46.1s	3
4	**Felipe Massa**	Ferrari	1h29m12.532s	2	1m46.314s	6
5	**Adrian Sutil**	Force India	1h29m13.362s	2	1m46.659s	8
6	**Nico Rosberg**	Mercedes	1h29m16.627s	1	1m47.885s	14*
7	**Michael Schumacher**	Mercedes	1h29m19.816s	1	1m47.874s	21^
8	**Kamui Kobayashi**	BMW Sauber	1h29m20.946s	2	2m02.284s	17
9	**Vitaly Petrov**	Renault	1h29m28.119s	2	No time	23
10	**Vitantonio Liuzzi**	Force India	1h29m39.099s	4	1m48.68s	12
11	**Pedro de la Rosa**	BMW Sauber	1h29m40.287s^^	4	2m05.294s	24^^
12	**Sebastien Buemi**	Toro Rosso	1h29m44.163s	4	1m49.209s	16**
13	**Jaime Alguersuari**	Toro Rosso	1h29m53.725s	3	1m48.267s	11
14	**Nico Hulkenberg**	Williams	43 laps	2	1m47.053s	9
15	**Sebastian Vettel**	Red Bull	43 laps	5	1m46.127s	4
16	**Heikki Kovalainen**	Lotus	43 laps	3	1m50.98s	13
17	**Lucas di Grassi**	Virgin	43 laps	1	2m18.754s	22
18	**Timo Glock**	Virgin	43 lap***	3	1m52.049s	20***
19	**Jarno Trulli**	Lotus	43 laps	1	2m01.491s	15
20	**Sakon Yamamoto**	HRT	42 laps	2	2m03.941s	19
R	**Fernando Alonso**	Ferrari	37 laps/spun off	3	1m47.441s	10
R	**Jenson Button**	McLaren	15 laps/accident	0	1m46.206s	5
R	**Bruno Senna**	HRT	5 laps/suspension	2	2m03.612s	18
R	**Rubens Barrichello**	Williams	0 laps/accident	0	1m46.602s	7

FASTEST LAP: HAMILTON, 1M49.069S, 143.647MPH/231.178KPH ON LAP 32 • **RACE LEADERS:** HAMILTON 1-44
* 5-PLACE GEARBOX CHANGE PENALTY ** 3-PLACE PENALTY FOR IMPEDING ROSBERG *** 5-PLACE PENALTY FOR IMPEDING YAMAMOTO ^ 10-PLACE PENALTY FOR IMPEDING BARRICHELLO IN HUNGARIAN GP; ^^ 10-PLACE PENALTY FOR ENGINE CHANGE

Lewis Hamilton powers his McLaren through Eau Rouge with Jenson Button next up in second.

preferential treatment from their teams.

Certainly, Renault found performance with its latest F-duct but, helped by Button's retirement, Kubica ran in second place for much of the race. Then, untypically, the Pole blew his chance by overshooting his pit box and the delay let Webber claim a second place he'd keep to the finish.

ITALIAN GP

The Belgian GP appeared to have shuffled the title race in Lewis Hamilton's favour, but he negated that at Monza with an over-eager move on the opening lap and was left to watch Fernando Alonso usurp his team-mate Felipe Massa to win for Ferrari on home ground.

The F-duct continued to be a distraction and a confusion even to the leading teams and McLaren's first two days at Monza were proof of this. Jenson Button opted to run with the F-duct and a commensurately large rear wing. Lewis Hamilton took the opposite approach, with no F-duct and the smallest wing profiles possible. It was a case of opposite approaches and Button appeared to have got it right as he qualified second, with Hamilton fifth.

With all his rivals starting with low wing profiles, Button wasn't going to be able to live with their cars on the straights. All he could hope for was that he would get ahead of them and hold them up. Which, after an excellent start, he did, demoting pole-sitter Fernando Alonso before the first chicane.

Perhaps inspired by this, and having already got past a slow-starting Mark Webber, Hamilton felt that he too should have a go. The Ferraris were close together as they approached the second chicane, but Hamilton got himself closer still and aimed for a gap up the inside of Massa that was always going to close. He was too far back to make it work, had his front right suspension snapped by impact with the Brazilian's left rear, drove onto the first of the Lesmos and had to retire in the gravel trap, chastened. Later, he quipped that that was one way to lose a championship. Having all race to reflect on this can only have enhanced the thought that a little caution might have been wise. Yet, within a few days, he was advised by the team not to change his approach. The difference would be that he did what he did when he had the points lead and in Singapore he would be leading the chase.

Button was upset to be called in first for his second stop, with Alonso pitting a lap later and emerging ahead. Button questioned the decision over the radio, but the team assured him that it had chosen the faster option. Whether they were right or wrong, the fact that his stop took 0.8s longer

Fernando Alonso discovered that, if there's one race to win as a Ferrari driver, it's this Monza.

MONZA ROUND 14
Date: **12 September 2010**
Laps: **53** • Distance: **190.592 miles/306.729km** • Weather: **Dry and bright**

Pos	Driver	Team	Result	Stops	Qualifying Time	Grid
1	**Fernando Alonso**	Ferrari	1h16m24.572s	1	1m21.962s	1
2	**Jenson Button**	McLaren	1h16m27.51s	1	1m22.084s	2
3	**Felipe Massa**	Ferrari	1h16m28.795s	1	1m22.293s	3
4	**Sebastian Vettel**	Red Bull	1h16m52.768s	1	1m22.675s	6
5	**Nico Rosberg**	Mercedes	1h16m54.514s	1	1m23.027s	7
6	**Mark Webber**	Red Bull	1h16m55.848s	1	1m22.433s	4
7	**Nico Hulkenberg**	Williams	1h16m57.384s	1	1m23.037s	8
8	**Robert Kubica**	Renault	1h16m58.6s	1	1m23.039s	9
9	**Michael Schumacher**	Mercedes	1h17m09.52s	1	1m23.388s	12
10	**Rubens Barrichello**	Williams	1h17m28.575s	1	1m23.328s	10
11	**Sebastien Buemi**	Toro Rosso	1h17m29.628s	1	1m23.681s	14
12	**Vitantonio Liuzzi**	Force India	1h17m30.678s	1	1m25.774s	19
13	**Vitaly Petrov**	Renault	1h17m43.491s	1	1m23.819s	20*
14	**Pedro de la Rosa**	BMW Sauber	52 laps	1	1m24.044s	16
15	**Jaime Alguersuari**	Toro Rosso	52 laps	2	1m23.919s	15
16	**Adrian Sutil**	Force India	52 laps	2	1m23.199s	11
17	**Timo Glock**	Virgin	51 laps	1	1m25.934s	24*
18	**Heikki Kovalainen**	Lotus	51 laps	1	1m25.742s	18
19	**Lucas di Grassi**	Virgin	51 laps	1	1m25.974s	21
20	**Sakon Yamamoto**	HRT	51 laps	1	1m27.02s	23
21	**Jarno Trulli**	Lotus	46laps/gearbox	1	1m25.54s	17
R	**Bruno Senna**	HRT	11 laps/hydraulics	0	1m26.847s	22
R	**Lewis Hamilton**	McLaren	0 laps/accident	0	1m22.623s	5
R	**Kamui Kobayashi**	BMW Sauber	0 laps/gearbox	0	1m23.659s	13**

FASTEST LAP: ALONSO, 1M24.139S, 154.013MPH/247.861KPH ON LAP 52 • RACE LEADERS: BUTTON 1-36, ALONSO 37 & 39-53, MASSA 38
* 5-PLACE GRID PENALTY, ** STARTED FROM THE PIT LANE

than Alonso's made all the difference.

Webber could climb no higher than sixth, having been stuck behind Nico Hulkenberg, but he at least left Monza with

the championship lead, having pulled five points clear of the sidelined Hamilton, while Alonso, Button and Vettel all moved closer in this tremendous five-way battle.

SINGAPORE GP

Self-belief was coursing through Fernando Alonso's veins after he beat Sebastian Vettel to pole. Then, once he'd led all the way for his second straight win for Ferrari, he reckoned that he could become World Champion for a third time.

The ultimate way to build confidence in sport is to establish momentum. If winning on Ferrari's home ground wasn't enough to make Fernando Alonso believe in himself, then making it two on the trot certainly was.

The streets of Singapore are nothing if not different from everything else the drivers face each year, as it's hot, humid and bumpy, with crazy kerbs at the chicane, to mention nothing of the racing being held after dark as the rest of city life potters by. Through all this came Alonso and grabbing pole was one of the key moments of his campaign, especially with Red Bull-favouring circuits to follow.

Sebastian Vettel, Lewis Hamilton and Jenson Button would line up next, ahead of a less convincing Mark Webber. Like this, the grid suggested a shaking up of the order. Yet all behaved well at the start as Alonso led into Turn 1 from Vettel. Button was briefly up to third, but instantly demoted by Hamilton.

They were soon able to back off as a safety car period was triggered as debris from Vitantonio Liuzzi's Force India had to be cleared after he was clattered by Nick Heidfeld's Sauber. Webber took this opportunity to pit, putting him onto a different strategy from his rivals.

With overtaking literally not an option, the order stayed as it was all the way to the planned pit stops, starting with Hamilton coming in on lap 28. A lap later, Alonso, Vettel and Button came in.

They had just settled back into the race when the safety car was needed for a second time as Kamui Kobayashi had crashed his Sauber out of Turn 18 and Bruno Senna had hit it.

At this point, Webber had moved into third as his rivals pitted, and so he was the target for a passing move by Hamilton when the safety car withdrew and Webber was slowed by Timo Glock's Virgin. Hamilton powered past on the outside. Although half

SINGAPORE ROUND 15
Date: **26 September 2010**
Laps: **61** • Distance: **191.972 miles/308.95km** • Weather: **Hot and humid**

Pos	Driver	Team	Result	Stops	Qualifying Time	Grid
1	**Fernando Alonso**	Ferrari	1h57m53.579s	1	1m45.39s	1
2	**Sebastian Vettel**	Red Bull	1h57m53.872s	1	1m45.457s	2
3	**Mare Webber**	Red Bull	1h58m22.72s	1	1m45.977s	5
4	**Jenson Button**	McLaren	1h58m23.963s	1	1m45.944s	4
5	**Nico Rosberg**	Mercedes	1h58m42.973s	1	1m46.443s	7
6	**Rubens Barrichello**	Williams	1h58m49.68s	1	1m46.236s	6
7	**Robert Kubica**	Renault	1h59m20.138s	2	1m46.593s	8
8	**Felipe Massa**	Ferrari	1h59m46.876s	1	no time	24
9	**Adrian Sutil**	Force India	2h00m05.995s*	0	1m48.899s	15
10	**Nico Hulkenberg**	Williams	2h00m06.37s*	0	1m47.674s	17**
11	**Vitaly Petrov**	Renault	60 laps	0	1m48.165s	12
12	**Jaime Alguersuari**	Toro Rosso	60 laps	1	1m47.666s	11***
13	**Michael Schumacher**	Mercedes	60 laps	2	1m46.702s	9
14	**Sebastien Buemi**	Toro Rosso	60 laps	1	1m48.502s	13
15	**Lucas di Grassi**	Virgin	59 laps	2	1m51.107s	20
16	**Heikki Kovalainen**	Lotus	58 laps/fire	1	1m50.915s	19
R	**Timo Glock**	Virgin	49 laps/hydraulics	1	1m50.721s	18
R	**Nick Heidfeld**	BMW Sauber	36 laps/collision	2	1m48.557s	13
R	**Lewis Hamilton**	McLaren	35 laps/collision	1	1m45.571s	3
R	**Christian Klien**	HRT	32 laps/hydraulics	1	1m52.946s	22
R	**Kamui Kobayashi**	BMW Sauber	30 laps/spun off	0	1m47.884s	10
R	**Bruno Senna**	HRT	29 laps/collision	1	1m54.174s	23
R	**Jarno Trulli**	Lotus	27 laps/hydraulics	3	1m51.641s	21
R	**Vitantonio Liuzzi**	Force India	1 lap/collision	0	1m48.961s	16

FASTEST LAP: ALONSO, 1M47.976S, 105.097MPH/169.138KPH ON LAP 58 • RACE LEADER: ALONSO 1-61
* 20-SECOND PENALTY ** 5-PLACE GRID PENALTY *** STARTED FROM THE PIT LANE

Fernando Alonso kept Sebastian Vettel behind his Ferrari to make it two wins in succession.

a car length clear, Webber was on the inside line and they clashed as he came into Turn 7. Two races, no points.

Webber was able to continue, and to boost his points advantage, but there was nothing that he could do to catch the leading duo. Equally, there was nothing that Vettel could do to overtake Alonso.

102

Everyone said that Red Bull Racing would dominate proceedings at Suzuka, and it did, with Sebastian Vettel putting himself right back in the hunt for the title as he raced to his third win of 2010, but Mark Webber extended his points lead by finishing in second place.

Suzuka is always a challenge and the drivers were left fretting as Saturday was a near-total washout. Qualifying had to be shifted to Sunday and that cranked up the pressure on all involved, but it did nothing to stop the Red Bull Racing duo filling the front row.

Sebastian Vettel lined up ahead of Mark Webber, as he needed to do if he was to start chipping into the Australian's points lead. The German's hopes were boosted at the start when Webber made a poor getaway and Robert Kubica fired his Renault into second place. This might have enabled Vettel to make his break, as the Pole was then expected to delay Webber, but the race went straight into a safety car period as two accidents marred the start and the first corner. Nico Hulkenberg was slow off the line and Vitaly Petrov powered past him, but then cut across the Williams driver's nose, putting both out as the Russian slammed into the outside wall.

Then, down to Turn 1, Felipe Massa found himself on the grass and clattered into the fast-starting Vitantonio Liuzzi as he rejoined. Still, at least they got that far, as Lucas di Grassi slammed his Virgin into the barriers on his reconnaissance lap.

Kubica wasn't a factor when they were released to race at full speed again, though, as his right rear wheel had fallen off.

So, Webber was able to stick with Vettel, but, ultimately, he was unable to pass him. Still, the 18 points for second place left him with a 14-point lead with three races to go.

Fernando Alonso was on strong form at Suzuka and placed third for Ferrari. He looked likely to be pressured by Lewis Hamilton, but a gearbox problem slowed the 2008 World Champion and McLaren's apparent plans to use the late-stopping Jenson Button to back the first three into his path came to naught. Button eventually passed the slowing Hamilton for fourth.

Michael Schumacher had a more competitive race and claimed sixth, but this

Sporting a new helmet livery for the occasion, Vettel signals that he's *itchi ban* (number one).

SUZUKA ROUND 16

Date: **10 October 2010**

Laps: **53** • Distance: **191.224 miles/307.746km** • Weather: **Sunny and dry**

Pos	Driver	Team	Result	Stops	Qualifying Time	Grid
1	Sebastian Vettel	Red Bull	1h30m27.323s	1	1m30.785s	1
2	Mark Webber	Red Bull	1h30m28.228s	1	1m30.853s	2
3	Fernando Alonso	Ferrari	1h30m30.044s	1	1m31.352s	4
4	Jenson Button	McLaren	1h30m40.845s	1	1m31.378s	5
5	Lewis Hamilton	McLaren	1h31m06.918s	1	1m31.169s	8*
6	Michael Schumacher	Mercedes	1h31m27.256s	1	1m31.846s	10
7	Kamui Kobayashi	BMW Sauber	1h31m31.361s	1	1m32.427s	14
8	Nick Heidfeld	BMW Sauber	1h31m36.971s	1	1m31.187s	11
9	Rubens Barrichello	Williams	1h31m38.169s	1	1m31.535s	7
10	Sebastien Buemi	Toro Rosso	1h31m40.129s	1	1m33.568s	18
11	Jaime Alguersuari	Toro Rosso	52 laps	2	1m33.071s	16
12	Heikki Kovalainen	Lotus	52 laps	1	1m35.464s	20
13	Jarno Trulli	Lotus	51 laps	1	1m35.346s	19
14	Timo Glock	Virgin	51 laps	2	1m36.332s	22
15	Bruno Senna	HRT	51 laps	1	1m37.270s	23
16	Sakon Yamamoto	HRT	50 laps	1	1m37.365s	24
17	Nico Rosberg	Mercedes	47 laps/accident	1	1m31.494s	6
R	Adrian Sutil	Force India	44 laps/oil leak	1	1m32.659s	15
R	Robert Kubica	Renault	2 laps/wheel	0	1m31.231s	3
R	Nico Hulkenberg	Williams	0 laps/accident	0	1m31.559s	9
R	Felipe Massa	Ferrari	0 laps/accident	0	1m32.321s	12
R	Vitaly Petrov	Renault	0 laps/accident	0	1m32.422s	13
R	Vitantonio Liuzzi	Force India	0 laps/accident	0	1m33.154s	17
NS	Lucas di Grassi	Virgin	-/accident	-	1m36.265s	21

FASTEST LAP: WEBBER, 1M33.474S, 138.968MPH/223.647KPH ON LAP 53 • RACE LEADERS: VETTEL 1-24, 39-53; WEBBER 25; BUTTON 26-38
* 5-PLACE GRID PENALTY

ought to have gone to Mercedes team-mate Nico Rosberg, except that his left rear wheel came off and he crashed.

Kamui Kobayashi had a spectacular race for BMW Sauber as he pitted late then worked his way past a number of cars to make it back to seventh, with the hairpin his most notable place for overtaking.

KOREAN GP

It was doubted that the new track would be ready in time. Then it was doubted that anyone would be able to beat the Red Bulls. Finally, it was doubted that the rain would relent, but the Red Bulls retired, the rain eased and Fernando Alonso was triumphant for Ferrari.

The paint was literally drying as the teams had their first sight of Yeongam, but the drivers were soon impressed with the new circuit and everyone got down to learning the track. As expected, it was the Red Bulls to the fore, with the talked-about upswing from McLaren not occurring. Indeed, it was Fernando Alonso who got closest in qualifying, with Lewis Hamilton fourth and Jenson Button off the pace in seventh.

As if there wasn't enough pressure on the five championship contenders before, the rain then started and kept on coming. So drenched was the circuit that the race had to begin behind the safety car, no doubt to the delight of pole-man Vettel, meaning that he would therefore be safe from attack into the tight first corner.

After three laps behind the safety car, the field was brought to a halt back on the starting grid. It was too wet but at least the laps covered would issue half points. Another start was attempted an hour later in the gloom. This too was behind the safety car, but the drivers were released to go racing after 17 laps and Vettel eased clear.

Hamilton was passed by Mercedes' Nico Rosberg into Turn 3. His misfortune was nothing next to Webber's, though, for the Australian dropped his Red Bull through Turn 12 at the second time of asking, bounced off the wall and collected Rosberg. So out came the safety car again as Alonso advanced to second and Hamilton to third.

Vettel was able to control proceedings from the front of the ball of spray and the next notable change came when Michael Schumacher demoted a clearly struggling Button. Pitting earlier than his rivals for a fresh set of inters brought Button out behind a gaggle of cars, some of whom weren't going to stop again.

Another safety car period brought everyone else in for their stops. Alonso slightly overshot his pit crew and the time lost let Hamilton into second. However, as

they were released again, Hamilton ran wide at Turn 1 and Alonso took the place back. Then, on lap 45, Vettel pulled off with engine failure and Alonso was able to make

it three wins from four starts to take the championship lead.

Schumacher was fourth and Vitantonio Liuzzi at last landed a result, with sixth.

YEONGAM ROUND 17

Date: **24 October 2010**

Laps: **55** • Distance: **192.108 miles/309.168km** • Weather: **Heavy rain**

Pos	Driver	Team	Result	Stops	Qualifying Time	Grid
1	**Fernando Alonso**	Ferrari	2h48m20.81s	1	1m35.766s	3
2	**Lewis Hamilton**	McLaren	2h48m35.809s	1	1m36.062s	4
3	**Felipe Massa**	Ferrari	2h48m51.678s	1	1m36.571s	6
4	**Michael Schumacher**	Mercedes	2h49m00.498s	1	1m36.95s	9
5	**Robert Kubica**	Renault	2h49m08.544s	1	1m36.824s	8
6	**Vitantonio Liuzzi**	Force India	2h49m14.381s	1	1m38.955s	17
7	**Rubens Barrichello**	Williams	2h49m30.067s	1	1m36.998s	10
8	**Kamui Kobayashi**	BMW Sauber	2h49m38.699s	1	1m37.643s	12
9	**Nick Heidfeld**	BMW Sauber	2h49m40.917s	1	1m37.715s	13
10	**Nico Hulkenberg**	Williams	2h49m41.661s	2	1m37.62s	11
11	**Jaime Alguersuari**	Toro Rosso	2h49m44.956s	1	1m37.853s	15
12	**Jenson Button**	McLaren	2h49m50.749s	1	1m36.731s	7
13	**Heikki Kovalainen**	Lotus	54 laps	1	1m41.768s	21
14	**Bruno Senna**	HRT	53 laps	2	1m43.283s	24
15	**Sakon Yamamoto**	HRT	53 laps	1	1m42.444s	23
R	**Adrian Sutil**	Force India	46 laps/crash damage	1	1m37.783s	14
R	**Sebastian Vettel**	Red Bull	45 laps/engine	1	1m35.585s	1
R	**Vitaly Petrov**	Renault	39 laps/accident	1	1m37.799s	20*
R	**Timo Glock**	Virgin	31 laps/crash damage	0	1m40.748s	19
R	**Sebastien Buemi**	Toro Rosso	30 laps/accident	1	1m38.594s	16
R	**Lucas di Grassi**	Virgin	25 laps/accident	3	1m42.235s	22
R	**Jarno Trulli**	Lotus	25 laps/hydraulics	2	1m40.521s	18
R	**Mark Webber**	Red Bull	18 laps/accident	0	1m35.659s	2
R	**Nico Rosberg**	Mercedes	18 laps/accident	0	1m36.535s	5

FASTEST LAP: ALONSO, 1M50.257S, 113.919MPH/183.335KPH ON LAP 42 • RACE LEADERS: VETTEL 1-45; ALONSO 46-55
* 5-PLACE GRID PENALTY

Conditions were treacherous and the race was delayed, but it all came Fernando Alonso's way.

Fernando Alonso couldn't live with the pace of the Red Bulls, but the Spanish Ferrari driver did all he could and finished in a vital third position to leave Interlagos with an eight-point championship lead over Mark Webber, who trailed his team-mate Sebastian Vettel home.

Five drivers arrived at Interlagos still in contention for the World Championship. By the end of the race, that was down to four, with Jenson Button falling by the wayside. Ferrari's Fernando Alonso had the biggest smile, as he was still ahead on points, by eight.

When the title fight reaches this stage, none of the contenders wants anything that can turn proceedings into a lottery, so Alonso, Red Bull's Mark Webber and Sebastian Vettel and McLaren's Button and Lewis Hamilton were not too pleased when it rained ahead of qualifying. Then, with just five minutes of the top 10 shoot-out left, a dry line began to appear and Williams rookie Nico Hulkenberg timed his change to slicks to perfection and drove beautifully to take his first pole, and Williams's first for five years. That he did so by 1.1s shows how great the lap was.

Vettel was second on the grid and knew that his best hope of winning rested on passing Hulkenberg before the first corner, then putting the German between himself and his title rivals. In dry conditions, this he did, but Webber was quickly up to second and both were helped as the Williams driver delayed Hamilton and Alonso.

Hamilton found his McLaren offering little grip, ran wide at the start of lap 2 and was soon back to fifth. He and Alonso would soon demote Hulkenberg, who always knew that he would be a sitting duck in the dry, but it took until lap 7 for the Spaniard to take third place, by which point the Red Bulls were well clear, with Vettel 9.5s ahead of Alonso. Hamilton had to wait until the Williams pitted, and this combined with his lack of grip meant that his outside title hopes were diminishing fast.

Button, who'd qualified only 11th, knew that he had to do something clever to climb the order and was duly the first to pit, on lap 11. And it worked, as he rose to fifth when those ahead pitted, and was right up with Hamilton, who'd started fourth.

Sebastian Vettel edges down the inside of pole-sitter Nico Hulkenberg to take the lead.

BRAZIL ROUND 18

Date: **7 November 2010**

Laps: **71** • Distance: **190.067 miles/305.884km** • Weather: **Hot and humid**

Pos	Driver	Team	Result	Stops	Qualifying Time	Grid
1	Sebastian Vettel	Red Bull	1h33m11.803s	1	1m15.519s	2
2	Mark Webber	Red Bull	1h33m16.046s	1	1m15.637s	3
3	Fernando Alonso	Ferrari	1h33m18.61s	1	1m15.989s	5
4	Lewis Hamilton	McLaren	1h33m26.437s	2	1m15.747s	4
5	Jenson Button	McLaren	1h33m27.396s	2	1m19.288s	11
6	Nico Rosberg	Mercedes	1h33m47.123s	3	1m19.486s	13
7	Michael Schumacher	Mercedes	1h33m55.259s	1	1m16.925s	7
8	Nico Hulkenberg	Williams	70 laps	1	1m14.47s	1
9	Robert Kubica	Renault	70 laps	1	1m16.552s	7
10	Kamui Kobayashi	BMW Sauber	70 laps	1	1m19.385s	12
11	Jaime Alguersuari	Toro Rosso	70 laps	1	1m19.581s	14
12	Adrian Sutil	Force India	70 laps	1	1m20.83s	22*
13	Sebastien Buemi	Toro Rosso	70 laps	1	1m19.847s	19*
14	Rubens Barrichello	Williams	70 laps	3	1m16.203s	6
15	Felipe Massa	Ferrari	70 laps	3	1m17.101s	9
16	Vitaly Petrov	Renault	70 laps	2	1m17.656s	10
17	Nick Heidfeld	BMW Sauber	70 laps	3	1m19.899s	15
18	Heikki Kovalainen	Lotus	69 laps	1	1m22.378s	20
19	Jarno Trulli	Lotus	69 laps	1	1m22.25s	18
20	Timo Glock	Virgin	69 laps	1	1m22.13s	17
21	Bruno Senna	HRT	69 laps	1	1m23.796s	24
22	Christian Klien	HRT	65 laps	2	1m23.083s	23
NC	Lucas di Grassi	Virgin	62 laps	3	1m22.81s	21
R	Vitantonio Liuzzi	Force India	49 laps/accident	1	1m20.357s	16

FASTEST LAP: HAMILTON, 1M13.851S, 130.518MPH/210.049KPH ON LAP 66 • RACE LEADERS: VETTEL 1-24, 27-71; WEBBER 25-26
* 5-PLACE GRID PENALTY FOR IMPEDING AT PREVIOUS RACE

There was nothing that Webber could do to pass Vettel, much as he would have liked to to boost his title hopes, and so he had to settle for second, although he was made to sweat a bit when Vitantonio Liuzzi crashed late on bringing out the safety car. Fortunately, there were seven lapped runners between him and Alonso for the restart.

Fernando Alonso arrived at Yas Marina as the clear championship leader. Yet as Sebastian Vettel broke clear, a safety car period accounted for the hopes of Alonso and Mark Webber, and Vettel did the rest to become the youngest ever World Champion.

As the dust settled after qualifying, it became clear that long-time points leader Mark Webber had left himself with a mountain to climb to become Australia's first World Champion since 1980. He knew that he had to start from the front row if he was to have a hope of overhauling Fernando Alonso's eight-point lead. The Ferrari driver had qualified third, but Webber was back in fifth. He was going to need a miracle.

Webber's team-mate Sebastian Vettel, who was a further seven points behind, was thus able to start dreaming, as he'd qualified on pole for the 10th time in the year's 19 rounds. He was fast away at the start, too, holding off a firm challenge from Lewis Hamilton through Turn 1.

Webber failed to make up a place at the start, but he was delighted to see that Jenson Button had moved the second McLaren past Alonso for third.

Then the safety car was triggered as Michael Schumacher rotated his Mercedes at Turn 6 as team-mate Nico Rosberg looked to go down his inside. All behind managed to avoid him save Vitantonio Liuzzi, whose Force India rode up and onto the Mercedes.

This is where the race changed its course, as several drivers towards the front end of the field pitted immediately to change to the option tyres that would be durable enough to take them to the end of the race. Rosberg was one such and Petrov another.

With the first three running comfortably, although without much hope of overtaking, as this circuit simply doesn't offer much occasion for any, Alonso was feeling content in fourth place, as that would be enough to make him champion, regardless of whether any of the drivers ahead of him won. As long as Webber was behind him and he fell no lower than fourth, he didn't care. So, when Webber pitted and was then delayed on his return by Jaime Alguersuari, Ferrari realised that a regular stop ought to put Alonso back out in front. So they called him in and it

YAS MARINA ROUND 19

Date: **14 November 2010**

Laps: **55** • Distance: **189.81 miles/305.470km** • Weather: **Sunny and dry**

Pos	Driver	Team	Result	Stops	Qualifying Time	Grid
1	Sebastian Vettel	Red Bull	1h39m36.837s	1	1m39.934s	1
2	Lewis Hamilton	McLaren	1h39m46.999s	1	1m39.425s	2
3	Jenson Button	McLaren	1h39m47.884s	1	1m39.823s	4
4	Nico Rosberg	Mercedes	1h40m07.584s	1	1m40.589s	9
5	Robert Kubica	Renault	1h40m15.863s	1	1m40.78s	11
6	Vitaly Petrov	Renault	1h40m20.357s	1	1m40.901s	10
7	Fernando Alonso	Ferrari	1h40m20.634s	1	1m39.792s	3
8	Mark Webber	Red Bull	1h40m21.08s	1	1m39.925s	5
9	Jaime Alguersuari	Toro Rosso	1h40m27.038s	1	1m41.738s	17
10	Felipe Massa	Ferrari	1h40m27.705s	1	1m40.202s	6
11	Nick Heidfeld	BMW Sauber	1h40m28.388s	1	1m41.113s	14
12	Rubens Barrichello	Williams	1h40m34.523s	1	1m40.203s	7
13	Adrian Sutil	Force India	1m40m35.162s	1	1m40.914s	13
14	Kamui Kobayashi	BMW Sauber	1h40m36.395s	1	1m40.783s	12
15	Sebastien Buemi	Torro Rosso	1h40m40.015s	1	1m41.824s	18
16	Nico Hulkenberg	Williams	1h40m41.6s	1	1m41.418s	15
17	Heikki Kovalainen	Lotus	54 laps	1	1m43.712s	20
18	Lucas di Grassi	Virgin	53 laps	1	1m44.51s	22
19	Bruno Senna	HRT	53 laps	1	1m45.085s	23
20	Christian Klien	HRT	53 laps	1	1m45.296s	24
21	Jarno Trulli	Lotus	51 laps/rear wing	1	1m43.516s	19
R	Timo Glock	Virgin	43 laps/gearbox	0	1m44.095s	21
R	Michael Schumacher	Mercedes	0 laps/accident	0	1m40.516s	8
R	Vitantonio Liuzzi	Force India	0 laps/accident	0	1m41.642s	16

FASTEST LAP: HAMILTON, 1M41.274S, 122.676MPH/197.428PH ON LAP 47 • **RACE LEADERS:** VETTEL 1-24, 40-55; BUTTON 25-39

Fernando Alonso became trapped behind Vitaly Petrov's Renault and watched his hopes fade.

worked. But they ended up behind Rosberg, Kubica and Petrov, so fourth place became seventh and eighth for Alonso and Webber, ending their hopes as Vettel won.

This was the first time that Vettel had held the points lead. And, in clinching the title at the age of 23 years and 134 days, he beat Hamilton's 2008 record by 165 days.

Leaving it late, Sebastian Vettel celebrates in Abu Dhabi after becoming the youngest World Champion in Formula One history.

FINAL RESULTS 2010

POS	DRIVER	NAT.		ENGINE	R1	R2	R3	R4
1	SEBASTIAN VETTEL	GER		RED BULL-RENAULT RB6	4P	RP	1	6P
2	FERNANDO ALONSO	SPA		FERRARI F10	1F	4	13	4
3	MARK WEBBER	AUS		RED BULL-RENAULT RB6	8	9F	2PF	8
4	LEWIS HAMILTON	GBR		McLAREN-MERCEDES MP4-25	3	6	6	2F
5	JENSON BUTTON	GBR		McLAREN-MERCEDES MP4-25	7	1	7	1
6	FELIPE MASSA	BRA		FERRARI F10	2	3	7	9
7	NICO ROSBERG	GER		MERCEDES MGP W01	5	5	3	3
8	ROBERT KUBICA	POL		RENAULT R30	11	2	4	5
9	MICHAEL SCHUMACHER	GER		MERCEDES MGP W01	6	10	R	10
10	RUBENS BARRICHELLO	BRA		WILLIAMS-COSWORTH FW32	10	8	12	12
11	ADRIAN SUTIL	GER		FORCE INDIA-MERCEDES VJM03	12	R	5	11
12	KAMUI KOBAYASHI	JAP		BMW SAUBER-FERRARI C29	R	R	R	R
13	VITALY PETROV	RUS		RENAULT R30	R	R	R	7
14	NICO HULKENBERG	GER		WILLIAMS-COSWORTH FW32	14	R	10	15
15	VITANTONIO LIUZZI	ITA		FORCE INDIA-MERCEDES VJM03	9	7	R	R
16	SEBASTIEN BUEMI	SUI		TORO ROSSO-FERRARI STR5	16	R	11	R
17	PEDRO DE LA ROSA	SPA		BMW SAUBER-FERRARI C29	R	12	NS	R
18	NICK HEIDFELD	GER		BMW SAUBER-FERRARI C29	-	-	-	-
19	JAIME ALGUERSUARI	SPA		TORO ROSSO-FERRARI STR5	13	11	9	13
20	HEIKKI KOVALAINEN	FIN		LOTUS-COSWORTH T127	15	13	NC	14
21	JARNO TRULLI	ITA		LOTUS-COSWORTH T127	17	NS	17	R
22	KARUN CHANDHOK	IND		HRT-COSWORTH F110	R	14	15	17
23	LUCAS DI GRASSI	BRA		VIRGIN-COSWORTH VR-01	R	R	14	R
24	TIMO GLOCK	GER		VIRGIN-COSWORTH VR-01	R	R	R	NS
25	BRUNO SENNA	BRA		HRT-COSWORTH F110	R	R	16	16
26	SAKON YAMAMOTO	JAP		HRT-COSWORTH F110	-	-	-	-
27	CHRISTIAN KLIEN	AUT		HRT-COSWORTH F110	-	-	-	-

108

RACE RESULTS FOR BOTH DRIVERS: i.e. FIRST AND SECOND LISTED AS 1/2, WITH THE TEAM'S BETTER RESULT LISTED FIRST

1	RED BULL-RENAULT	4/8	9/R	1/2	6/8
2	McLAREN-MERCEDES	3/7	1/6	6/8	1/2
3	FERRARI	1/2	1/2	7/13	4/9
4	MERCEDES	5/6	5/10	3/R	3/10
5	RENAULT	11/R	2/R	4/R	5/7
6	WILLIAMS-COSWORTH	10/14	8/R	10/12	12/15
7	FORCE INDIA-MERCEDES	9/12	7/R	5/R	11/R
8	BMW SAUBER-FERRARI	R/R	12/R	R/R	R/R
9	TORO ROSSO-FERRARI	13/16	11/R	9/11	13/R
10	LOTUS-COSWORTH	15/17	13/R	17/R	14/R
11	HRT-COSWORTH	R/R	14/R	15/16	16/17
12	VIRGIN-COSWORTH	R/R	R/R	14/R	R/NS

SCORING

1st	25 points
2nd	18 points
3rd	15 points
4th	12 points
5th	10 points
6th	8 points
7th	6 points
8th	4 points
9th	2 points
10th	1 point

SYMBOLS AND GRAND PRIX KEY

D DISQUALIFIED **F** FASTEST LAP **NC** NON-CLASSIFIED **NS** NON-STARTER **P** POLE POSITION **R** RETIRED **W** WITHDRAWN

R5	R6	R7	R8	R9	R10	R11	R12	R13	R14	R15	R16	R17	R18	R19	TOTAL POINTS
3	2F	R	4	1P	7P	3PF	3PF	15	4	2	1P	RP	1	1P	?
2	6	8	3	8	14F	1	2	R	1PF	1PF	3	1F	3	7	?
1P	1P	3P	5	R	1	6	1	2P	6	3	2F	R	2	8	?
14F	5	1	1P	2	2	4	R	1F	R	R	5	2	4F	2F	?
5	R	2	2	3F	4	5	8	R	2	4	4	12	5	3	?
6	4	7	15	11	15	2	4	4	3	8	R	3	15	10	?
13	7	5	6	10	3	8	R	6	5	5	17	R	6	4	?
8	3	6	7F	5	R	7	R	3	8	7	R	5	9	5	?
4	12	4	11	15	9	9	11	7	9	13	6	4	7	R	?
9	R	14	14	4	5	12	10	R	10	6	9	7	14	12	?
7	8	9	10	6	8	17	R	5	16	9	R	R	12	13	?
12	R	10	R	7	6	11	9	8	R	R	7	8	10	14	?
11	13	15F	17	14	13	10	5	9	13	11	R	R	16	6	?
16	R	17	13	R	10	13	6	14	7	10	R	10	8P	16	?
15	9	13	9	16	11	16	13	10	12	R	R	6	R	R	?
R	10	16	8	9	12	R	12	12	11	14	10	R	13	15	?
R	R	11	R	12	R	14	7	11	14	-	-	-	-	-	?
-	-	-	-	-	-	-	-	-	R	8	9	-	17	11	?
10	11	12	12	13	R	15	R	13	15	12	11	11	11	9	?
NS	R	R	16	R	17	R	14	16	18	16	12	13	18	17	?
17	15	R	R	21	16	R	15	19	R	R	13	R	19	21	?
R	14	20	18	18	19	-	-	-	-	-	-	-	-	-	?
19	R	19	19	17	R	R	18	17	20	15	NS	R	NC	18	?
18	R	18	R	19	18	18	16	18	17	R	14	R	20	R	?
R	R	R	R	20	-	19	17	R	R	R	15	14	21	19	?
-	-	-	-	-	20	R	19	20	19	-	16	15	-	-	?
-	-	-	-	-	-	-	-	-	-	R	-	-	22	20	?

1/3	1/2	3/R	4/5	1/R	1/7	3/6	1/3	2/15	4/6	2/3	1/2	R/R	1/2	1/8	498
5/14	5/R	1/2	1/2	2/3	2/4	4/5	8/R	1/R	2/R	4/R	4/5	2/12	4/5	2/3	454
2/6	4/6	7/8	3/15	8/11	14/15	1/2	2/4	4/R	1/3	1/8	3/R	1/3	3/15	7/10	396
4/13	7/12	4/5	6/11	10/15	3/9	8/9	11/R	6/7	5/9	5/13	6/17	4/R	6/7	4/R	214
8/11	3/13	6/15	7/17	5/14	13/R	7/10	5/R	3/9	8/13	7/11	R/R	5/R	9/16	5/6	163
9/16	R/R	14/17	13/14	4/R	5/10	12/13	6/10	14/R	7/10	6/10	9/R	7/10	8/14	12/16	69
7/15	8/9	9/13	9/10	6/16	8/11	16/17	13/R	5/10	12/16	9/R	R/R	6/R	12/R	13/14	68
12/R	R/R	10/11	R/R	7/12	6/R	11/14	7/9	8/11	14/R	R/R	7/8	8/9	10/17	11/14	44
10/R	10/11	12/16	8/12	9/13	12/R	15/R	12/R	12/13	11/15	12/14	10/11	11/R	11/13	9/15	13
17/R	15/R	R/R	16/R	21/R	16/17	R/R	14/15	16/19	18/R	16/R	12/13	13/R	18/19	17/21	0
R/R	14/R	20/R	18/R	18/20	19/20	19/R	17/19	20/R	19/R	R/R	15/16	14/15	21/22	19/20	0
18/19	R/R	18/19	19/R	17/19	18/R	18/R	16/18	17/18	17/20	15/R	14/NS	R/R	20/NC	18/R	0

2011 FILL-IN CHART

DRIVER	TEAM	Round 1 – 13 Mar BAHRAIN GP	Round 2 – 27 Mar AUSTRALIAN GP	Round 3 – 10 Apr MALAYSIAN GP	Round 4 – 17 Apr CHINESE GP	Round 5 – 8 May TURKISH GP	Round 6 – 22 May SPANISH GP	Round 7 – 29 May MONACO GP	Round 8 – 12 Jun CANADIAN GP
1 SEBASTIAN VETTEL	Red Bull								
2 MARK WEBBER	Red Bull								
3 LEWIS HAMILTON	McLaren								
4 JENSON BUTTON	McLaren								
5 FERNANDO ALONSO	Ferrari								
6 FELIPE MASSA	Ferrari								
7 MICHAEL SCHUMACHER	Mercedes								
8 NICO ROSBERG	Mercedes								
9 ROBERT KUBICA	Renault								
10 VITALY PETROV	Renault								
11 RUBENS BARRICHELLO	Williams								
12 PASTOR MALDONADO	Williams								
14 ADRIAN SUTIL*	Force India								
15 PAUL DI RESTA*	Force India								
16 KAMUI KOBAYASHI	Sauber								
17 SERGIO PEREZ	Sauber								
18 SEBASTIEN BUEMI*	Toro Rosso								
19 JAIME ALGUERSUARI*	Toro Rosso								
20 JARNO TRULLI	Team Lotus								
21 HEIKKI KOVALAINEN	Team Lotus								
22 NARAIN KARTHIKEYAN	HRT								
23 TBA	HRT								
24 TIMO GLOCK	Virgin Racing								
25 JEROME D'AMBROSIO	Virgin Racing								

SCORING SYSTEM: 25, 20, 15, 10, 8, 6, 4, 3, 2, 1 POINTS
FOR THE FIRST 10 FINISHERS IN EACH GRAND PRIX

* Leading candidates at the time of going to press.

Round 9 – 26 Jun EUROPEAN GP	Round 10 – 10 Jul BRITISH GP	Round 11 – 24 Jul GERMAN GP	Round 12 – 31 Jul HUNGARIAN GP	Round 13 – 28 Aug BELGIAN GP	Round 14 – 11 Sep ITALIAN GP	Round 15 – 25 Sep SINGAPORE GP	Round 16 – 9 Oct JAPANESE GP	Round 17 – 16 Oct KOREAN GP	Round 18 – 30 Oct INDIAN GP	Round 19 – 13 Nov ABU DHABI GP	Round 20 – 27 Nov BRAZILIAN GP	POINTS TOTAL

111

Red Bull Racing had the pace in 2010, but more rule changes mean that this year could be a different story.

The publishers would like to thank the following sources for their kind permission to reproduce the pictures in this book.

Lester Brown: 97

Getty Images: /Guillaume Baptiste/AFP: 93

LAT Photographic: 37, 52, 59TR, 61C; /Charles Coates: 2-3, 11, 12, 13, 16, 26, 31, 40, 42, 43, 45, 53, 54, 100; /Glenn Dunbar: 10, 19, 21, 24, 30, 32, 33, 34, 35, 46, 88, 91; /Steve Etherington: 8-9, 18, 28, 48, 49, 55, 57, 62-63, 92, 95, 99, 101, 102, 106, 107; /Andrew Ferraro: 14, 17, 22, 23, 27, 29, 38, 39, 47, 50, 51, 56, 61BL, 86-87, 89, 90, 96, 98, 103, 104, 105; /Drew Gibson: 20, 41; /Alastair Staley: 25; /Steven Tee: 4, 6-7, 15, 36, 44, 61BR, 84-85, 94, 112

Courtesy of Silverstone Circuits Limited: 58-59

Sutton Motorsports: 61TL

Every effort has been made to acknowledge correctly and contact the source and/or copyright holder of each picture and Carlton Books Limited apologises for any unintentional errors or omissions that will be corrected in future editions of this book.